Praise for *Holistic Trauma Healing*

"Jackie's comprehensive yet accessible writing style makes complex techniques like EMDR and trauma-informed yoga approachable for all readers. The book's integration of psychology, allopathic medicine, and complementary healing modalities is both inspiring and easy to follow, offering valuable insights and exercises. ... Jackie's dedication shines through in this book, making it an essential resource for anyone seeking a holistic approach to trauma recovery."

—**CASIE FARIELLO**, CEO of Other Parents Like Me and founding member of Parenthood Ventures

"Jackie's book is an incredible resource for those who are tired of getting bogged down in the science of trauma and are left without any healing prescriptions. ... These techniques are backed by science, but the focus is on transmuting trauma into an opportunity for growth and expansion. Jackie is there every step of the way."

—**CHRISTY ABATE**, co-owner of the Angel Cooperative and the Angel Wing, Reiki and Karuna master, priestess of the Rose Lineage, retreat leader, facilitator, and yoga teacher

"Jackie utilizes her numerous areas of expertise to provide the reader with a place to explore, educate, and heal. Each chapter is an in-depth and detailed guide to processing trauma emotionally, as well as physically. ... This book contains a plethora of self-growth knowledge, reflections, and practices."

—**ALEXA SERVODIDIO**, LCSW, EMDR therapist, author, radio and TV host

"In the world of trauma healing, there is not one path or one magic pill. It is a journey unique to each person. Reading Jackie's book will open your eyes to a variety of possibilities and Jackie's warm and friendly personality shows through as she presents options and information to help your healing."

—**BOB BUTERA**, PhD, director of Comprehensive Yoga Therapy at YogaLife Institute and author of *The Yoga Life*

"A highly accessible, empathetic, and valuable guide on how to thrive and not just survive trauma and significant stress. Jackie addresses the pain in our bodies, hearts, and minds with a mix of traditional and alternative approaches to growth and healing. She lays out the nature, evidence, and value of these tools and invites us to find our own individual healing combo by taking what we want and leaving the rest. The beauty is that many of her resources are free and DIY."

—VANESSA ELIAS, owner and founder of Thrive with a Guide, support group facilitator for National Alliance on Mental Illness (NAMI), and certified parent coach

"With so many books about healing it's difficult to find one written in such a way that it brings together physical, metaphysical, mental, and emotional methods in an integrative, comprehensive way. Jacqueline has done that and more! Even if you haven't experienced extreme trauma, this book is for you—it is an honest and personal approach to help you facilitate your own healing!"

—MELANIE BARNUM, author of *Real Life Intuition*

"With practical exercises and research-backed techniques, *Holistic Trauma Healing* is a comprehensive guide to mind-body recovery. Author Jacqueline Jackson combines her personal healing experience with over two decades of professional expertise to offer the ultimate guide for anyone seeking practical and accessible ways to complement traditional medical treatments, explore new self-care practices, or support clients healing from stress, anxiety, or trauma."

—HEATHER ROSS, family recovery coach, *Living While Loving Your Child Through Addiction* podcast

HOLISTIC TRAUMA HEALING

About the Author

Jacqueline Jackson is passionate about writing and sharing yoga and complementary healing modalities to support your recovery journey. She currently works as a writer, yoga practitioner, and group facilitator with the online network Other Parents Like Me. Jackie is an experienced registered yoga teacher (ERYT-500) and Continuing Education Provider (YACEP) with Yoga Alliance since being certified in 2001. She completed her year-long comprehensive yoga therapy certification in 2013 and her trauma-informed yoga certification in 2016. She is a lifelong learner and a member of the International Association of Yoga Therapists (IAYT).

She shares her books, meditation, therapeutics, stress reduction, and lifestyle management skills to thousands in a variety of schools, studios, clubs, corporations, retreats, and teacher trainings. Her debut as an author is *Urge Overkill: A Story of Breaking Free*, a self-help book on overcoming domestic violence from her days working at a domestic violence and rape shelter.

Jackie offers individual consultations; private, group, and corporate classes; workshops; and retreats both online and in person. Her specialties include prenatal yoga, structural yoga therapy, trauma-informed yoga, mindfulness-based stress reduction (MBSR), and other meditations. She is a Reiki Master in the tradition of Dr. Mikao Usui.

Sign up for her newsletter and receive a free practice video from Integrative Healing. Find her online at www.jacquelinejackson.net.

HOLISTIC TRAUMA HEALING

Strategies to Integrate the
Body, Mind, and Spirit

JACQUELINE JACKSON

LLEWELLYN
WOODBURY, MINNESOTA

FIRST EDITION
First Printing, 2025

Book design by Rebecca Zins
Cover design by Kevin R. Brown
Interior art by Llewllyn Art Department

Llewellyn Publications is a registered trademark of Llewellyn Worldwide Ltd.

Library of Congress Cataloging-In-Publication Data
Pending
ISBN 978-0-73877-955-3

Llewellyn Publications
A Division of Llewellyn Worldwide Ltd.
2143 Wooddale Drive
Woodbury, MN 55125-2989

www.llewellyn.com
Printed in the United States of America

GPSR Representation:
UPI-2M PLUS d.o.o., Medulićeva 20, 10000 Zagreb, Croatia,
matt.parsons@upi2mbooks.hr

This book is dedicated to my amazing friend and mentor Marcelle Soviero and my beloved family: Jack, Ethan, and Cole. Thank you for all your love and support. It is also dedicated to you, dear reader, and to all who benefit from it.

Heartfelt appreciation to the Llewellyn staff for supporting me in making my dream come true. Thank you to Kat Neff, for introducing me to Llewellyn and for her support with publicity. Thank you to Becky Zins, who did the initial design and edit. Thank you Stephanie Finne, for helping me with the rest of the editing, and to Sammy Peterson, for finalizing the design.

May this be more than just a book; may it be an engaging interactive experience with potent techniques, a road map to support you in your healing process, and a tool kit to use while finding inner strength to promote well-being and serenity.

Ten percent of the profits from this book will go to the Center for Motivation and Change: https://motivationandchange.com/.

CONTENTS

INTRODUCTION

Two words that describe our lives in the United States could be *stress nation*. A global pandemic, political upheaval, gun violence, an opioid epidemic, widespread layoffs, and the challenges of 24-7 connectivity have ramped up the pressure to be a perfect storm of stress, anxiety, and trauma. We are a nation in need of healing. There is only so much we can consume, only so many medications we can take, and only so many operations we can undergo to deal with all these forms of our fear.

The goal of this book is to support our traumatized, stressed-out nation starting with ourselves and proactively seek ways we can holistically heal our stress, anxiety, and trauma—especially our trauma, both individual and collective. How? Experientially, through the exploration of integrated healing practices. My quest has been to access my inner strength and powers of healing and to share it so others may find theirs. This has been my saving grace in healing from domestic violence and cancer as well as being a caregiver for loved ones who struggle.

These experiences led me to seek the healing methods you will find in this book. Too often in my experience, we or someone close to us get a diagnosis. Desperately, we deal with insurance and see the different specialists, who weigh in. We are left with many disparate parts from experts, with all their subsets and specializations, who might fail to see and synthesize the latest research information that is available. We are left wading through the contrasting information, trying to make sense of it even as we are in the midst of a health crisis! As we know, stress does not aid healing.

When we are fighting for our lives, we will battle by all means necessary to save ourselves or our loved ones. This is a tool kit from which we can draw from expert research to move forward in our healing journey. That's where I hope to lend support from my personal experience and research to integrate information for the layperson. This offering aims to give you access to many of the available options. Instead of pitting talk therapy against bodywork, an integrative approach honors the symbiotic relationship between the two. Talking about trauma may clarify the narrative, but it's through bodywork that we can rewrite the physiological responses imprinted by trauma.

For all those interested in holistic healing and creating a personalized self-care tool kit for themselves, I share this. It's for those, like me, who are looking for solace and hope in feeling empowered by yoga, breathwork, meditation, and holistic healing modalities. As a member of the International Association of Yoga Therapists and a group facilitator with the national parent support network Other Parents Like Me, I work to create connection, space, and community through shared experience and resources. My intention is to share do-it-yourself (DIY) exercises, stress reduction, and lifestyle management techniques (many of which you will find throughout this book) to various populations online and in person through teaching, workshops, support groups, and as a speaker/facilitator. Since 2001 I have been writing newsletters and articles and have been featured in newspapers, magazines, and online publications. Prior to this I gained corporate experience in sales, marketing, management, and social work.

Since 2001 I have been honored to teach yoga and meditation to thousands of people. In the same way that yoga is all about integration of body, mind, and spirit, the following trauma resources can be combined for a holistic approach. As an ongoing student and teacher, I am trained to teach the modalities of the chakra system, trauma-informed yoga, and Reiki as a master Reiki practitioner in the Usui lineage. While a good amount of the following material comes from research, I use myself as the proverbial guinea pig through direct experience in the bulk of the offerings—that is, through therapies such as eye movement desensitization and reprocessing (EMDR), cognitive behavioral therapy (CBT), dialectical behavioral therapy (DBT), and somatic experiencing (SE). If you're sketchy on the details of these, don't worry. Their full overviews will come up shortly in their respective chapters.

Trauma Stats

In 2024, the National Council on Community Behavioral Health reported 70 percent of us here in the United States have experienced some type of traumatic event at least once in our lives—that's 223.4 million Americans. The report went on to say, trauma is a risk factor in nearly all behavioral health and substance use disorders. To those who fall within these stats, this book is for you. Sure, these stats may sound overwhelming, and it is alarming. There is good news with a note of caution here.

Please know that there are also positive reports that people can and do regularly recover from trauma. For example, in the United States right now we have 22.35 million people in recovery from addiction. Impressive! People can and do get better every day. Power to the people!

When people experience trauma of all sorts, they may never be exactly the same as before. It's like a coat hanger that is bent to fish out a drain. It can go back to its original shape but not the exact same shape. Our experiences change us. We are always changing. The only constant is change. Later on, we will also see how our experiences change our actual brains. But first, in chapter 1, we will see about how resultant growth is possible.

This is not to sugarcoat or deny anyone their experience. We definitely don't want that to be an excuse for those around the traumatized to look away, brush it off, or say things like *Buck up!* It is a call to hold space for our individual and collective trauma and realize our tremendous healing capabilities so we can tap into them. The following top trauma interventions, together with complementary modalities, provide options that are proving effective in preventing many long-term effects of trauma. Take heart that awareness is a starting point in the healing process. I also find the willingness to be open enough to do the work has proven to be hugely beneficial. Throughout the following chapters, you will find "In Practice" exercises to directly connect with the offerings. I encourage you to keep a journal in this exploratory process to get the most out of it.

1

The ABCs of Body-Mind Trauma Treatment

When there is trauma, the head goes up
in the clouds but the body keeps the score.
We need to get back into the body to heal.

TRAUMA EXPERT BESSEL VAN DER KOLK

Unfortunately, most of us will experience a trauma at some point in our lives, and as a result, some of us will experience debilitating symptoms that interfere with daily life. Almost everyone has some sort of suffering they'd like to alleviate or release, right? If it doesn't serve your soul, let's figure out how to face it so you might let it go or somehow transform it. The goal is to identify the issue, then learn ways to deal with it once you understand it more.

The thing about trauma is that it differs widely between each of us according to our personal experiences. We probably agree every unpleasant experience is not trauma. Certainly not all of us who experience a potentially traumatic event will actually become psychologically traumatized. Traumatic experiences often involve a threat to your life or safety, but any situation that leaves you feeling overwhelmed and isolated can be traumatic, even if it doesn't involve physical harm.

At its core, trauma is an overwhelming, gut-wrenching psychological and emotional response to an event or an experience that is deeply distressing or disturbing. It also could possibly be the subjective childhood experience of feeling abandoned. Since trauma is completely subjective, what causes one person to be traumatized does not always have the same effect on another, even in the same circumstance. We see that it's not the objective facts that determine whether an event is traumatic; it's our subjective emotional experience of it. How *you* see it and what it means to you personally plays a big part. What matters is the impact the traumatic experience had on you and how it continues to affect your life. It's not what happened on the outside; it's what happened on the inside.

Embodiment

If we need to get back into our bodies to heal, then how we get to what is on the inside is what embodiment is all about. The term *embodiment* means the connection of the body and mind and comes from somatic therapy. In positive psychology it is called the act of healing through movement. I am fascinated by the term *embodiment* on different levels, and not only as it relates to my ongoing yoga practice and my relationship with my body. I am also struck by the enormity and importance of it as a process for easing trauma as well as a whole host of other challenging emotions.

You can "embody mindfulness" as a skill and build this ability using your intention and mind-body associations by setting aside time to focus your attention on your breath and body sensations as related to traumatic events or stress. You can use it to explore how pain can be transformed by the alchemy of your attention and creativity. You will see this as a theme throughout the entire book, so please make note of the embodiment practices that speak to you.

Post-Traumatic Stress Disorder (PTSD)

You may be wondering how to determine if a trauma requires clinical intervention. Post-traumatic stress disorder (PTSD) is a mental health condition triggered by a terrifying event. Symptoms may include flashbacks, nightmares, and severe anxiety, as well as uncontrollable thoughts about the event (Mayo Clinic Staff 2018). This is not to diagnose but highlight the prevalence of PTSD and post-traumatic stress (PTS), a common, normal, and often adaptive response to experiencing a traumatic or stressful event, which is not classified as a mental illness. The point is to reduce the fear factor it may conjure up. Trauma will not likely go away if it is not identified or dealt with. There is no one-size-fits-all solution, so let's take an exploratory approach to recovery. A common sign of healing you'll see throughout this book happens when you realize you did the best you could in a tough situation, and you are now able to feel safe, like the trauma is behind you.

Generational Trauma

Can trauma be passed down? Consider generational trauma, repeating a cycle of trauma from your ancestors or carrying the heavy burden of trying to break it. This type of trauma that does not end with the individual is also known as transgenerational trauma. Families that have experienced unresolved trauma in the past—such as war, displacement, abuse, mental illness, and addiction—may continue to pass on dysfunctional coping mechanisms and negative worldviews to succeeding generations. It seems pain travels through family lines until someone is ready to heal it in themselves. One person can serve as living proof that all can get stronger. As we heal ourselves, we help our families, which helps them get stronger. By going through the agony of healing, we no longer have to live in it or pass on the trauma to the generations that follow. It is worth the work to free ourselves of the darkness of trauma (Dixon 2021).

Here is an example. My friend's mother, Ella, was abandoned by her mother as a child. When this happened, Ella was sent to live in a boarding house by her father until she came to the United States from Germany alone at age fourteen. She didn't speak the language and eventually went on to work in the restaurant industry, where eventually she met her husband.

Ella passed the trauma along to my friend and her siblings when she left her late husband, taking two of her five kids with her and her new husband, under the guise of going on vacation. The drama continues with Ella's estrangement from four of her children, who are unable to forgive this and her abusive behavior. I am going to back up here. Just to be clear,

Tips to Break the Cycle of Generational Trauma

If you are a parent, it's crucial to go through the generational traumas healing in addition to opening up conversations with your children, cousins, grandkids, etc. about your lived experiences.

- Have a discussion with your parents or other close family members about their experiences and coping mechanisms.

- Observe any ingrained patterns, attitudes, or stories from your family that you still perpetuate.

- Discuss these issues with a dependable friend, relative, or therapist, and think about finding another means of coping or communicating.

- Develop understanding and sympathy for your family and the difficulties they faced. Take note that many of our predecessors sacrificed a lot of their time and effort for us to live better lives, despite their shortcomings.

no one should put up with abuse. As someone who has dealt with domestic violence, I made a vow to myself that I won't take abuse again, so that is not what I am suggesting here.

The point is that the next generation is impacted by trauma. As a result, a few of Ella's grandchildren have decided to believe Ella is just a terrible person unworthy of communication, without understanding the role of generational trauma. My therapist helped me with talking points for my kids on the subject. We can love someone from afar if it is not healthy to be close to them. And we can change the story we tell to focus on family resilience versus labeling someone as bad. Despite Ella's mistakes, a broader perspective would be that Ella worked hard to give her kids a better life than she had. Yet she repeated the abandonment trauma with them, and now some of them are poisoned with unforgivingness and possibly poised to pass it on to the next generation. What can be done, and how might you apply it to your situation?

- Create a new story about your family, yourself, and the world that you want your kids to believe and embody.

- Trauma victims have two options. They either keep repeating the pattern, or they can find a way out by inventing a new story. This occurs when family members speak up and deal with any hurt, pain, or abuse from the past.

- Look for signs of healing like being able to see your parents as human beings and understand how trauma impacted their parenting.

Forms of Trauma

Did you know that trauma presents itself in different ways? It can have an impact on how you express your emotions, which is one of the most frequent ways that it manifests. Denial, rage, grief, and emotional outbursts are some of the frequent emotional signs and symptoms of trauma. Trauma victims may channel their intense feelings away from themselves and toward other people, including friends or family, which is why trauma is challenging for loved ones. It is hard to help someone who pushes you away!

Understanding the emotional side effects of trauma might make the healing process a little easier. Emotional trauma symptoms include self-blame, survivor guilt or shame, and decreased interest in everyday activities. Enduring trauma even affects how we think and may result in things like

- nightmares, flashbacks, or reexperiencing the trauma

- difficulty with memory, concentration, and making decisions

- attention deficit issues

Physical signs of trauma can be just as genuine and worrisome as those of illnesses or injuries. After a traumatic event, it's important to take preventative measures to manage stress levels and any trauma symptoms. You might observe indicators such as fatigue, poor concentration, anxiety, being unable to cope in certain circumstances, and physical pain. Trauma also spills into our relationships and how we interact with others. It can look like issues of regular conflict with others or a tendency to become isolated or detached. It can also manifest as difficulty trusting others and feeling betrayed.

Balancing the Nervous System

Many expert perspectives believe what you might intuitively already know: that the basis of trauma recovery is all about offsetting the trauma by balancing your nervous system to help it calm down. If you do not get the chance to digest and release the resulting sense of shock experienced throughout the mind-body system, it is difficult, if not impossible, to balance your neurological systems. You could risk staying in a persistent state of intense physiological and psychological-emotional anxiety if that doesn't happen. This frequently takes the form of what is called hyper (over) or hypo (under) aroused states.

Let's break it down. Hyperarousal is an amped-up state of being highly worried, anxious, and incessantly searching the environment for potential threats while remaining in a hypervigilant state of high alert regardless of the situation. You guessed it: This reaction is known as the flight or fight response. Hypoarousal, on the other side, is a flat state in which you might feel shut down, lethargic, apathetic, melancholy, disassociated, or disengaged. It could present as blanking out, being unable to remember anything for a period of time. Maybe you experience a blurred or distorted sense of reality. This is the freeze or fawn response, which leaves you feeling empty, numb, or paralyzed.

If you are not as familiar with the lesser-known fawn trauma response, it is a form of people-pleasing in which you immediately try to please in order to avoid any conflict. In either of these hypoaroused responses, you may lose the ability to efficiently process inputs. Shutdown of the brain's prefrontal cortex, which is responsible for decision-making, interferes with our capacity for logical thought and frequently results in feelings of dysregulation, or the inability to appropriately regulate our emotions.

Post-Traumatic Growth (PTG)

I have found it helpful and important to understand that those who have experienced trauma are not only capable of surviving it but also the experience itself may function as a catalyst to inspire positive transformation. You might be wondering how that is possible. It's called post-traumatic growth (PTG), or positive change that occurs as a result of overcoming a traumatic experience or significant life crisis. The term *PTG* was coined in 1996 to describe an important phenomenon that gives hope (Calhoun et al. 2017). PTG is the experience of your development, at least in some areas, to surpass what was present before the struggle with crisis occurred. You may have since experienced changes that are viewed as important and that go beyond the status quo.

What helps me shift my perspective in working to heal my own trauma is to zoom out to see the big picture of focusing on the nuggets of wisdom I've gained through my recovery process. Turns out I am not alone. Between 30 to 70 percent of those who experienced trauma also felt they could identify positive change and growth coming out of the traumatic experience. They described profound changes in their view of relationships, how they see themselves, and their philosophy of life.

Maybe you have heard the adage that struggle can create strength. Just to be clear, this is certainly not meant to imply that traumatic events are good. They are not, but for many, life crises are a part of life's struggle. You are not given the choice between suffering and growth on the one hand and no suffering and no change on the other. It is how you work and grow your ability to cultivate what is known as a growth mindset. I learned about this concept at my kids' elementary school, and it immediately rang true. A growth mindset perspective thrives on challenge and sees failure as a springboard for growth. It's all about stretching your existing abilities rather than seeing setbacks as evidence of unintelligence.

Depending on the various sources being drawn from, there are commonalities in post-traumatic growth. Here are some I have personally experienced in the classroom of life and with those whom I have worked with and known. This kind of growth may enhance your appreciation for life and your relationships with others, open you to new possibilities in life, help you tap into your personal strength, and invoke spiritual change. Post-traumatic growth is a favorable transformation that happens as a result of overcoming a traumatic event or major life crisis. Even so, I wouldn't wish trauma on anyone.

The Post-Traumatic Growth Inventory (PTGI)

There's even a measurement for examining "the beneficial effects of trauma" called the post-traumatic growth inventory (PTGI), which gauges how some survivors of traumatic events come to value improvements in their philosophy of life, connections with others, and perceptions of themselves, all of which were hard-won through building coping mechanisms (Collier 2016). An example of someone high on the PTGI scale is Viktor Frankl, the neurologist and psychiatrist who wrote *Man's Search for Meaning*, which chronicled his experiences as a prisoner in Nazi concentration camps during World War II. In it he describes his psychotherapeutic method that involves identifying a purpose in life to feel positive about. I'd say he is purposely shifting his focus. You need something to live for, especially in dire situations.

Frankl said that for some in the death camps, their reason for living was to eventually get revenge on the guards; whatever works. Developing new interests, being willing to feel emotions, and having a greater sense of self-reliance and more compassion for others are among the twenty-one items on the PTGI scale. Interestingly, it was discovered that women typically report more advantages than men do, and more beneficial changes are reported by those who have gone through traumatic events than by those who have not. The PTGI has to do with optimism and extraversion—you know, being gregarious and outgoing; apparently that helps! The scale seems to be useful in assessing how successfully survivors of trauma rebuild or reinforce their understandings of themselves, others, and the significance of events.

Ten Basic Principles for Healing

If you are ready to take responsibility for your health and well-being, you may appreciate the tenets set forth by internationally recognized healer, author, and television host Inna Segal, who is also the creator of Visionary Intuitive Healing®. This system includes working with the mind, deleting negative thoughts and belief systems, and tuning into your higher consciousness for healing. Her work has been influential to me and an ongoing part of my healing process. I find the mindset to be important. Remember, healing means wholeness and to remediate or cure. To heal on all levels, we might try all of the following intuitive yet often neglected fundamentals of healing that Segal mentions in *The Secret Language of Your Body*:

> **Commit to Making Your Health a Priority.** You can explore this idea of putting yourself and your truth (*satya* in Sanskrit) in chapter 2. Recognize yourself as a valuable individual who deserves complete recovery and well-being. Self-care is a theme throughout this book. Be receptive to discovering the underlying causes of your illness and misery. Instead of taking medicine or turning off your body, work on letting go of any negativity that may be causing your ailment. Letting go is not erasing a memory or ignoring the past; it is no longer reacting to things that used to

make you feel tense. It is releasing the energy attached to certain thoughts. I think of it like a bubble rising up in water from the depths of my being: it surfaces, pops, and releases old, stuck energy. Do this by paying attention to your body's signals and making the appropriate adjustments.

Feel Your Feelings Rather Than Keeping Them Buried. We will delve into this concept in chapter 3 on the chakras, especially the sacral chakra for processing emotions, and through the body-work/somatic experiencing of chapter 6 when we explore pendulation. Experiencing sensations might be uncomfortable, so many people think about them instead. Use them as an opportunity to expand and reach your ideal weight, release pain, create change, and remove the armor that keeps you from experiencing health, peace, and joy. Do this instead of shutting them down by being distracted, watching screens, eating junk food, smoking, drinking, using drugs, bingeing, or doing anything else.

Breathe Consciously. Breathwork is offered in all the chapters throughout this book. We often take shallow breaths, which keeps our bodies tight and inactive, and makes them work harder. You become more aware of your body, develop intuition, calm your mind, and purify your blood when you breathe slowly, deeply, and mindfully. As the breath moves energy throughout your body, you also feel more energized with a sense of well-being.

Eat Healthfully and Consciously. This is part of the yoga in chapter 2, as it pertains to purity, or *saucha*. Most of us are aware of what makes up a healthy diet. However, in our hectic and stressed-out lives, it is easy to turn to fast food, which typically has high levels of fats, sugar, caffeine, and hazardous chemicals. Plus, a lot of us often eat hurriedly and on the move, without paying attention to what we are eating or actually tasting and appreciating our food. Horking down chips while bingeing Netflix is not helping! Our bodies have the chance to recover and renew fast and readily when we take the time to prepare healthy food that we eat slowly and chew deliberately.

Move Your Body. See chapters 2 and 6 on yoga and bodywork for more. We might express our dissatisfaction with feeling uninspired, overweight, and unhappy. We all have the power to develop an exercise regimen that will help us reach and maintain a healthy weight to us get stronger, healthier, leaner, and fitter. You may feel better about yourself, enjoy your body, have more energy, detoxify, and recover by exercising regularly. Plan an enjoyable exercise regimen such as walking, swimming, going to the gym, dancing, yoga, martial arts, surfing, tai chi, or whatever floats your boat!

Listen to Your Body. This is a form of embodiment you will find throughout the book especially with yoga, somatic experiencing, and eye movement desensitization and reprocessing (EMDR). Recognize when it is okay to work, play, and enjoy yourself. Which cycles are you on? When are you at your best? What can you do to make your life more productive? When we ignore our body's messages, stress, tension, worry, aggravation, anxiety, then sickness start to develop. Pause for a short bit every several hours to check in. Stretching, deep breathing, or even a quick meditation can make the difference between feeling fatigued, trapped, and anxious versus healthy, creative, and tranquil.

Be Creative. Take a deep dive into this with the expressive arts exercises in chapter 7. You can unwind, enjoy yourself, and discover amazing things while you are being creative. It offers the chance to study, grow, and identify your strengths. A creative person is frequently more inspired, innovative, and resourceful. Find enjoyable activities that allow you to express your creativity so that you can live fully.

Add More Color to Your Life. Check out the color therapy associated with this in chapter 3. We can feel light, energetic, and cheerful or heavy, despondent, and exhausted depending on the color we wear or surround ourselves in. Learn about the characteristics of the colors that make you feel good, then add them to your life. This could entail painting your walls a soothing shade of green for a calming effect. Consider sporting a bold orange dress or yellow shirt to feel alive or bringing flowers inside for further rejuvenation during the winter. Make whatever it is colorful.

Make Gratitude Your Attitude. This reframe is associated with chapter 5 on the cognitive reframe in cognitive behavioral therapy (CBT), dialectical behavioral therapy (DBT), and positive psychology. Instead of obsessing over what you need or lamenting your limitations, concentrate on all the wonderful things you have in your life. Keep in mind that what you give your attention to will expand. If you concentrate on your problems, they will get worse. Where your intention goes, your energy flows.

Make Laughter a Priority. Do you think you need an occasion to laugh? The advantages of laughter are so enormous that many all over the world take part in "laughter clubs," which make laughing for the sake of laughter their credo. Laughter yoga that teaches particular laughter techniques exists. This style of yoga was developed based on the idea that forced laughter has similar physiological and psychological advantages to spontaneous laughter. Usually done in groups, it involves lots of eye contact and light-hearted interaction amongst players. I can vouch for the relief it offers; it really helped me enjoy some belly laughs.

Resilience

Never give up. This has been a helpful mindset and theme throughout my life when I feel defeated. It worked back when I did sales and has helped in parenting, learning, yoga, healing, and pretty much all my endeavors. Try one more time and it just might work or at least help me turn a corner. For me, the motto sums up resilience, or your capacity to not give up, to hold fast, keep going, mend, and recover from difficulties. It is a kind of flexibility, toughness, and ability to spring back from and deal with adversity.

Case in point is the struggle and tenacity of Louis Zamperini in his biography and movie *Unbroken*. Zamperini was a troubled young man who transformed into an Olympian runner who then went on to survive the unimaginable: first a plane crash, then the near-death experience of being set adrift on a life raft for months, only to end up in a series of brutal POW camps. He survives it all, returns a hero, and even learns to skateboard at age eighty! There are general factors of resilience common to people like Zamperini that include assertiveness, believing in ourselves and our ability to solve problems, and learning to live with uncertainty. Then there is self-awareness, a positive outlook, and empathy for others, as well as having goals and aspirations.

Resilience can also be thought of as the ability to strike a balance between working to be independent while also being willing to depend on others for support. It's about being open to support or even treatment as needed. We need each other for support but must be our own superheroes and saviors. Sometimes, with maladaptive coping strategies like compulsive behaviors and addiction, we must save ourselves from ourselves and seek professional support. There is wisdom in knowing our limits. Simply talking about a situation with a friend or a loved one won't necessarily make our troubles go away, but it does allow us to share our feelings, get support, receive positive feedback, and come up with possible solutions to our problems.

Resilience could look like the appropriate use of needed prescription drugs or alternative remedies and modalities (such as those offered in this book). It also could be abstinence from drugs, workaholism, gambling, bingeing, or other triggers, aka reminders or sensitivities of past painful experiences. It could also be a sense of obligation or purpose toward yourself or others, like when you share your experiences in the hopes that others are able to empathize and receive comfort or inspiration. This was what brought to me write this book, work at a domestic violence and rape shelter, do social work, and work on a mental health network. We know that where our attention goes, so our energy flows as we become magnificent manifesters. Setting deliberate intentions or objectives is key for focus. Our culture and temperament have an impact on the specifics.

Resilience Is an Inside Job

Like happiness, resiliency is said to be an inside job. Ask yourself what helps you lighten or light up? Then do that thing as much as possible. For me, it's been laughter. It really is my best medicine. Often we take ourselves far too seriously, and in doing so we edge out the secret of harmony on our planet, which is living in joy. What if laughter is sacred and its essence is nirvana? Then a heart filled with gaiety and laughter is a heart filled with the essence of heaven or bliss.

When I got a cancer diagnosis, I felt a dark cloud come over me, so I decided to combat it with comedy. Relentlessly I listened to comedy. It was a busy time and I was getting ready to move. As I was prepping the house for showings while caring for my two young boys, I consumed lots and lots of Comedy Central radio. I'd have my iPhone in my pocket to listen as I cleaned. Science has shown what we already know in our hearts: Laughter is the body's natural painkiller, allowing the body to release endorphins (*Psychology Today* 2022).

Laughter has other documented benefits as well. In the shorter term, it activates and releases your stress response and soothes built-up tension. Now you know that laughter builds resilience and humor helps keep everyday irritations in perspective. Most (not all) problems are pretty small when you consider the big picture. Here is a resilience joke with gallows humor from Woody Allen: "Life is full of misery, loneliness, and suffering, and it's all over much too soon." As we often joke on the mental health network, sometimes even dark humor can be a pressure release.

The Resiliency Zone

The resiliency zone is when your mind and your body are in a state of well-being. It's when you are in a good headspace and best able to deal with life's challenges. It is the in-between space, or equilibrium, between emotional extremes. It is the middle ground between the ups and the downs. Stress can bump you out of your resiliency zone into your high or low zone. You don't want to be too high on the scale (where you feel anxiety, edgy, pain, or anger) or too low (where you get stuck in depression, numbness, fatigue, and isolation). When you are in your resiliency zone, you can handle the stresses that happen during the day and react with the best part of yourself. In the resiliency zone, you can come from a place of calm, self-trust, and skill—always my biggest goals.

Resourcing for Resiliency

You can try resourcing, which is finding and using things that comfort you. Cue the laughter for those like me who find laughter to be the best medicine. Use resources or tools to help you get back into your resiliency zone. That enables you to move from a place of stress to a place where the adrenaline, cortisol (or stress hormone), and all of the body chemicals stored from trauma can be released. Living with addiction or grief from a long-term trauma, such as illness or the death of a loved one, can disrupt the resting state of your nervous system. Finding strategies to discover the means to restore your sense of self and create a new identity is all about getting into the resiliency zone. As an example, try the safe space meditation in chapter 5.

Healthy Habits for Resilience

Self-care on all levels is the consistent key to recovery. It has many forms and can include taking a step back, spending time alone, asking for help, putting yourself first, setting boundaries, staying home, asking for what you need, and forgiving yourself. When life knocks us down, we may isolate ourselves and forget that nurturing close relationships can help us find support. Staying focused on goals, priorities, and actively living according to our values by regularly thinking about them are all linked to higher resilience.

Emotional Resilience

Emotional resilience is when you can tap into realistic optimism, even when dealing with a crisis. Realistic optimists believe in their power to make good things happen in rough conditions. Basically, it is understanding that the road to success won't be easy, and it leads to greater success because it forces you to take action. Enter my neighbor and trauma therapist Bonnie Rumilly, who worked to treat victims of 9/11 and the victims' families of the Sandy Hook elementary school shooting as well as her ongoing work with first responders. Rumilly has immersed herself into the world of trauma healing from a psychology standpoint, and it has opened her up to the usefulness of complementary practices, such as mindfulness, that can be used to augment and balance it.

Rumilly feels that resiliency is a mix of nature versus nurture, that each individual is unique and complex, and that every situation is different. Like her, I have seen people find strength and purpose in starting agencies or companies and helping others. Some people have the ability to hone in on advocacy work. In our experience, people heal when they can find a way to channel or focus their pain and energy to help others.

IN PRACTICE
Getting into the Resiliency Zone

Finding freedom from constant reactive patterns in your outer world may feel like escaping from a jail cell. When you work to get into your resiliency zone, you are essentially freeing your mind! Here's how to shift your perception in order to change the narrative.

Steps for Finding Your Resiliency Zone

- Modify how you view adversity by seeing what it has to teach you.

- Develop gratitude.

- Engage in self-care.

- Play or laugh it out.

- Develop relationships that are caring and supportive.

- Donate to others, whether it be time or donations.

- Practice meditation and yoga.

- Spend some time outside.

- Practice self-love and self-compassion.

. . . .

*Do you have other ideas? Write them in your
journal or experiment in your own way.*

Other Resilience Factors

In her work, Rumilly has gained insight into healing trauma, and she found that the number one factor in determining resilience with her clients has been the ability for them to build strength and grow through challenges. "When people are in a vulnerable place, resilience can be cultivated and growth can occur. For example, in losing a loved one," said Rumilly when I interviewed her. "The most resilient people evolve over time and are able to integrate a new normal with learned coping skills and new sources of strength. This is what we refer to as post-traumatic growth."

Some may just call this toughness. *Tough times make tough people* is another adage that speaks to a growth mindset. This could happen if you are able to process it in a way that leads you to change and flexibility. Resilience is also the process of adapting well in the face of adversity, trauma, tragedy, threats, or significant sources of stress such as family and relationship problems, serious health problems, or workplace and financial stressors.

Choose Joy

If joy has disappeared from your vocabulary, maybe it's time to get it back! The key is to take charge of your recovery and experiment with what works for you. This is a hands-on, experiential practice. My friend Marcelle and I like the adage *choose joy* whenever possible and especially when things feel dire. Yes, I know that sometimes sounds absolutely absurd and annoying. In the parent support groups, we joke about butterflies, rainbows, and unicorns in the face of challenging issues. But what if we could actually do that? Of course, if you are dealing with serious trauma, you may

· · · · · ·

Three Therapist Tips for Building Resilience

1. To the best of your ability, look for social connectedness such as support groups and peer support. It is extremely beneficial to be with those who share similar feelings and experiences. This helps you learn the important truth that you are not alone.

2. Develop a new hobby or a long-forgotten passion. It could be knitting, rock climbing, fishing, or an old childhood pastime. Learn to use it as a coping skill. For me, it is singing to offset my throat issues, so I joined a competitive barbershop chorus and am learning to find my voice.

3. The more coping skills and self-care strategies at your disposal, the more present you become. There is no one way for all, so I hope you will find helpful options in this book!

need intervention first or as a complement to that. Like life, choosing joy can be a process. A journey to joy, if you will.

Emotional Guidance Scale

When you are ready, consider that you can choose your state of being. Instead of feeling trapped by life's conditions, freedom is the realization that you are the only jailer of your life. Everything you do is a choice, and you have the option to choose again. A second before a thought takes hold, you have a choice of whether to go with it or not. I like reaching for a better feeling thought. I draw from the Emotional Guidance Scale outlined in Esther and Jerry Hicks's book *Ask and It Is Given: Learning to Manifest Your Desires*. For me, this has been a helpful tool for lifting myself out of lower vibrations.

Here is how it works: The Emotional Guidance Scale is a list of commonly felt emotions, ranging from joy, appreciation, freedom, love, and empowerment (the highest) to fear, despair, desperation, grief, and powerlessness (the lowest). The middle ranges include boredom, pessimism, frustration, and disappointment, amongst others. To feel better, identify where you are on the emotional scale and intentionally reach for better-feeling thoughts that lead to better-feeling emotions. Like in therapy, the idea is that feeling the emotion is important. Then the focus shifts to discovering thoughts that give feelings of relief, which is even better. Once you're stable in a new emotion, you've moved up the scale. Then you continue the practice of reaching for a better-feeling thought and moving up the scale to a higher-vibration emotion.

If I am in despair, for example, I can choose disappointment instead, which is a step up the emotions ladder. From there, I can choose a more neutral feeling and maybe eventually move up to acceptance and hope. You can climb up the ladder of emotions, which can eventually even lead to joy.

Now I am adding another idea to consider if you are open. Consciously climbing the ladder to choosing joy is a way of expressing the Hermetic philosophy quote, "As within, so without; as above, so below; as the universe, so the soul." The Hermetic tradition explores the relationship between the individual (microcosm) and the universe (macrocosm). To me, the quote suggests that who I am on the inside will be reflected in the world around me through the filter of my mind, emotions, and experience. Therefore, if whatever we think or accept consciously will be the circumstances of our lives, why not put out an intention to work for joy, hope, or what we want to invite into our reality? Then we can see ourselves as deliberate, intentional creators of our reality rather than victims of circumstance. This is important when dealing with trauma because trauma implies a lack of choice. Let's take back our power and boost our resilience.

Institutionalized Resilience: The Spartan Mentality

The Spartan mentality is at the extreme end of the building resilience continuum. The city-state of Sparta was renowned for its warrior culture, independent women, and military might. The classic history of Sparta, written by the ancient Greek writer Plutarch, claims that Spartan society purposefully made life difficult for children. Why? To instill resilience so that their kids might learn to value the little things. This was done via the agoge, the training system that Sparta's would-be warriors entered at the age of seven, when they were taken from their homes. It was brutal. Fighting between boys was encouraged, and the older boys willingly participated in beating the younger boys to toughen them. They learned to fight, endure pain, and survive through their wits. Self-denial, simplicity, the warrior code, and loyalty to the city-state governed their lives. Food theft was also promoted. Who wouldn't be tempted to replace their meager daily serving of soup with stolen snacks? There was a catch: If you were discovered, you received a beating. It was unforgiving.

However, Plutarch claimed that if the children could survive without food, they would learn to fight while starving and would appreciate any food they were given. They were such warriors that when they learned of an enemy at the city gates, they did not ask how many there were; they'd only ask where the enemy was. In other words, they were going to defend the city no matter the cost, no questions asked. That is some serious training.

IN PRACTICE
Three Spartan Tactics to Boost Resilience

Some daily Spartan habits are surprisingly routine and relatively easy to implement. We can use Spartan principles to boost our mental resilience in modern life.

Physical Fitness. A Spartan workout would begin with weightlifting for strengthening. Running, riding, and mountain climbing for endurance would all be included. Finally, there are exercises that increase resistance, such as going barefoot in the snow or hiking through soggy, rainy terrain—you know, like the modern Spartan races people pay money to do.

Cold Plunge/Cold Showers. Either is a great practice to train your resilience to suffering and is a key element of developing Spartan mental toughness. Building up your body's tolerance for cold water is a simple way to prepare your brain to handle other challenging conditions. Unconsciously, you are aware that forcing yourself to endure unpleasant feelings will eventually increase your tolerance.

Face Your Fear. The Spartans never let their fears grow in the background. They always had to confront them, and this confrontation secured their courage and mental strength. Instead of letting your fears gain momentum, you can learn about them and eventually face them. As an example, you might be afraid of talking to your boss about a pay raise. As long as you refrain from talking to your boss, the fear will grow in the background and the possibility of a pay increase will pass. Your intentions and plans will have been weakened by the fear. Instead, you could begin by making small moves. Although you might not want to bring up the compensation increase right away, you can engage your boss in a regular conversation instead. In this way, you gradually but steadily chip away at your fear. It will eventually vanish entirely.

Institutionalized Resilience:
Military Training

The 2024 National Veteran Suicide Prevention Annual Report states currently in the United States, we have 17.2 veterans dying by suicide each day, with veterans being one and a half times more likely to die by suicide than civilians. Because of dire statistics like these, military resilience training has been researched by the government since the 1970s and is now used to support military personnel and their families in the development of mental, physical, emotional, and behavioral toughness. These training sessions are designed to help soldiers cope with adversity, adapt to change, and overcome challenges to improve mental health and performance.

As part of the University of Pennsylvania's Positive Psychology department (whose faculty includes the Positive Psychology founder Martin Seligman, whom you will meet in chapter 8), these trainings were developed to teach resiliency skills. One example is teaching the ability to recognize false ideas. This is about using critical thinking skills with a questioning approach to encourage reflective, independent problem-solving. This draws from cognitive behavioral theory. It has been established that resilience can be learned, and cognitive behavioral therapy offers useful teaching methods for preventing depression.

Part of the instruction also concentrates on strengthening your relationships through the use of affirmative dialogue, which is choosing words that are encouraging and supportive. This training also relates to making compliments specific and using helpful language and responses. This includes relying on honest, respectful, and supportive communication.

Military Mindfulness Training

Standing at attention isn't the same as paying attention. Mindfulness trains soldiers how to use meditation to stay present, avoid attention lapses, and mentally prepare for dangerous missions. The benefits extend to soldiers returning from combat as well as those who are preparing to deploy. Mindfulness has been shown to improve resilience, enhance performance, and help prevent the development of stress-related mental health issues.

IN PRACTICE
Resilience Skills for Mental Toughness

These evidence-based abilities build cognitive and emotional fitness, strength of character, and strong relationships for the military—and the rest of us.

Optimism. This is the skill of noticing and expecting the positive. It is about taking purposeful action to focus on what you can control.

Mental Agility. This is the ability to look at situations from different perspectives and think creatively with mental flexibility.

Emotional Control. Notice and accept your emotions to manage and improve them. Realize the impermanence of your emotions. Witness and observe your emotions with kind attention and patience, giving them the space to morph—and, in many cases, completely evaporate.

Inquire and Investigate. Self-management is how you cultivate your ability to control or redirect any disruptive emotions and impulses you become aware of. It's all about adapting to changing circumstances.

Mental Rehearsal with Positive Imagery. Practice and see yourself achieving skills you want. Use this thought process with your five senses to either create or re-create an experience in your mind. You can also call this mental rehearsal, mental practice, and visualization. It is a form of internal simulation training.

Anxiety and Physical Arousal Regulation (Breath Control). The simplest of all relaxation strategies is slow diaphragmatic breathing, similar to that used in meditation and yoga. We know that breathing in this way can have many benefits. The most obvious one is the immediate effect upon your physiology/body sensations. When you are getting stressed, you will notice how your heart rate increases and your breathing becomes shallow and sporadic. Concentrating on your breathing and aiming to slow it down will reduce your heart rate and make you feel calmer and more in control.

Goal Setting. To set your focus and build confidence, use SMART goals, which stands for specific, measurable, action-oriented, realistic, and timed. Once you have a general goal in mind, apply the principles of SMART goals to focus on how to reach it.

Connection. This is the skill of building and keeping trusted, strong relationships.

Strength of Character. Try harnessing the ability to use your strengths to engage authentically, align with your values, and overcome obstacles. It is not just self-improvement; I think of it as a way to be true to myself.

IN PRACTICE
Forgiveness Journaling

Forgiving someone who has hurt or traumatized you can be incredibly difficult. But imagine your higher self offering you a message: release your anger and resentment so that healing can begin. What if your inner wisdom encouraged you to let go of irritation and rage? It's completely valid to feel angry—your emotions are real and justified. Still, consider the toll that holding on to anger takes on your well-being.

Forgiveness doesn't mean saying, "What you did was acceptable." It means choosing to drop the heavy burden of pain caused by someone else's actions. Holding on to resentment is like drinking poison and expecting the other person to suffer. In reality, unforgiveness harms you the most, keeping you tied to the pain. And often, the hardest person to forgive is ourselves. No matter who it's about, keep in mind that you're forgiving for your own sake—because forgiveness sets you free. You might imagine your higher self guiding you to let go of resentment, especially if you're open and willing to ask for that help. Perform the following:

- Ask yourself who or what have I been unable to forgive?

- Ask your higher power to help you release unforgivingness.

- Imagine your burdens and unforgivingness being carried away or lifted from you.

- See it floating up, up, and away—goodbye and gone forever!

. . . .

Imagine what it would feel like to forgive and be relieved and cleansed of the poison of unforgivingness. Do you have other ideas? Write your responses in your journal.

2

Channel Your Inner Yogi with Therapeutic and Trauma-Informed Yoga

*Yoga helps people reclaim their bodies by providing
a container in which they can feel their feelings.
It gives people a sense of time, which is missing
in response to trauma. We could say to ourselves,
"Today sucks, but tomorrow is a new day."*

TRAUMA EXPERT BESSEL VAN DER KOLK

Besides helping us weather the storms of good and bad days, yoga can work wonders for your body and calm your mind. Yoga spans thousands of years, making its way from the East to the West, and all types of yoga have brought about healing and spiritual transformation. Yoga is a great example of embodiment therapy, as it's literally a mind-body practice. It has even been found that yoga significantly reduced PTSD symptoms with a comparable effect to the well-researched approaches of therapy and medication.

Yoga may improve functioning by helping traumatized people tolerate physical and sensory experiences associated with fear and helplessness. It increases your emotional awareness and you affect tolerance, or the awareness of how much of your emotions you can tolerate, sit with, or feel without needing to do something to shut them off (Emerson et al. 2014, 559–65). Yoga practice focuses on your breath and specific postures to reach a peaceful state, so you might say that yoga has been healing various traumas for thousands of years, yet there is typically a difference in yoga therapy practice versus a studio or gym yoga class. It is not just exercise or a workout.

What Are Yoga Therapeutics?

These days people walk into my yoga classes saying they were sent by their doctors for all kinds of issues. Experts supporting yoga as a complementary practice makes sense since its ultimate goal is to lead you to self-mastery and self-realization. Sounds therapeutic, right? While all yoga is potentially therapeutic and healing, yoga therapy is focused on you as an individual and applying specific yogic tools such as postures/exercises, breathwork, and meditation techniques to address your physical, mental, and emotional needs. The yogic therapeutics model of health works to address every aspect of your life instead of considering each body part or system separately, as is typical in allopathic medicine. It is a good complement to mental and physical health in treating the whole individual, which is a positive and preventive shift in our health-care system.

Case in point is the crossover work of Amy Weintraub, founder of the Life Force Yoga Healing Institute and pioneer in the field of yoga therapy and mental health. Weintraub trains therapists and students in the use of yogic techniques such as guided imagery, affirmation, and targeted breathing practices to meet and balance moods. I adore the way she explores how these yoga-based therapies, which have a solid, evidence-based foundation, can be used for successful treatments in certain mood or mental states through her clinical stories and anecdotes.

Yoga Therapy: Isn't All Yoga Therapeutic?

When hearing the relatively new term "yoga therapy," people often ask whether all yoga is therapeutic. It is a good question and one that I get all the time as a yoga therapist. The short answer is it depends on how it is taught and if you feel safe and supported.

The whole purpose of doing the poses is to dispel stress and trauma from your body so you can calm your nervous system down enough to quiet your mind and heal. A good yoga teacher may prompt you to feel your emotions, be present, and just breathe through it. A yoga therapist and some clinical therapists with integrative practices might also employ both yogic breathing practices and poses for mood management as well as share mudras, imagery, affirmations, and help bring yoga off your mat and into your everyday life.

Both methods may use specialized meditation techniques such as the ancient practice of yoga nidra (psychic sleep) and the modern iRest, a combination created by psychologist and yoga scholar Richard Miller. Of course, clinical therapists have a whole host of additional psychological modalities, some of which I'll break down and integrate with complementary practices throughout the pages of this book. Many of us first learn about yoga through its physical practices, but a common misconception is that it's all about stretching or movement. Yoga therapy can help you whether you can't move at all or are quite active. A general public yoga class can certainly ease everyday aches, pains, and mood complaints. Whether one-on-one or in a small group, yoga therapy aims to go much further because it is tailored to you as an individual.

Yoga therapy is the opposite of one size fits all. You've heard the slogan *No pain, no gain*? It has no room in yoga therapy, which is more like *No pain, no pain*—quite the opposite! For me, this is the best approach for all kinds of yoga practice. After all, the yoga sutras on which the practice is based say that the practice is meant to be adapted to the individual. Originally, it was taught one-on-one. At its core, this age-old system of harmonizing the body with the mind and breath using physical poses, breathing exercises, and meditation is a process of self-discovery.

Roots of Yoga Therapy

The yogic perspective is that we are multidimensional beings who should examine all pain as having its source in a lack of understanding of ourselves, which you'd explore in therapy and yoga practice. It is about getting to know ourselves, our hidden gifts, and the underlying programming that either does or does not support us.

When we know our bodies well, we can find tools to be free of physical pain. For example, pain in the chest could be muscular, neurological, cardiovascular, or respiratory. The idea is that once we get to know our emotional nature completely, we can direct our attention to the state of just being present to immediate feelings objectively to remove the pain of the past. When we lean into our emotions, let them come up for acknowledgment, and attend to them, they can transform and give us messages we need to hear or help us heal.

The aim of both yoga and therapy is to enable you to find wholeness in your life, where you do not feel like you are constantly trying to fit broken pieces together. Yoga's core teachings are a deep dive into understanding your motivations and behavior for insights into your psychological conditioning and transformation. We know therapy does the same and is more clinical. Yoga, like therapy, allows you to see your conditioned way of life and teaches you how to let go of the patterns that aren't working. Then you can positively transform yourself and, from that, maybe even inspire others too.

One yogic technique that therapists teach is cognitive behavioral therapy, which is used to reality check our thinking in order to identify our limiting thoughts so we can choose more empowering ones. The same principle can be found in Patanjali's *Yoga Sutras*, a collection of 196 Sanskrit sutras (verses) dated from 500 BC on the theory and practice of yoga. Specifically, sutra 2.33 states: "When disturbed by negative thoughts, opposite (positive) ones should be thought of." The act of replacing negative thoughts is also called *pratipaksha bhavana* in Sanskrit.

For example, when caught up in feeling fear, we can shift our focus to calm and safety or the expansive healing energy of love. I'd also add that if it is impossible to replace the negative with a positive, try to put a positive alongside the negative thinking. We will find mindfulness in therapy. In both therapy and yoga, we are taught to feel our feelings. We let them wash over us and not try to push them away (there's that affect tolerance again). We sit in the pain and give it our attention. *No mud, no lotus, may I be at peace in the muddy water* type of thinking.

This is counter to the tendency to grasp at things that are pleasurable and push away things that are painful. We may think, *I don't want to feel depressed, so I am going to find relief at the bottom of a whiskey bottle.* The next day the depression is still there—and also a hangover and even more anxiety, right? Processing feelings and emotions helps us work them out, so our awareness is key. When we have anxiety and trauma, we tend to live focusing on past difficulties and future worries. Mindfulness can help us stay present in the current moment with our feelings and emotions even when we are uncomfortable—maybe especially then.

We can learn to accept our feelings, move through them, and in turn grow from them. The past is over and cannot be changed, the future is not here, but the present is always accessible in the here and now. Since depression is being stuck in the past and anxiety is anticipating the future, we come to know that right now we can decide how we want to react to what is happening. It's like how the meditation master Thich Nhat Hanh would question the reality of these anxious tendencies: "Right now there are no bombs breaking through the ceiling. No one is chasing me. Right now I can breathe in and out. Right now I am okay."

In other words, we can be present, and we do not need our flight, fight, or freeze mechanism unless the situation demands it. Unless there is something to react to, right now we can take a breath and pause to be less reactive. We can check in to how we are feeling, decide what we need at this moment, and take action. Maybe we just need to take a nap, to cry, to take ten breaths, to stand and stretch, or to get some fresh air. Maybe we need an action plan. Take a pause and ask yourself what you need right now. As an example, I just drank water as I sat at my desk working on a deadline.

Yoga for Balancing an Unregulated Nervous System

In yoga and therapy, we want to balance an unregulated nervous system. To do this, consider how a healthy nervous system operates. Imagine you worked all day, came home, and crashed on the couch. You're beat. You're body lets go and relaxes. You feel the weight of your body sink into the couch, and you might exhale a sigh of relief. In this way, your nervous system adapts to being at home. It begins to release the pent-up stress from the day. Within a few minutes, your energy starts to return. You begin to feel energized. A pleasant evening forms in your mind.

A Healthy Nervous System . . .

is one that bounces back and manages our energy well. Under conditions of life challenges and stressors, an influx of hormonal energy is triggered to enable us to take action. When we're ready to relax, the nervous system then clears that energy. When healthy, it regulates or manages the amount of incoming stimulation with a corresponding amount of energy release. When your nervous system is regulated, you can shift easily from high arousal (anxiety, stress, or stimulation) to low arousal (boredom or relaxation). You can more easily move from neutral states into those of joy and contentment. Regulation in human beings is the way the nervous system handles stress and emotions. More generally, it's the way it manages your energy.

An Unhealthy Nervous System . . .

reacts differently to the same scenario as above. Instead of unwinding for a few minutes on the couch and getting your second wind, you remain tired. The stress of the day hangs there all night long, and you have nothing left from which to live your life. The next day, you get up and start the same cycle all over again. Your life has become very small. You're living in a depleted state. An unhealthy nervous system is a dysregulated nervous system that will unconsciously and physically hold on to the work stress in the muscles and fascia (the connective tissue throughout the body). The hormones triggered by the stress response make individuals with dysregulated nervous systems feel wired or hyper yet exhausted at the same time. They may even carry this tension into their sleep or have problems sleeping.

All this might mean you'll have a hard time managing your emotions. There's no buffer zone for you to consider how you'd like to respond. As a result, you're more likely to impulsively react. Of course, this is not always helpful and can cause problems. Don't worry if you sometimes lose it. It happens, right? Maybe the goal can be to embrace failure in those moments. Missteps and roadblocks are ultimately an opportunity to learn, pivot, and restart with a new perspective. We can help ourselves become more resilient to trauma, stress, and anxiety if we have the opportunity to process or work through it. We already know that someone who has experienced trauma may have challenges with connecting to what is going on inside their bodies at any moment while their head goes somewhere else, but there are things we can do to help ourselves.

Yoga Therapy Tips for Self-Care in the Healing Process

- Lean on your support system by finding your people with shared experience.

- Turn to your spirituality and surrender the things you can't control.

- Find meaning in your challenges by seeing what you can learn from them as best you can.

- Read about others' experiences that resonate with you.

To me this speaks to the essence of yoga as a practice because it is not as much about being a "good person" as it is about being good to yourself by checking in to see what is needed to support yourself in the present moment. You do this in the poses so that it ultimately spills over into the rest of your life. To go back to the question of all yoga being therapeutic, I'd say the above-mentioned tips can be part of your lifestyle management and stress reduction. These two factors differentiate yoga therapy from typical yoga classes. Of course, there can always be exceptions, especially as our collective awareness rises.

Yoga for trauma is finding connection between your body and your mind. Trauma is not just an event that took place sometime in the past; it's an experience that leaves an imprint on your mind, your brain, and your body, which is why it's said that trauma is often more about your response to an event rather than the event itself. When experiencing trauma, you may dissociate or disconnect from your body. Yoga can help you reestablish your mind-body connection. If you don't, you may respond in unproductive ways. To create safety, the nervous system deals with perceived danger by automatically sending out cortisol, your stress hormone.

In the long term, your body's safety tactic of ramping up anxiety often causes disruption and unease, especially if this state persists even after the danger has passed. This can look like overreactions and high physiological responses that do not match your situation. Trauma is also described as being stuck in gut-wrenching, heartbreaking emotions and unbearable physical sensations. Yoga helps with that. Consider when you get into a yoga pose and are asked to hold the pose for five breaths before coming out of the pose. It gives you the sense that this too will pass. Really, it's a form of containment to feel your feelings in small doses so as not to be overwhelmed by them.

And then there is this: In van der Kolk's research, he found that yoga was more effective than medication in treating trauma and even had more beneficial effects. Maybe meditate before you medicate? Maybe both? If you need both, use all the modalities at your disposal. Like best-selling author Glennon Doyle quipped, "Jesus loves me, this I know, for he gave me Lexapro." Medication is a lifesaver for some people. There is no one right way. You must forge your own path. It's important to find your individual healing combo. How? By being proactive. That is a huge determining factor in healing. I think we have to find ourselves by thinking for ourselves in order to do that. By all means necessary, we must discover what works for us. Pull out all the stops! To get on our road to recovery, we want to have as much information as possible and tools to draw on.

Healing takes time. It is not linear. Please keep in mind, dear reader, you can go back and forth in your process. Once you move through stages, you can still move back through them again. If you know this, it's easier to accept it when you find yourself taking one step forward in your healing

. . . . .

but then two steps back, so to speak. Your mending will ebb and flow. You can't rush your healing.

Ideally, healing is like a spiral when you revisit some old issue, only the second time you circle around, it becomes an upward spiral. This time you have a higher vantage point of lived experience and a chance to choose again how to deal with it without falling into old patterns. You can use this revisiting process as an opportunity to see how far you've come on the road to recovery and wholeness.

In the meantime, create space, pathways, and the truth of well-being as your birthright and natural state of being. See yourself as whole, healed, and complete. This is a journey to fearlessness and liberation. What if you are closer to freedom than you think? Take the next best step and give yourself a lot of slack and grace—that is, compassion and permission to forgive your faults, to be imperfect. It's okay not to be okay and to fall apart sometimes, assuming you avoid hurting yourself or anyone else. Each time you make room for present awareness in yoga, from facing the physical challenge of holding a posture or confronting difficult emotions or thought patterns, you learn to accept and embrace sensations in your body and your mind. Because these may have been previously interpreted as threatening, it can be a kind of titration. Imagine it as surfing a wave of intense feelings, sensations, and emotions with the goal of riding them out.

Yoga helps me be with my feelings. It enables me to reinterpret them in the present and release them when they feel stuck or in a loop. This is why yoga is called the practice of liberation. It is finding freedom from old patterns or habits.

In Sanskrit, these patterns are called *samskaras*, the subtle impressions left by our past actions. Samskaras are the foundation of our physical, mental, and emotional habits, shaping us in both positive and negative ways. They can be energy blocks created by past experiences and sensitivities. They can be self-destructive patterns, such as those linked to low self-esteem. The word *samskara* comes from *sam* (meaning complete or unified) and *kara* (meaning action or cause). In addition to general patterns, they also represent personal impressions, thoughts, and behaviors that together shape our conditioning. The more we repeat these patterns, the stronger they become, creating deep grooves that are hard to break. Samskaras can be positive, such as the selfless acts of someone like Mother Teresa, or negative, such as the harmful thought patterns that fuel self-doubt and toxic relationships. Negative samskaras are the things that hold us back from positive growth and change.

While yogis call them *samskaras*, neurophysiologists call them *neural pathways*. They are grooves in the neuroplasticity of our brains. It is exciting to know these pathways literally can be reconfigured and rewired as we create new habits with practices such as yoga and meditation, along with the others we explore throughout this book.

The body is the place where all memory resides. All of our stories are stored in our physicality, morphing our personality, socialization, posture, relation with gravity, and the quality of the connective tissue of our our bones and muscles. This includes our body's elasticity, tension, and strength. If changes to our body are due to nonphysical stress such as loss of a job, the body will still react with emotionally based pain. This type of pain can lead to a shortening of muscle fibers and result in feeling stress and tension.

Swami Vivekananda said that the body reveals the consciousness. By changing our consciousness, we can change our bodies. The hatha yoga stance is that by making a difference in our physiology, we can make a difference in our consciousness. Just as our posture can vastly improve with yoga poses, once unhelpful paradigms are released, this allows us to open to the joy of living more fully. Plus, if you've yet to try yoga, know this: There's a post-yoga class bliss that keeps many coming back! I want a T-shirt that says *I'm here for the savasana* (savasana is the final resting pose).

Trauma is widespread, yet its invisible tentacles sometimes reach even farther. The Recovery Village, a national drug rehab center, estimates that about 80 percent of people with PTSD have a co-occurring psychiatric disorder in their lifetime; nearly 50 percent of people with PTSD have a co-occurring substance use disorder; and major depressive disorder affects 30 to 50 percent of people with PTSD (Gonzales 2022). We see the widespread impact and implications of PTSD and all types of traumas on the mental health of a large part of our society. Now throw in the estimated 36 million Americans practicing yoga to see how the necessity of trauma-informed yoga is rising. The good news is that modern practitioners have created specialized yoga practices to quantify the effectiveness of yoga as a therapeutic tool for trauma. These have evolved into two similar-sounding terms that have different approaches.

Trauma-Informed Yoga (TIY)

A specialized form of yoga for trauma is called trauma-informed yoga (TIY). It assumes that everyone has experienced some level of trauma or significant life stress—we did just get through a global pandemic—which adds an element of the unknown. To address this, the TIY approach rests on a set of principles that supports a sense of safety, support, and inclusivity for all who walk through the door. Its aim is to build resilience by connecting you with inner resources that help you work through your discomfort, understand your experience, and separate your feelings from your actions.

You don't need to be a soldier or have PTSD to benefit from the encouraging TIY style. It uses invitational language and gives more modifications and options than most yoga classes. The TIY antidote to being traumatized or for general anxiety is to empower you to feel in charge of your body and your experience. In the TIY experience, specialized instructors offer all these options, which serve to return the sense of control over your body. This is because it is a choice that is often lost in trauma. Keep in mind that yoga in the United States has been criticized for generally being too aggressive. In my experience, this is unfortunately true.

I remember going to Dharma Mittra's class in New York City and overhearing one student ask another, "Do you practice yoga once or twice a day?" That seemed like some other-level pressure to me. Yet I realize there is certainly a practice for every body; a gymnast may need a more athletic practice than most people. Regardless of preferences and opinions, my rule of thumb is if you feel agitated in a yoga class, that means it is too aggressive and it is time to back off. Most yoga teachers would agree, though I would like to see it emphasized more.

Teacher Talk in a TIY Class

TIY has its own language. If you were to walk into this type of class, you might encounter these types of suggestions:

- "If you would like, raise your arms here or place them together in front of your heart."

- "Come to the general shape of the pose, try this alternative, modify like this, or feel free to sit this one out" type of speech.

- "In your own time," "Fold or twist any amount," and "Stay here five more breaths or finish when you feel done" are options.

- The option to close your eyes, lower your gaze, or let your eyelids be heavy if you'd rather not close your eyes implies free will.

In TIY we avoid using generalizations like "sadness and anger live in the hips" or other phrases that imply a blanket experience. Instead, the goal is providing background and elaborating on the reasoning behind it. I might explain how numerous dense nerve bundles are located in the hips and connect to the brain so we frequently store a variety of emotions there. As we practice a hip-opening pose, it's usual for a range of feelings or experiences to surface. Investigate how you feel and what it means to you. Choice is encouraged even in this situation by letting the individual decide what working a hip opener means to them.

TIY Tools for Creating Safety

If you are looking for TIY yoga, please know that it uses tools. It does this by placing a lot of focus on creating safety in the physical practice space for a trauma-informed environment. There are sitting options for relaxation, or savasana. There is no wrong way of doing this! The main goal is to be present, breathe, and be in the body. Different uses of music, props, lighting, and the room setup are modified.

- The use of straps is optional or not offered, as it could be triggering for students who were bound or are in recovery from drug use.

- The teacher tries to be the first to the class to greet each student at the beginning, making them feel comfortable and welcomed.

- During class the teacher tries to be where students can see them to avoid anyone feeling startled or snuck up on.

- The teacher may stay in the front rather than walk around.

- The room and mats are set up so everyone can see the door, though once this is done the teacher generally allows people to choose where they set up rather than directs them to move.

- The teacher may avoid turning lights completely off or tell students before dimming them. They get consent first for everything.

- Mats may be in a semicircle so no one has anyone behind them.

- There are few physical assists or adjustments, if any. Permission would need to be granted prior to the teacher physically assisting or adjusting participants. Touch is powerful and could be triggering for those who have experienced trauma. Touching is generally not recommended in TIY.

Because TIY seeks to reach underserved populations, it has tools for accessibility. The goal is to meet you where you are at, both literally and figuratively. Examples of audiences might be a domestic violence shelter, an eating disorder clinic, prison, or recovery facilities. TIY classes are typically not stereotypical yoga people wearing Lululemon tights, and practice is often less vigorous than public yoga studio classes. The class could include Indigenous and culturally or linguistically diverse people. They may be recipients of specialized care and those recently discharged from hospital settings. It could also include those with poor medical access or people in rural and remote areas. These underserved groups may include older males and younger people with long-term, persistent, or serious health problems. Other considerations include the following:

- There are places where people may actually be sleeping outdoors or on the ground and the people may be wearing non-yoga clothes such as jeans because that is all they have.

- Participants may have physical constraints greater than those typically facing regulars at yoga studios.

- TIY classes usually have less focus on yoga's spiritual aspects than in a public setting, as this could come off as preachy and be divisive.

- The teachers are looking to connect with the participants, who are likely not used to Sanskrit terms, chanting, chakras, or other more esoteric aspects of yoga.

My trauma-informed yoga training was through an organization called United We Om®. We were taught that, as yoga teachers, we were not there to heal or help. Rather, the goal was to connect to participants so that they might look for and find something within themselves.

Participants are encouraged, therefore, to reach in and find their own source of strength, not use a teacher as a crutch. The idea is to teach that calm, peace, or strength is within them. The point is showing love, connection, and value with participants. United We Om® teachers choose to work with underserved populations with whom they may have a connection or a shared experience. We practiced creating a specific introduction so that we could share what is human and relatable about ourselves without talking about war stories or revealing too many personal details.

For example, when I've worked with those in safe houses through my local domestic violence crisis center, I've introduced myself as follows: "Hi, I'm Jackie, and I survived domestic violence. I am here because yoga saved my life. I find that the breathing and yoga techniques help me move forward with more ease. I don't know what my life would be like without it. I want to share what has been useful for me, and hopefully you will find some tools that will be useful for you."

The practice is based on the growing understanding that trauma takes a heavy toll on the body and the brain. When the body absorbs and anticipates trauma, we are likely to experience hyperarousal, hypervigilance (persistent fight or flight states, a symptom of PTSD), and an inability to self-soothe. At the same time, our bodies respond by shuttering or dampening sensation. They avoid stimuli, and our bodies become numb. TIY teaches us to quiet our minds and regulate our physical responses. This calms our emotions. The goal is to enable us to recognize and tolerate physical sensations so we regain a feeling of safety inside our bodies.

Watch for Triggers in Yoga

Triggers are basically overly intensive reactions to more or less everyday events, like the unexpected loud noise that makes you jump. Traumatic memories are implicit, autonomic, and unconscious. Our triggers are stored in an unconscious, fragmented form with no sense of order or connection even to themselves. Yet they can be easily activated by sensory inputs in the present moment, causing us to intensely experience reminders of something that happened to us in the past. When we feel activated, or some may use the word *triggered*, it is more than just being mildly annoyed. For those with a history of trauma, encountering something that brings back memories of that trauma can make it feel like they are reliving the original experience in real time.

There are types of trauma triggers to beware of when practicing asanas. Case in point: Having our head down in a yoga pose with our arms back could evoke a memory of being arrested or mistreated with our wrists in handcuffs. Poses that imitate a traumatic event we have experienced should be avoided. We can choose to take the safer alternative or sit this one out. If

What Your Triggers May Be Telling You

Anger tells you when a fundamental need is being ignored or dismissed.

Shame invites you to practice giving yourself love and acceptance.

Jealousy shows you what you want for yourself and where you feel "less than."

Judgment or criticism of others shows you where you judge yourself.

Depression shows you when your soul is not being nourished in how you are living your life.

Overwhelm invites you to pause and release the things you do not need to do.

Exhaustion invites you to put boundaries in place to stop you from overextending yourself.

Dissociation tells you when you are feeling unsafe and invites you to return to your body and ground.

you are working through your own trauma—say you are a veteran or a victim of domestic violence—please understand that "being triggered" is part of a pattern of feeling the sensation of being off-balance, aka physiological disequilibrium, as clinicians would say.

These symptoms could be things like anxiety, muscle tension, and anger. For one person it could be feeling overwhelmed or out of control; for another it may feel like pain and sadness. Really, it could be anything that prompts an increase or return of these or other associated symptoms linked to your trauma. For example, a person recovering from a substance use disorder may be triggered by seeing someone using their drug of choice. The experience may cause intense returned cravings and even relapse.

In Practice
Yoga Therapy/TIY Sequence

Now that you are aware of the precautions, you have the option to try TIY for yourself. This practice is for trauma, anxiety, low self-esteem, poor body image, and distress. It was inspired by Mukunda Stiles's *Structural Yoga Therapy* and my own take from my yoga therapy training at the Yoga Life Institute. The focus is on courage tempered with gentleness, balanced postures, forward folds, twists, and upward-reaching poses.

1. **Alternate Nostril Breathing**. See breathwork directions on page 64.

2. **Contemplation.** Notice that contemplation has the word "temple" rooted within it. We can think of our body as a temple where we house the divine light within, a sacred space inside us. Let's practice paying attention on purpose to our thinking in this space. This can literally be done in a special space set aside for this or just an inward focus. This is an invitation to invoke a sense of wonder and objective curiosity.

3. **Mountain Pose with Equal Breathing.** Mountain is useful for getting a good foundation and sets the standard for

embodiment. It is a cornerstone pose with articulations that can be found in every other yoga posture. Inhale for the count of four and exhale for the count of four.

4. **Standing Warm-Up Half Sun Salute (three times).** This movement is self-directed based on your breath, which gives you a sense of control over your body, practice, and experience.

5. **Tree Pose with Roots Visualization.** Tree is beneficial for grounding your base into the earth like the somatic grounding technique we will explore in chapter 6. This is key to offsetting trauma, which leaves people with their head in the clouds. Tree helps when you feel scattered.

6. **Warrior I to Warrior III Prep.** This flow enables people to find their strength from within and channel their inner warrior. It entails a pose and counterpose.

7. **Down Dog.** This weight-bearing posture builds inner strength at your core and requires engagement in your shoulders and arms, which strengthens them. It is an inversion that brings a fresh blood supply into the brain for mental clarity and stretches the backs of your legs.

8. **Cobra Pose/Locust Post (six times).** This throat-opening pose can help when our throats become locked, which often happens in trauma when one is afraid to speak their truth.

9. **Child's Pose.** This back body stretch is a great home base to return to for comfort and inner child work. As an option, visualize one's body as a baby nestled within the confines of a thousand-petalled lotus or within white light, safe and peaceful.

10. **Half Seated Forward Fold.** This back body stretch is an introspective, inward-turning pose to help people adjust to exploring their inner landscape for the duration of the pose.

11. **Reclined Half Twist.** This pose is used for wringing out the tension from the spine like a wet washcloth. Inhale length into your spine, exhale your belly in, and release detritus that no longer serves.

12. **Plow, or Legs up the Wall/Waterfall Pose.** This inversion rests the heart and stretches the hamstrings. It is good for many issues with the legs, including varicose veins, and hemorrhoids and injuries that are helped by elevating your legs. It literally changes your vantage point to see a new perspective on the world. Imagine a waterfall of vibrancy flooding down your legs, into your torso, and out through your extremities. It is flushing out anything that no longer serves.

13. **Three-Part Breathing.** Inhale to fill the belly, ribs, and chest from the bottom of the torso to the top. Exhale to contract the chest, ribs, and belly from the top back down to the bottom. (See detailed practice on page 50.)

14. **Autosuggestion: Delete Fear and Download Love.** All emotions can be reduced to either fear or love. Observe where you feel fear and tension in your body. Visualize and imagine the violet flame of transmutation floating down from the source as a luminous sphere. Watch it burst over the crown of your head and flow down, over, and through your entire body, all the way down to a cellular level. It is deleting all programs of fear. Breathe them out. Imagine a download of love flooding in. Breathe in the expansive healing energy of love as if it were a type of sparkling spiritual caulking that smooths and coats your entire being. Continue breathing in love and breathing out fear until this feels complete. Say, "[Your name] is free of fear and filled with love." Feel yourself healing or healed. Repeat until you feel clear.

IN PRACTICE
Three-Part Breathing (Dirga Pranayama)

Start with a straight spine and focused attention on your breath moving within your body.

- Inhale: Breathe into and inflate your belly, ribs, and chest, sitting tall.

- Exhale: In descending order, feel your chest, ribs, then belly relax back in toward your spine.

- Continue at your own pace, gradually letting the three parts of the breath flow smoothly without pausing for full and complete inhalations and exhalations.

- Continue for up to five minutes, or for as long as you feel comfortable.

When practiced correctly, dirga pranayama will invigorate and rejuvenate your mind, body, and spirit. Be mindful to avoid forcing your breath or breathing too deeply. It's important for your lungs to feel comfortably full, but not strained. Let your breath be easy and smooth. If your breath becomes strained or you start to feel dizzy or anxious, stop the exercise and let your normal breathing pattern return.

The Issues Are in the Tissues

It is said in yoga and somatics that the issues are in the tissues. This is a scientific fact. Whether you struggle with trauma, anxiety, depression, an eating disorder, or another mental health challenge, being fully alive means being connected with all of who you are in your body and mind. According to this theory, consciousness is embodied, making the ability to tune in to your body one of the most useful skills you can develop as a human. Developing your capacity to pay attention to your body, interpret its signals, and utilize that knowledge to control how you feel about yourself and your life is key to managing the difficulties associated with your mental health. The art and science of trauma therapy, bodywork, and yoga all support this.

Given how important your body is to you remaining on earth, it makes sense that it should play a role in healing. In the West, we have spent decades relying solely on the "thinking mind" to help us make decisions, obtain clarity, and try to solve our issues. Our minds are incredible, as we all know. It's a useful, frequently underutilized resource. More and more, research demonstrates that our emotions and memories are stored in our bodies, not our thoughts. And that brings us back to this book's central premise: We can't think our way through conditions that are rooted in our hearts.

We can't heal pain that's spread all over our bodies just by accessing our thinking minds. Of course, that helps, but it does so mostly *in conjunction* with body awareness. Whether we struggle with painful memories that hold us back, anxiety that has us mentally constructing doomsday, or maybe depression that has us blue and lethargic, it could be we live in a body with which we are at war. Whatever the case, the cause of our pain lives in our body *and* our minds.

My Life as a Yoga Junkie

I have my own history of trauma that I thought was over, but it came out when I first started yoga teacher training in 2001. It was not a trauma-informed style, and I went all in with the physical practice. My fellow trainee Joe and I joked that we were yoga junkies, waking up each day wondering where we could take a class, as if it was a fix. There were others in our training who shared our obsession. Nothing wrong with that, except my perfectionist, type A reaction to it.

I physically pushed myself to the limit and immediately began dropping weight and getting obsessed with the scale. I became self-conscious about the physicality of the practice, as I came from a desk job to the athleticism of Ashtanga yoga. Eventually, I learned to listen to my body and adapted a practice and a teaching style that was intuitively invitational and accessible. In the process, I learned that I was suppressing my anxiety and trauma by masking it with activity, food, productivity, and alcohol. The vulnerability of the practice evoked a trigger for my anxiety. Mind you, this was subtle, and it took a while to gain these insights.

When I cut back on the activity and the alcohol, the food bingeing became a challenge. It was like Whack-A-Mole. Beat one compulsive behavior down and up pops another! Turns out this is a common theme in recovery. The good news is I am becoming more aware of my sensitivities and learning to sit with my emotions rather than mask them. It is uncomfortable as hell yet freeing and helpful at the same time. It may be hard work to face my trauma but it's better than stewing in it! If I had known about TIY back then, it would have been very useful to me in learning about myself and being able to decipher what my body was telling me. I might have come to understand sooner what was happening and been better able to work through my triggers. I was curious, but I didn't know what I didn't know, you know? My goal is still awareness with calm curiosity. I want to come from a place of skill and peace while learning to trust myself. I want to be a healed healer.

Trauma-Sensitive Yoga

I want to do a quick mention of a very specialized trauma yoga called trauma-sensitive yoga, aka Trauma Center Trauma Sensitive Yoga (TCTSY). The name was coined by David Emerson in 2003 at the Center for Trauma and Embodiment at the Justice Resource Institute in Massachusetts. It is a specific clinical program taught under the care of a clinical practitioner. This empirically validated clinical intervention is for complex trauma, chronic treatment-resistant trauma, and PTSD. Emerson advises, "It's a serious clinical intervention and an adjunctive aspect of a broader psychodynamic therapy," he says. "Part of the protocol at the center is that everybody has to be in therapy."

"Trauma-sensitive yoga is best used with people who specifically experience interpersonal trauma, aka traumas perpetrated by people on other people, that take place within relationships. It may include incest survivors and victims of child abuse, neglect, torture, or captivity," says Emerson

(Emerson et al. 2009, 123–8). TCTSY is also helpful for veterans because there are similarities between their being stuck or feeling trapped and what happens with kids and adults who grow up or get trapped within abusive environments. TCTSY is modified to accommodate a trauma-sensitive yoga class similar to TIY with an emphasis on making choices and community. The purpose is to improve the participants' situation or change things to better suit them as individuals.

There is acknowledgment that some of the poses they are invited to try may not actually work for their unique body. For many students, the invitation in both approaches allows people to make choices that feel brand new and even radical to them. They may have never before been empowered in this way. Ultimately the goal is to gain intuitive knowledge of the natural flow in and out of emotions, to realize their impermanence, and to open to deeper experiencing as a healing process.

Looking for Trauma-Informed Teachers?

In laying out standards to differentiate yoga from yoga therapy, we see there are distinctions, and two organizations are trying to define them for us. The Yoga Alliance (YA) and the International Association of Yoga Therapists (IAYT) are two separate nonprofit, membership-based trade and professional organizations for yoga teachers and yoga therapists, respectively. Their voluntary, paid registries recognize teachers and schools who've received a certain standard of yoga and yoga therapy teacher training.

Each organization requires a different amount of training for certification. Twenty years ago, the YA created standards for yoga teachers that required each registered yoga teacher to have a minimum of two hundred hours of teacher training. Recently, after years of developing their own training standards for yoga therapists, the IAYT has a requirement for a minimum of one thousand hours of training to become certified. See the bibliography at the end of the book for links to teachers and organizations.

Yoga Philosophy

Here is where yogic philosophy comes in. The goal of the yoga therapeutic practice is to make a buffer zone, some room for you to consider a response that is more helpful. Along with these are yogic guidelines, dubbed the Eight Limbs of Patanjali's *Yoga Sutras*, for living a meaningful and purposeful life. Each stage is preparation for the next, although we don't always experience them "in order."

You can begin the practice with any of the eight limbs, but Patanjali advises we start with the physical asana postures as a way into the practice to move from the more obvious to the more subtle. Whatever way you start is totally fine, of course! It's said that just as with an infant, all "limbs" and body parts grow concurrently, so in the eight-limbed path, we work on various limbs, at times simultaneously. Patanjali says that by following this path, ignorance (*avidya,* as it is known in Sanskrit) and the obstacles to bliss are removed. The first four stages (limbs) are the concentration on refining personality, gaining mastery over the body, and the development of energetic awareness. These aid in preparation for the second half. These next four stages (limbs) deal with the senses, the mind, and attaining higher states of consciousness.

Foundation of the Yoga Sutras

Patanjali focuses on an eight-limbed, or *ashtanga*, system of discovery. Note that there is also a yoga series you may have heard of called ashtanga that was brought to the United States by the late Pattabhi Jois. Patanjali's ancient system of yogic practices is designed to bring liberation from the patterns of the mind. In other words, the sutras aid and expand on the practice in gaining awareness and transformation.

In Yoga Sutra 1.2, Patanjali lays out the definition and purpose of yoga: *Yogash citta vrtti nirodha: yoga is the cessation of the modifications, or fluctuations, of the mind, aka the chatter.* It means the state of yoga, or quiet, is experienced in a mind that has no longer identified itself with its vacillating waves of perception, or constant babble. It's in the quiet mind, known as the state of yoga, that we achieve mental steadiness.

The Eight Limbs of Yoga

1. The five self restraints, or *yamas,* pertain to abstinences or restraints. Taking a cue from Nischala Joy Devi in *The Secret Power of Yoga*, you can shift the focus from what should be avoided in some of these to what can be created.

    Nonviolence/Ahimsa—avoid causing harm, pain, and judgment to ourselves and others. Do this by developing peace and harmony within.

    Truthfulness/Satya—speaking and living your truth based on love in thought, word, and deed. It means being true to yourself in all that you do.

    Non-Stealing/Asteya—freedom from coveting or taking things or ideas from others. Strive to be generous and grateful. This means not selling yourself or others short. Focus on strengths of self and others. Be mindful of how you spend your time and how much of others' time and energy you take up.

    Self-Restraint/Brahmacharya—moderation and finding middle ground in yoga postures and all activities you do for increased energy. Walk with your own sense of higher consciousness.

    Non-Hoarding/Aparigraha—freedom from greed and taking only what you need. It is how you can use appreciation and gratitude to magnify your abundance.

2. The observances, or *niyamas,* are rules of conduct toward ourselves.

    Purity/Saucha—cleanliness of the body and mind using simplicity and single-pointedness. It helps you create space by clearing out the clutter and excess in your physical space, your mind, and your body.

Contentment/Santosha—is about choosing your state of being and generating your own reality as you work toward your goals. It is like radical acceptance (which we will explore in chapter 8) because it is about how you can accept reality as it is in order to gain freedom.

Self-Discipline/Tapas—is a conscious life choice and fiery determination to meet your goals and burn off impurities that stand in the way of enlightenment. It is about having passion without attachment to any particular outcome.

Self-Study/Svadhyaya—this is self-reflection and introspection. It helps you awaken to all aspects of yourself that you may realize your true nature and real self. Be open to learn from whatever source gives insight, regardless of its origin in any particular race, culture, or creed.

Surrender/Ishvara Pranidhana—is about devotion and love. It is handing over your life and burdens to a Higher Power while standing in your personal power. It encourages you to pay attention to direction from within, as you work to affect change.

3. Asana is posture to make your body strong and rid it of tension for a more peaceful mind. Strive for body awareness with a balance of compassion and challenge. Seek a sense of steadiness in the poses.

4. Pranayama is breath control techniques and breath extension. Steady breath creates a steady mind and aids in energy management.

5. Pratyahara is sense withdrawal, a turning inward and conscious control of the five senses to reduce distractions for peace within.

6. Dharana is concentration and a single-pointed focus of the mind instead of multitasking. You practice drawing your mind back when it wanders off.

7. Dhyana is meditation or uninterrupted concentration or true stillness that is steady. It says release thought and action for a deeper level of being.

8. Samadhi is enlightenment and dropping the sense of self for a feeling of oneness, unity consciousness, and deep peace. It is a state of bliss, love, and freedom.

In the classical texts on yoga known as the *Hatha Yoga-Pradipika*, it is said that the most important aim of any yoga practice is the feature of asanas, especially the focus while in them that sets it apart from other forms of exercise. The point being that they should increase our mental calm and clarity.

Asana itself can be a form of meditation for mental focus if done mindfully. When this happens, *then the Seer* (our witness awareness or the *real us*) is revealed, resting in *its own essential nature* and one realizes the True Self. The goal is to merge the mind into the True Self and thus be true to one's self in how we think, the words we use, and the things we do. Ah-ha! This sounds like the *integrated sense of self* from therapy. It is about seeking the joy found in the experience of the self as our innate spirituality. Often, we don't realize that the joy we are looking for is experienced in the discovery of our True Self. Yoga *is* the study of self (svadhyaya). It is an ongoing process and a life's work. These practices complement the work of our mental health practitioners, using similar, sometimes overlapping techniques, like with mindfulness.

Somatic Yoga Practice as Movement Therapy

Speaking of overlapping techniques, we come to another movement-based therapy to explore called somatic yoga (SY). SY employs mind-body training to manage muscular pain, improve balance and posture, and increase ease of motion. Meet Thomas Hanna, the creator of clinical somatics, a practice for physical healing and pain reduction through mind-body connection, movement, and touch. SY is an offshoot of somatics, the Feldenkrais Method, the Alexander Techniques, Rolfing, tai chi, and yoga. They can all be considered somatics, or methods of bodywork (Eichenseher 2022).

Compared to regular yoga classes at your local studio, somatic yoga activity is slower and more thorough. While resting on the floor, you could practice pelvic tilts while tensing and relaxing the psoas muscle to help it release, which is an illustration of pandiculation that follows. SY retrains our brains to recognize and use the muscles in a different way. It is not a unique style of yoga. The idea is that developmental causes, established patterns, emotional stress, injuries, or trauma may cause our muscles to tighten up or become restricted. In order for these muscles to function more naturally and comfortably, the brain needs to be reeducated through small, progressive, and gentle actions. Want to try?

IN PRACTICE
A Mini Somatic Yoga Experience

Here we'll practice reclined spinal flexion and extension. Start in constructive rest, lying on your back with your knees bent hip-width apart. This practice can complement and strengthen your yoga, giving you a new tool to integrate your mind and your body. For beginners, it could serve as a gentle segue into the practice.

Let's take the subject of learning about your spine for inspiration here. In this position, I invite you to imagine or envision your spine as a starting point. Did you know our spine consists of thirty-three stacked vertebrae? The seven vertebrae of the cervical spine in your neck form an inward C shape. Moving down, tune in to the twelve vertebrae of the thoracic spine in your mid-back, which bend out slightly to make a backward C shape.

The five lumbar vertebrae in your low back bend inward to create a C shape. The sacrum consists of five fused vertebrae that make up the pelvic girdle. Finally, the coccyx, like a tail with its four fused vertebrae, is located at the base of your spine and attached to your pelvic floor muscles and ligaments. Now feel the distinctive spine of your own in this next step. These are questions to ask about your spine with an option of doing so from constructive rest pose and moving into bridge pose.

· · · · · ·

In bridge pose, exhale and press your feet and hands into the ground. Tuck your pelvis under with an option to lift your seat, head straight, then inhale and go back to first pose and ask yourself the following:

- How does my spine move?

- Where is the weight falling?

- How does my spine feel?

Somatic practices are all about getting to know yourself more intimately in a safe and informed practice. Your practice is meant to evolve to meet your ever-changing needs as a dynamic being. The intention is to bring you inward on a deeper level. Like TIY, it is all about reclaiming the ability to make choices about your body.

Everyday Enlightenment

It's true that the state of yoga occurs momentarily in many of us without training. Following periods of concentration, we may often report that we were performing a task (such as reading) in which we became perfectly still. It was noticeable that we lost all sense of time. During these periods of active meditation, access to our intuitive insights becomes available. As a result, we will instinctively understand how to manage ourselves in situations that formerly caused problems.

Patanjali defined this natural process as the state of yoga when he laid it out in the context of the eight limb guidelines. The objective is for these momentary quiet experiences to become part of our everyday living. We could also say this level of mental functioning is characterized by consistent focused attention. This is concentration that is interrupted and steady (dharana and dhyana respectively) and becomes available once we have successively recognized and conquered the lower levels of our incessantly chattering monkey mind. What we want is total absorption of the mind where it is focused so deeply that nothing else can penetrate it, which is pratyahara or withdrawal of the senses.

Healing with Breathwork/Pranayama

Ancient yoga texts also view disease as an imbalance in the flow of *prana*, or life force, in the body. The focus is on improving the functions of the body systems through the proper use of breathing to restore the life force energy to the affected body systems. In this way the yogic approach of applying breathing techniques as an intervention for body disorders or functions is considered to be of critical importance. There is mindfulness in breathwork. After all, breath is life. We come into existence on the physical plane on an inhale and we leave on an exhale. It is our constant companion throughout every moment of our lives. The best part is we can use it for calm, energy, or evenness. Tuning into it gives us feedback on the state of our nervous system and mind.

Did you know hospitals taught pranayama for COVID recovery? They don't call it by the Sanskrit name. It's accurately labeled *breathing techniques*. But really, what is more immediate than breathing? That's what makes it one of the top mindfulness techniques and one of my favorites. For me, mindfulness is the feel of cool water on a hot day. I've heard people complain the term *mindfulness* is overused. I'd say the practice is typically underutilized in modern life, especially with screen time and constant distractions, not to mention a culture of productivity and busyness. What's the antidote? A conscious decision to be present and in the moment-to-moment awareness without judgment. Useful, simple, practical.

Consciously breathing is a popular technique. Most of the time, we don't even know we're breathing because we don't need to. We breathe automatically and without notice. Switching over to a conscious breathing pattern instantly changes everything. We become focused on our breath, and in doing so, we begin to relieve the kind of anxiety that accompanies an unaware way of moving through the world. It's just a shift in perspective, yet it makes all the difference.

Many of us have an unhealthy pattern of holding our breath, especially when we're stressed. By getting the breath moving freely through the body, we can move that stress out of the body and relieve anxiety in the process. When you're feeling anxious, it's important to bring your attention immediately to your breath. We can use breath to tap into the life force energy within and surrounding us. The idea is that the universe is here to guide us and protect us in times of struggle. When we bring our awareness to our breath, we can connect to this sacred life force energy. Isn't that divine?

In Practice
Bumblebee Breathing Technique

Bumblebee breathing is a type of pranayama, or breath control, known in Sanskrit as *Bhramari*, or humming breath. It refers to using your voice to shift into steadiness to offset the effects of stress. Studies show nature sounds decrease cortisol and calm the nervous system.

Prepare by sitting up straight and comfortably.

Step 1: Take a deep breath in.

Step 2: Use your index fingers to plug your ears and make the sound "mmmm" as you hum and breathe out. A humming sound is produced during a slow exhalation with the lips pressed gently together. Make the sound as long as you can, then breathe in again and repeat. The goal is to try to find the level of pressure between them that creates the most vibration through your whole head from the sound.

Step 3: Do this for around eight breaths, paying attention to the reverberation in the bony part of your skull.

This humming sound is particularly effective in stimulating the vagus nerve, the main branch of the parasympathetic nervous system, which helps an over-aroused nervous system to reset, allowing us to relax.

IN PRACTICE
Box Breathing, or 4 x 4 Breathing Technique

Box breathing is a powerful and simple relaxation technique that aims to return breathing to its normal rhythm. This breathing exercise can help to clear your mind, relax your body, and improve your focus. Known as "the breath reset," or four-square breathing technique, it is easy to do, quick to learn, and can be a highly effective technique in stressful situations. People with high-stress jobs, such as soldiers and police officers, often use box breathing when their bodies are in fight-or-flight mode. This technique is also relevant for anyone interested in re-centering themselves or improving their concentration.

Before starting, sit with your back supported in a comfortable chair and your feet on the floor. Visualize your breath like a box with four equal sides.

Step 1: Close your eyes. Breathe in through your nose while counting to four slowly. Feel the air enter your lungs.

Step 2: Hold your breath inside while counting slowly to four. Try not to clamp your mouth or nose shut. Simply avoid inhaling or exhaling for 4 seconds.

Step 3: Begin to slowly exhale for 4 seconds.

Step 4: At the bottom of the breath, when the lungs are empty, hold for a four count.

Step 5: Repeat steps 1 to 3 at least three times. Ideally, repeat the three steps for four minutes, or until a sense of calm ensues.

If you find the technique challenging to begin with, try counting to three instead of four. Once you are used to the technique, you may choose to count to five or six.

Alternate Nostril Breathing

Alternate nostril breathing (ANB) is a yogic breath control practice known as *nadi shodhana pranayama* in Sanskrit, which translates to "subtle energy clearing breathing technique." It is good for facing fears. Say you suffer from agoraphobia, the fear of flying. ANB is good to use when you find yourself on an airplane. Like the previous breathing techniques, I find it has an immediate calming effect. This type of breathwork can be done as part of a yoga and meditation practice, or anytime when you need to offset anxiety and to help quiet and still your mind.

Benefits of alternate nostril breathing include

- relaxation of your body and your mind
- reduction of anxiety and blood pressure and lowers heart rate
- promotes overall well-being

These benefits, in turn, may help you to become focused and aware.

ANB Studies on Stress and Cardiovascular Functions: ANB is a good way to take your Zen off your yoga mat and has a lot of studies supporting it with measurable improvements in helping people to be mindful of the present moment and in lowering stress. This is evidenced by tests showing decreased levels of cortisol, the stress hormone. Cardiovascular function was improved using ANB by significantly lowering factors such as heart rate, respiratory rate, and blood pressure so you can use it to enhance your athleticism and lung function.

ANB Studies on Well-Being show a beneficial effect on blood pressure, heart rate, and vital capacity as well as on physical and physiological fitness-based performance. It also discovered that various yogic breathing techniques have many health advantages, including enhancements to active individuals' brain, pulmonary, and metabolic capabilities. It calms the nervous system as it raises breath awareness. Whatever your goals, try it.

IN PRACTICE
How to Do Alternate Nostril Breathing

Step 1: Sit in a comfortable position.

Step 2: Place your left hand on your left knee.

Step 3: Lift your right hand up toward your nose.

Step 4: Exhale completely and then use your right thumb to close your right nostril.

Step 5: Inhale through your left nostril to the top of the breath and then close the left nostril with your fingers.

Step 6: Open the right nostril and exhale to the bottom of the breath through this side.

Step 7: Inhale through the right nostril and then close this nostril.

Step 8: Open the left nostril and exhale through the left side.

Step 9: This is one cycle.

Step 10: Continue for up to five minutes.

Step 11: Always complete the practice by finishing with an exhale on the left side.

ANB Precautions: If you have a medical condition such as asthma or any other lung or heart concern, please consult your doctor. Adverse effects, such as shortness of breath, while doing the breathing technique indicate you should stop the practice immediately as well as feeling lightheaded, dizzy, or nauseous. If you find that the breathing is bringing up feelings of agitation or that it triggers any mental or physical symptoms, simply stop the practice and return to normal breathing.

In Practice
Calm Breathing Techniques

This type of controlled breathing is sometimes practiced as part of yoga. It is also used within meditation. However, controlled breathing can be practiced on its own without any fancy tools, detailed instructions, or the need for a therapist. All you need to do is change the length of your breaths.

Two-Count Breath is an easy breath that comes from my TIY training and is a good start that is safe for the largest segment of the population. The steps are:

- inhale for the count of two

- exhale for the count of two

Coherent Breathing's goal is to breathe at a rate of five deep breaths per minute. This helps slow the ANS, which generally translates to the count breath cycles that last for the count of six. Dr. Richard Brown, associate professor of Clinical Psychiatry at Columbia University, developed a comprehensive neurophysiological theory of the effects of yoga breathing on the mind and body to relieve anxiety, depression, trauma, and violence symptoms. The steps are:

- inhale for the count of six

- exhale for the count of six

4-7-8 Breathing Ratio, also known as the sedative breath, was developed by integrated medicine expert Dr. Andrew Weil. For this technique,

- inhale for four counts

- hold for seven counts

- exhale for eight counts

An important part of trauma recovery is for survivors to find support in recognizing and responding in a healthy way to their current physiological and psychological states. In TIY, the goal is for participants to notice that yoga can have both stimulating and soothing effects on both the physical and psychological-emotional levels. Balance can be encouraged in the nervous system through poses that incorporate both stimulating and calming postures. The aim is that we tune in to when we most feel safe, soothed, and secure.

Part of the skill of a trauma-informed teacher is to emphasize present-state awareness and offer opportunities for students to choose what brings them balance. Over time, students can build coping skills and make choices that support their transition from being over aroused or under aroused, to a more balanced state. Having a bad day? Want to release pent up tension? An example of how to discharge nervous energy, aka incomplete impulses related to CNS activation, is with the moving chair yoga combo of poses.

In Practice
Discharging Stress with the Moving Chair

The moving chair pose is done by standing with your weight distributed evenly between your feet, then bending the knees as if sitting into a chair with the weight at your heels. Keep knees aligned over your ankles straight forward and parallel with each other. Avoid letting your knees go over your toes. Reach your arms over your head with fingers stretched wide over your head.

> **Step 1:** Inhale and notice your front spine opening as you sink back into an invisible chair. Imagine grasping stress from around your body and mind and making fists of tension with your hands above your shoulders and head.

> **Step 2:** Exhale while folding forward; swing your arms out behind you and up over your head in a forward fold while releasing stress with your fingers outstretched. Sound off with a big "HA!" Be as

loud or as soft as you want. Do this several times or as long as you like before coming back to standing. Check in to see how you feel after having done the sequence six times.

Moving chair is an opportunity to bring your movement and breath together for a quick relaxation fix. Did you also know that the role of movement alone in correcting functional disorders is limited but when tied to the breath, the two work together for better results? Movement with breath is meditation in motion, a form of self-control, and paying attention for direction from within (aka isvara pranidhana). Keep in mind that you can use this to help alleviate various ailments, such as pain, hypertension, and insomnia. Now, there's growing evidence that modified yoga, when taught by specially trained individuals and best in conjunction with therapeutic support, can be a tool of empowerment and healing for those who have experienced trauma. Exchange the word *trauma* for *anxiety* to see why this practice is applicable to most everyone.

Holistic Approaches to Healing Trauma

No discussion of the distinctions between TIY and yoga therapy in a holistic approach to trauma would be complete without further synthesis of its ties and overlap to psychology.

Emotional Regulation

The ability to exert control over our emotional state is emotional regulation, the opposite of dysregulation. It may involve behaviors such as rethinking a challenging situation to reduce anger or anxiety. It could be working with signs of sadness or fear or focusing on reasons to feel happy or calm. Self-awareness is also all about attention and control since using them makes it easier to accept our full selves. Which is to say these are both the qualities we are proud of and those we want to develop.

When we are lacking a clearly defined sense of self it becomes tougher to know exactly what we want. Likewise, if we feel uncertain or indecisive when it comes time to making important choices, we can end up struggling to make any choice at all. Our ability to make decisions in life is greatly aided by having a strong sense of who we are. Knowing what originates from our own selves versus what comes from our programming or the outside, enables us to live genuinely, from minor things like favorite meals to major issues like personal values.

It is easier to regulate ourselves once we have spent time learning what our emotions, triggers, and sensitivities are and how we best deal with them. These are forms of being true to ourselves in speech, or satya. It is also about using self-restraint, or brahmacharya. This often boils down to keeping our cool by doing things that uplift us, such as venting to friends, journaling, exercising, and meditating. These are suggestions you might get in yoga or regular therapy. Another thing that helps in establishing a sense of presence is the use of emotional regulation aids, which could include practicing self-compassion by being kind to yourself, doing your favorite form of exercise, practicing mindfulness meditation, seeking therapy, or sleeping. Try it. Check in and ask yourself what do I need right now to feel better? Maybe it is channeling your creativity to resist mindless or compulsive behaviors. This conscious effort to reach a goal is determination, known as *tapas* in Sanskrit. Sometimes it is as simple as taking three consciously deep breaths.

Study of Self and Interoception

Like Socrates's advice to "Know thyself," the goal of yoga asks us to do the same by exploring our internal state, called interoception. This is your sense of signals that come from inside your body. It lets you know if your heart is beating fast, if you need to breathe more deeply, or if you need to use the bathroom. It lets you know if you are hungry, full, hot, cold, thirsty, nauseated, itchy, or ticklish.

Regions of your brain known as pathways of interoception are the key parts of the brain that seem to add up to your ability to experience the visceral (body, gut, nervous system, and deep inner feeling) part of yourself. This includes being able to feel your muscles contract or extend or to feel your feet on the ground. It is also an important part of the mind-body work for treating trauma. This focus is used to create an integrated sense of yourself so you can feel right, full, or a sense of presence. This sense can be enhanced in therapy and yoga. It is when you feel connected to yourself in a deeper way than normal. I think of it as contentment with your process, or santosha.

Modern Applications

Like the throb of trauma, there are aches and pains that surgery, physiology, or physical therapy cannot reach. Those who are in pain tend to inflict it on others. We can do it to ourselves through disappointment and carry these scars with us until they become us. To offset all this, Mukunda Stiles suggests we delve into a little self-discovery by asking ourselves three questions and reflecting on the one that sparks the most reaction, both mentally and physically.

1. What am I afraid of?

2. What am I angry about?

3. What am I holding on to?

We repeat this process over the course of ten minutes and watch carefully for the body's answers along with mental insights. He suggests "digging deeply with the questions and allowing yourself to open hidden doorways to your body's manner of answering you." In this exercise, my initial answers were that I find I am most afraid of the negation of myself and, ultimately, the death of myself and the ones I love. Much of my fear seems to be rooted in instinctual self-preservation tactics (aka maladaptive coping strategies) that don't work. Underneath my anger is fear. I am holding on to patterns that have roots in my childhood traumas, which I address in therapy and yoga practice. I will continue to work on healing myself to be a fully integrated person.

In moments of clarity, the real me is the part that is able to see all this and know that what I see is not me. With awareness there is a softening in my heart toward my inner child and toward the challenging parts that I'd rather disown. "The Self is empathetic," said Patanjali, who also recommends a deep dive into ourselves to uncover the True Self whose nature is compassion, love, and peace. When faced with situations totally outside our experience, sometimes the best we can do is meditate, reflect, and hand them over to the universe or to our higher consciousness, as we see it.

We may not always be able to be free of pain and suffering from events of the past but there is this from the *Yoga Sutras*, "The suffering from pain that has not yet arisen is avoidable [we can call this anxiety or future worrying or future tripping]. The cause of that avoidable pain is the close association of the Seer (us) with the Seen (current situation) so that one does not differentiate the True Self (the observer)." To me, this means we can reduce our suffering when we experience ourselves as the witness of challenging thoughts and know ourselves as the older, wiser part of ourselves that is able to watch, recall dreams, and is separate from our suffering. We can zoom in to our present-moment experience rather than focusing on the past or the future.

Mindfulness Practices

There are many ways to practice mindfulness. I will outline a couple here and include others in the bibliography at the end of the book.

Self-Compassionate Mindfulness

Self-compassionate mindfulness is invaluable for self-care and is a form of presence and empathy directed at ourselves. When I first heard about this term for being kind to ourselves in the face of perceived inadequacy, failure, and suffering, it immediately drew a parallel in my mind as a similar approach with yoga therapeutics. Both are forms of self-interest and concern. The phrase *self-compassionate mindfulness* was introduced to me by Dr. Kristen Neff in her book *Self-Compassionate Mindfulness: The Proven Power of Being Kind to Yourself.*

This self-kindness is a form of self-study and involves techniques for soothing and comforting yourself when suffering. It is realizing our common humanity, which involves recognizing that pain is an inevitable part of being human. This comes together with the awareness of being open to our pain and suffering in the moment.

This approach allows the gentleness, positivity, and upliftment of yourself that it takes to begin to transform and heal. It's impossible to improve your situation when your energy or vibration is low and you are beating yourself up, right? Passive self-compassion is what Neff likens on her website to "turning inward" (Neff 2024). It would look like someone who is experiencing burnout at work, who goes home to draw a hot bath and play relaxing music at the end of the working day. On the other hand, a more assertive or fierce act of self-compassion is what Neff likens to "acting in the world." For the same person it would be speaking up to their boss about taking some time off or cutting down their current workload. This is covered in Neff's second book, *Fierce Self-Compassion: How Women Can Harness Kindness to Speak Up, Claim Their Power, and Thrive.*

In short, self-compassion sometimes involves letting our bodies know everything is okay with warmth and tenderness (this a form of moderation, or brahmacharya). Other times it means figuring out what we need and ensuring those needs are met. In yoga practice, this could look like backing out of a pose when we feel agitated and simply taking a more passive position (ensuring non-injury/ahimsa). Or we may choose to be more active by speaking to the instructor or finding another class where we do feel safe.

Trauma-Sensitive Mindfulness

Along these lines is a specific meditation that can just be the discipline of being "mindful," in which case you simply pay attention to what you're paying attention to rather than trying to demolish or push away thoughts. Being mindful can sometimes seem contradictory. The goal is obviously to feel less stressed and anxious. If you have suffered trauma, this is particularly difficult to put into practice, as it can send you into a maze of uneasy emotions and ideas. Experts are aware of this paradox, which became trauma-sensitive mindfulness. "When we ask someone with trauma to pay close, sustained attention to their internal experience, we invite them into contact with traumatic stimuli—thoughts, images, memories, and physical sensations that may relate to a traumatic experience," says David Treleaven, author of *Trauma Sensitive Mindfulness.* "This can aggravate and intensify symptoms of traumatic stress, in some cases even lead to re-traumatization."

On the other hand, research suggests that engaging in mindfulness practices can help you more easily manage your brain activity, allowing you to stop worry or distressing thoughts. It's simpler to catch a thought that might make you feel bad before you even feel it when you're aware of what you're paying attention to. It slows you down so you can think before you act. Fortunately, there are a variety of mindfulness techniques that are effective for those who have endured trauma. They urge you to pay attention to your feelings and engage in other present-centered activities when practicing trauma-sensitive mindfulness. These techniques can be very quick, easy, and even pleasurable, like the one that follows.

IN PRACTICE
Mindfulness Eating: A Trauma-Sensitive Practice

To experience a trauma-sensitive practice, you can do a mindfulness eating exercise by grabbing a small, delicious snack that you associate with positive emotions, such as a grape or a piece of chocolate.

Step 1: Find a comfortable spot where you feel safe and at ease to practice eating mindfully and very slowly. Become aware of your breath. Invite your belly to rise on the inhale and to fall on the exhale.

Step 2: Look from the left side of your peripheral vision across your space to the right side of it, as you slowly turn your head side-to-side. Try this for a minute or more as you become aware of the objects in your space. Notice the textures, colors, shapes, and the way the light hits each of these. This moment will never be replicated again.

Step 3: Hold the food in your hand and observe its shape, color, and texture along with the way the light hits it in the moment. Notice the smell. Before taking a bite, notice any sensations in your mouth. Is there salivation? Is there a sense of hunger or anticipation?

Step 4: Take a Small Bite. Place the food in your mouth but pause before chewing. Notice the sensations of it in your mouth. Become aware of the temperature, texture, and any initial flavors you can name.

Step 5: Taste the food. Notice all of the different flavors you can label. Sweet? Bitter? Salty? Begin chewing slowly. How many bites does it take you to finish? Pay attention to the changes in texture and taste. How does the food feel as you chew? Does the flavor change?

Step 6: Reflect on your experience. If your mind wanders, gently acknowledge any thought without judgment and bring your focus back to the experience of eating. After swallowing, pause and notice any lingering sensations or emotions.

Step 7: Take an inventory and explore some more:

- How did the food taste and feel?

- What emotions or thoughts surfaced during your practice?

- Did you feel connected to your body's hunger and fullness cues?

- Were there any moments of discomfort or ease?

Step 8: Practice Self-Compassion. Remind yourself that this experience is about practicing mindfulness, not perfection. Notice how you felt and acknowledge that with kindness. It's okay to have mixed feelings. Celebrate any moments of mindfulness or awareness, no matter how small.

More Trauma-Sensitive Mindfulness Exercises

- Play your favorite music. Try to pay attention to details you've never noticed before.

- Walk while keeping track of your steps. How many steps do you take on the inhale? How about on your next exhale?

- Stretch out. Feel the sensations in your body and breathe out tension.

- Look around you and take note of the many sounds, textures, and colors.

Finding Middle Ground

Moderation is brahmacharya, or self-restraint, and was key in offsetting my yoga junkie mentality, the subject of my first book. Finding middle ground has been a mind-blowing improvement not only in the physical postures but as a goal in all that I do. It helps temper overindulgence or sacrifice to help us retain energy or prana for higher transformational work. This has evolved into a recurring theme I teach in all my classes. The goal is to be like Goldilocks in the poses—not too much, not too little but looking to find the *just right* place. It is always applicable because our threshold is always changing and evolving.

This is all about finding the place between where a little more would be too much yet a little less wouldn't quite be enough. How can we tune in to the body's innate intelligence while respecting our physiological gripping when we get to our edge? This is our body, aka our best friend, protecting us from injury.

We are invited to use our breath as our constant companion and guide to explore our edge on the inhale. Then on the exhale we back away from it until we can relax into the pose. This allows the trauma and stress to release and unravel as our skin loosens off our muscles and muscles ease away from our bones. In being present, as we continue to learn to be fully in our bodies, they will let us know where they hold sadness, gladness, pleasure, and pain. Maybe we can think of the practice of yoga as a time to feel loved, free, and fully alive. Can we be open to the variations of these feelings and allow the distinction between them to dissolve? Maybe we give ourselves permission to do less, be authentic, and work through powerful emotions as they come up?

These multiple questions all have the same answer: Yes. But only when we feel safe enough. That is, when we feel it is an accessible yoga practice where we feel in charge. In my experience, a lot depends on me making a connection between my body and my mind, to what is happening in the space, and if I trust the teacher. Self-acceptance through awareness over self-improvement is really the point of yoga for me. *It's the journey of the self, through the self, to the self,* according to the Bhagavad Gita, the best known of all the Indian scriptures and one of its most famous epic poems. It's said that a yoga class without any type of meditative quality or awareness isn't actually yoga. It's just exercise.

We want our yoga to help us become more aware of our bodies, minds, breath, and emotions by watching the processes in our bodies and minds as a witness. Meditation is an important yoga practice and one of the most powerful tools to help us find our inner selves, to calm/silence the mind, and to attain self-awareness. It's no surprise then that the practice of self-awareness is promoted by doctors, psychotherapists, coaches, healers, and all kinds of experts in the field of human potential development.

Self-awareness is considered a basis for both physical and psychological well-being. Both yoga and therapy are paths toward achieving this. Ultimately, the awareness that is gained in yoga would spill out past our mats and into our daily lives. A worthy goal! Personally, I don't have the headspace, time, or inclination to do something unless it is applicable and helpful to my everyday life. I am sure you don't either, dear reader. Reaching awareness is necessary in order to find the sweet spot during asana practice, in which the yogi shifts from focusing on the physical aspects of holding a pose into the mental clarity and stillness that the asana brings.

Focusing Techniques

Focusing techniques can bring you to center and back to the present moment. Here I outline two techniques that work for me.

Breathing Prompt

While at rest in corpse pose (savasana) try an additional technique that I like to add in the final rest at the end of yoga practice. It is not a breath ratio and does not entail achievement, so it is effortless but comes from the late BYS Iyengar, father of Iyengar yoga. Once relaxed, focus on your in and out breaths. Each time you inhale, as the air hits the inside of the lungs the individual consciousness recedes to make way for the Divine. On the exhale, the two merge. I love staying with this one for a while. This is the coming together of the lower with the higher self, which we call the state of yoga.

Gaze Point, Bandha, and Mudra

Besides the previous breathing technique, examples of some other tools for calm and steadiness are points of focus. Try the gaze point, or *drishti* for each pose. Steady gaze for a steady mind. This keeps the mind from wandering off. The internal locks, or *bandhas*, use specific muscle engagements for stabilization and to increase or direct your energy. Then there are the specific hand postures, or *mudras*, to direct your energy and attention. Steady gaze, internal strength, and intentional postures all contribute to a steady mind.

Autosuggestion Technique

Simply put, autosuggestion is positive self-talk. Émile Coué, a pharmacist and psychologist, created this psychological strategy at the start of the twentieth century. It is connected to the placebo effect. While Coué believed in medicine, he found that patients often fared better when he emphasized the likelihood of success. And yes, that's the kind of bedside manner I want from my doctor! When I first met my oncologist, she told me the facts of my case and that I would live forever. I had to smile. It helped to dissipate the dark cloud that the cancer diagnosis had brought on. It was just the kind of remark that endeared her to me even after I left her practice to join Sloan Kettering's survivor program. This is the promise of autosuggestion, as a type of uplifting self-talk used to help you control your ideas, feelings, or actions. The method is frequently applied during self-hypnosis. Of course, the good news is you don't need your doctor to do it because it is self-directed.

In a nutshell, autosuggestions are a very powerful technique for reprogramming your subconscious mind by suggesting a positive statement in the second-person as if addressing yourself. *Jackie is a critically acclaimed writer*, for example. Autosuggestions can be used alone or in combination with positive affirmations, depending on the beliefs you want to overwrite and how you feel about them. Autosuggestion is your body's way of communicating with itself. It functions by asking or telling your subconscious mind to alter your perception and conduct in order to get better outcomes. Negative language would therefore have undesirable outcomes, in contrast to how positive talk would produce beneficial results. This is a technique for instilling your exact desires in your subconscious.

Autosuggestion can be used for self-healing, letting go of negative emotions, and processing positive ones in their place. Breath, movement, feelings, touch, and imagery are combined creatively. By actively eliminating the harmful emotions or programming, the idea is to download the opposite feeling and then invite in the healthier emotions. If you think about it, you are utilizing autosuggestion all the time, so always try to be kind to yourself. Too often, we are our own worst enemies and frequently blame ourselves unjustifiably and in ways we would never dare to judge another person. Never be critical of yourself because by doing so, your subjective mind will unintentionally get a negative autosuggestion, which it will eventually embrace and adopt as its own.

Try this. If you notice your inner critic bringing you down, sincerely apologize to yourself as you would to someone else. Then replace your negative autosuggestion with a constructive one.

IN PRACTICE
Autosuggestion

Here are some autosuggestions to try. Feel free to customize!

- [Your first name], you are so loved. Everybody loves and cares for you.

- [Your first name], you have the whole universe on your side. Everything is going your way.

- [Your first name], you are such a confident person. You are so strong and intelligent.

- [Your first name], I think the best of you. I accept you in every way.

- [Your first name], it is so wonderful to see you in your natural, joyful state.

- [Your first name], you are such a wonderful person.

Affirmations

Affirmations may be considered as a type of autosuggestion or positive self-talk. A positive affirmation is a helpful statement best stated in the positive, present tense, and in the first person, such as *I am prosperous, I am healing, I am getting stronger every day.* A positive affirmation is similar to a kind word. Use them to boost your self-esteem and make you feel good. They can help you to challenge and overcome self-sabotaging and negative thoughts. As you repeat them often and believe in them, you can start to feel positive changes. For example, evidence suggests that affirmations can help you to heal, to perform better at work, to play an instrument, or to improve in athletics. I have a whole bunch of them on sticky notes around my office and stuck to my meditation altar that I use every day. It has been life changing.

Affirmations aid you in letting go of negative emotions, and processing positive ones. Breath, movement, feelings, touch, and imagery are combined creatively. By actively eliminating the bad emotions or programming, the idea is to download the opposite feeling and then invite in the healthier emotions. As the Buddha said, "The mind is everything. What you think, you become." This is a way to become the conscious choosers and creators of our lives. You may want to create your own affirmations. Craft them to be meaningful and inspiring to you.

Affirmation vs. Mantra

While affirmations are a declaration that complements who you are as a person or confirms who you want to be, mantras are sacred sounds that attune your energy to the power and meaning of the word or phrase. There's been several references in this book to mantra so far, so let's dive deeper. Did you know that the word *mantra* originated from the Sanskrit language and means "the thought that liberates and protects"? That means that a mantra is a thought or word(s) said out loud that quiets your mind and allows it to focus on an intention.

Mantras prepare you for meditation and provide a quiet mind by gently training the mind to find the stillness in repetition and to attune to a higher consciousness. I always say that mantra is like a rowboat to help you traverse the rocky waters of your mind. How? By cancellation. The mantra replaces your thinking and your thinking cancels your mantra so you are left with silence. Mantra helps control the chattering mind.

Embody Your Mantra

If you really want to integrate practices, try a moving mantra embodiment practice with yoga. Knowing the healing value of your physicality, we return to the ongoing theme of embodiment. You can use mantra to add another dimension to your healing toolbox by physically and verbally expressing it simultaneously. This is something I do as another layer to my yoga, or it could be done in walking meditation, dancing, etcetera. Use your imagination and creativity. It's fun! For example, you could pick an

English mantra such as *Peace* or you can use your own customized affirmation from the affirmation exercise. In chapter 8, you will have a chance to try Sanskrit and Buddhist mantras.

IN PRACTICE
Embody Your Mantra

In matching your breath with your movement, you create a meditation in motion in yoga. You can "embody mindfulness" with a meaningful mantra to embody your intention for physical manifestation. Let's try it with a half sun salute for the moving part. Ready?

Step 1: Stand in mountain pose and state your mantra.

Step 2: Inhale your arms up and state your mantra.

Step 3: Exhale and fold forward, repeating your mantra.

Step 4: Inhale and rise up halfway, repeating your mantra.

Step 5: Exhale and fold again and repeat your mantra.

Step 6: Inhale and rise up to stand back in mountain with your hands pressed together over your heart and repeat your mantra.

3

Healing Through the Body's Energy Centers/Chakras

The body is the vehicle, consciousness the driver.
Yoga is the path and the chakras are the map.

**CHAKRA GURU ANODEA JUDITH, AUTHOR, THERAPIST, BODY/
MIND INTEGRATION, SOMATIC THERAPY, AND YOGA TEACHER**

Your seven body chakras, or "wheels of light," are energy points or centers aligned with your spine that can energize or soothe your body to affect your emotional and physical well-being. Pronounced with a *ch* sound, the chakras are thought to be spinning disks or concentrations of energy that correspond to bundles of nerves and major organs. Learning how energy moves through the chakras, you can begin to invite it to flow freely through your body for healing and greater health. The life-force energy that flows through the chakras is called *prana* in Sanskrit; it's called *chi* as in "tai chi" from Traditional Chinese Medicine; and in Japanese it's *qi* as in "qigong." All these traditions point to the same thing: that you need this life-force energy to flow in a balanced way without it getting stuck or moving too quickly for your overall well-being.

Your energy system is another mind-body tool to assist in your search for wholeness. Carl Jung advised that the attainment of wholeness requires one to stake one's whole being and that nothing less will do. There can be no easier conditions, no substitutes, and no compromises. Working with the chakras can deepen your self-knowledge. For the chakras, yoga employs internal practices of mantra, pranayama, and meditation. The beauty is that all of this you can and must do for yourself versus relying on a practitioner.

If this esoteric spiritual concept offends your intellect, perhaps consider the following chakra work to be a psychological support option from your holistic tool belt. At least to begin. Maybe it can be a gateway, a process of self-discovery. Who knows? You may even become enticed to delve deeper into the layers of self with this modality.

Given the importance of the chakras, it is good to have the ability to clear out congestion and align them. You might think of this light energy as inherent goodness, well-being, or a glow radiating from points running along your spine going from the base to the crown of your head. Some even say there are 114 different chakras or more, but the seven main ones are the body chakras most often referenced in the West. In traditional yogic wisdom, they are described as energy vortexes in your body, corresponding to key organs, bundles of nerves, and other regions of your energetic body that have an impact on your emotional and physical well-being. They are believed to be spinning disks of energy that function best when open and aligned.

At their best, these convergences of energy, both in your body and on the paths out of it, enhance efficiency. On the other hand, they create blockages or can be sources of illness and disease in your body and mind (Stelter 2023). What if this ancient philosophy of the chakra healing system provided wisdom for modern life on how you can best care for your psychological and physical health by using them? Each of these seven main chakras has a corresponding number, name, color, keynote, and health focus. These features will be useful when we get to the practice portion. At their heart, the chakras of the body are what Hindu spiritual traditions describe as seven centers of concentrated metaphysical energy that are known as your subtle, or etheric, body. They are the part of your makeup you cannot see but you can feel as energy in the space around your body.

Chakras for Eternal Youth

Some, like Peter Kelder, go so far as to say that the chakras are the fountain of youth. In his best-selling book from 1998, *The Ancient Secret of the Fountain of Youth*, Kelder's idea is that your chakras control and are key to preserving your health and vitality. He says that your chakras control your endocrine system's seven glands, which in turn control all your bodily activities. This includes the aging process. If this intrigues you like it did me, he offers yoga poses to do each day in about ten minutes, if you streamline them. I'd say the average person would find them accessible, outside of the spinning part, which is tough if you suffer from vertigo.

These poses are used to maintain the good health and rapid rotation of the chakras so that your vital life energy can pass through your endocrine system. According to Kelder, in a healthy body, the chakras rotate at high speeds, allowing prana, or etheric energy, to flow upward through your endocrine system. The flow of vital energy is, however, impeded or obstructed if one or more of these vortexes start to slow down, which he says is simply another name for illness.

Chakras: The Little Brains of the Body

Although the chakra system may be popular among yoga practitioners, it is often regarded as myth in scientific communities, mostly because scientists in the West have conducted very little research on the topic. Yet research *is* emerging. If you are curious about chakra research in your energy system, check out Dr. Joe Dispenza's program *Blessing of the Energy Centers* on his *Rewired* series offered on Gaia TV. In it he equates coherence, or a state in which all the parts of the seven body chakras operate together, as a means to create wholeness. Dispenza says you can think of each chakra as an individual center of information or clusters of neurological networks he calls mini-brains. Each has its own specific energy that carries a corresponding level of consciousness, its own emission of light expressing very specific information. Each also has its own individual glands, hormones, chemistry, and individual network of neurons.

Dispenza reasons that if each one of those centers has its own individual brain, then each also has its own individual mind in which each receives, processes, or expresses energy. When they are blocked, they no longer produce a healthy neurological mind to send the necessary signals to the associated parts of the body where these centers connect. When those mini-brains become coherent or balanced, they send logical messages through the organs, tissues, and cells to each area of the body that's related to the corresponding center. Dispenza says that when the parasympathetic nervous system (again, your rest and digest mechanism) is switched on, the chakras are able to be clear and that creates order in your nervous system for healing.

In other words, balanced chakras send clear messages to the rest of your body and cells for healing so that you can reprogram your ANS with your mind-body connection. He is saying that thinking and feeling or using your mind can activate your neurological centers. They work together. You can then see how powerful your thoughts are and that they do create your reality. Dispenza's mind-body research proved the connection in a study where subjects were directed to only think of enlarging their biceps. These thoughts did have a measurable effect in comparison with those in the control group who did not focus their thoughts on muscle growth. Dispenza's meditation method for tuning in to your own energy and enhancing well-being aims for coherence in each chakra. He feels that these body sites are much more than just chakras. At each of these sites, specific endocrine glands are situated, each with a separate brain.

He says you can achieve coherence in each of your energy centers by tuning in, establishing coherence, and delivering chakra healing throughout your entire body intentionally. In turn, you may stimulate your autonomic nervous system, calm down your brainwaves, and rewire yourself through guided meditation. Be sure to set your intention when working with your chakras.

Physicality of the Chakras

We know experimental research on the chakras is limited, yet several scholars link the chakras with anatomical locations and functions in your physical body, which you can see below. Check out the correlations between the seven body chakras and how they relate to the glands of your endocrine system. Researchers then reasoned that the function of the associated endocrine gland must have something to do with the spiritual, psychological, psychosomatic, and physiological functions attributed to the chakra as follows (Pope 2018):

CHAKRA CENTER	RELATING TO BODY'S GLANDS
Root	**Gonads/Ovaries** govern sexual reproduction
Sacral	**Adrenals** regulate metabolism and the stress response
Solar Plexus	**Pancreas** regulates your digestive system
Heart	**Thymus** builds immunity defenses
Throat	**Thyroid** controls metabolism, growth, and more
Third Eye	**Pineal** regulates sleep and wakefulness
Crown	**Pituitary** regulates bodily functions such as growth

Anatomical Theories of the Chakras

Looking at the chakras as they correspond to the physical structures in your body is what clinical neuropsychologist Richard Maxwell offers with his Anatomical Theory of the Chakras. This model for comprehending the chakras focuses on gap junctions, which are the connections and channels between the cytoplasm (think cell gel) of two nearby cells that allows communication between them. According to Maxwell's theory, all of these spine-based, centralized, communication networks of your body are controlled by the chakras (Gibson Ramirez 2024). They inform each other on many levels.

Functional Theory of the Chakras

Rather than controlling a specific part of your body, another theory links your chakras with your brain-body structures that provide your conscious mind with information about your CNS and its processes. This is according to Joseph Loizzo, Assistant Professor of Clinical Psychiatry in Complementary and Integrative Medicine at Weill Cornell Medical College. His work compares and connects modern maps of the CNS with maps of the subtle body in an attempt to explore the subtle body through CNS function. He calls this meditative mind-brain-body integration (Loizzo 2016).

Loizzo's Model of Chakras Corresponding to CNS

Here's how Loizzo lays out how the chakras can be cross-referenced with maps of the CNS:

CHAKRA CONNECTION	TO CNS MAPS
Crown Chakra	**Neocortex**, or the center for higher brain functions such as perception, decision-making and language
Third Eye Chakra	**Prefrontal Cortex**, which governs cognitive control functions such as impulse inhibition and cognitive flexibility/adaptability
Throat Chakra	**Limbic System**, involved in our behavioral and emotional responses, especially behaviors you need for survival
Heart Chakra	**Midbrain**, which governs motor movement and auditory/visual processing

Chakra Connection	To CNS Maps
Solar Plexus Chakra	**Pons** (part of the brain), which regulates your breathing and REM sleep that processes information and consolidates memories
Sacral and Root Chakras	**Medulla Oblongata,** which controls autonomic activities such as heartbeat and respiration

Note that Loizzo feels that scientists cannot empirically assess this theory because the technology to prove this has yet to be discovered. It doesn't exist yet.

Psychological Theory of the Chakras

Though the chakra system grew from Eastern philosophy, one of my favorite new age authors, Dr. Anodea Judith, interpreted the texts and made the knowledge more accessible for the rest of us. As founder and director of Sacred Centers, Judith is considered one of the country's foremost experts on the combination of chakras and therapeutic issues. She is known as the guru of the interpretation of the chakra system for the modern lifestyle.

I love how her work embodies an integrated approach. Her popular book *Eastern Body, Western Mind: Psychology and the Chakra System as a Path to the Self* impressed on me the layers I could excavate in doing the chakra work as it related to my emotional and mental constitution. Judith sets out healing strategies of the chakra system using the framework of psychology. Like all good trauma experts, she emphasizes the importance of getting into the connection of your body and mind for healing. She explained, "To lose our connection with the body is to become spiritually homeless. Without an anchor we float aimlessly, battered by the winds and waves of life."

She inspired me to work through being uncomfortable in my own process, to turn inward, to contemplate my own strengths and weaknesses.

This journey led me to find alternate approaches to growth. Judith compares the various maps of psychological development, including Freud's, Piaget's, Erikson's, and Reich's models.

The Chakra System Related to Maslow's Hierarchy of Needs

Remember Maslow's Hierarchy of Needs, where your most basic needs (food, water, and shelter) need to be met before you can work your way up toward meeting the higher needs of self-actualization? Judith relates chakra theory to these psychological development stages by outlining the order of needs that you must satisfy in order to develop and grow into the next stage. I appreciate how she adds another layer of integration for deeper understanding. Here's how Judith correlates Maslow's needs-based ladder with the chakras:

THE CHAKRA SYSTEM RELATES TO . . .	MASLOW'S HIERARCHY OF NEEDS CORRESPONDS WITH THE . . .
Physiological Needs	Root Chakra
Safety Needs	Sacral Chakra
Belonging	Solar Plexus Chakra
Self-Esteem	Heart Chakra
Self-Actualization	Throat Chakra
Transcendence	Third Eye and Crown Chakras

The Chakra System Related to Psychosocial Development

Judith also relates the chakra system to Erick Erikson's stages of psychosocial development. The idea is that your personality develops in a kind of predetermined order from infancy to adulthood. This affects your well-being, as you can see in the next chart. Basically, Erikson's theory outlines eight stages of psychosocial development from infancy to late adulthood. At each stage, you face a conflict between two opposing states that shapes your personality. Successfully resolving the conflicts leads to virtues such as hope, will, purpose, and integrity. Challenges in these stages lead to outcomes of mistrust, guilt, role confusion, or despair. Don't worry, these stages can be resolved successfully at a later time. Maybe this can be done through mind-body work and many of the ideas presented in this chapter. The strong suit of this theory is how it can provide a useful framework for mental health providers treating patients facing major life adjustments or developmental turning points (McLeod 2024).

The Chakra System Relates to . . .	Erickson's Psychosocial Development
Root and Sacral Chakras	The Trust vs. Mistrust stage (if needs are dependently met, the infant develops trust)
Solar Plexus Chakra	The Autonomy vs. Shame and Doubt stage (toddlers exercise will and learn to do things for themselves or they doubt themselves)
Heart Chakra	The Initiative vs. Guilt stage (preschoolers learn to initiate tasks and carry out plans or they feel guilty about plans to be independent)
Throat Chakra	The Industry vs. Inferiority stage (children learn the pleasure of applying themselves to tasks or they feel inferior)
Third Eye Chakra	The Intimacy vs. Isolation stage (teens test roles and integrate into a single identity or are confused) and /or the Generativity vs. Self-Absorption stage (the middle-aged develop a sense of contributing to the world or not)
Crown Chakra	The Integrity vs. Despair stage (the older person looks back over their life and feels a sense of satisfaction or lack)

Judith goes on to relate chakra theory to a number of other psychological theories of development, such as Piaget's stages of cognitive development and Freud's psychosexual stages. Really, the main difference between chakra theory and psychological theories of development is that chakra theory correlates growth to energy stored and held in the body. In this way, Judith shows how viewing development through the lens of the chakras is more holistic, embodied, and attuned to the mind-body connection.

She adds another dimension to those original psychological models. Because of this, some scholars proposed chakra theory as a stand-alone model for growth-oriented development that is distinct from traditional psychological views of development.

I also appreciate that Judith applies the chakra system to important modern, social realities. She delves into issues like those we address on the mental health network, such as addiction and other compulsive behaviors. She also explores codependence, family dynamics, sexuality, and personal empowerment. In working with the chakras, you might also think of them as both transmitters and receptors. The idea is the frequency at which you emit energy will match the frequency of what you receive in your life. It's like the Law of Attraction idea that everything is energy. If you match the frequency of the energy you want, you can better help create that reality for yourself. Let's explore this.

Areas of Opening

Would you like to attune to the messages of your body chakras? In your journey through your chakras, you may encounter openings that could be internal, external, physical, emotional, and spiritual in nature. Here's an example. An internal opening could be when you work to mend your broken heart from a loss. Maybe that wall you previously built around it to protect yourself comes down as you heal. In turn, you learn to trust again.

Chakra charts are widely available, but here is a breakdown in the terms I learned in yoga teacher training and in various workshops throughout the years. Think of your back body as protective, like a shell. The back of your body represents yang, will, and masculine aspects. It is all about defense, invulnerability, action, or even inaction. The front of your body is yin, the feminine aspect of your emotions, feeling, spirit, and vulnerability.

There's more. The right side of your body holds energies that are closely associated with what you might define as the traditional masculine traits. Generally, masculine characteristics such as assertiveness, determination, decisiveness, and the ability to move forward create positive energies. Other masculine traits, such as aggressiveness, obstinance, impulsivity, and recklessness may carry negative energies. Likewise, there are good and negative energies connected to typical feminine traits. Positive traits include generosity, thoughtfulness, compassion, and nurturing. Negative traits include instability, frailty, and contentment with the status quo. Sometimes it might be challenging to move ahead in life because of an emphasis on the past.

Although our communities may still urge youngsters to focus on the traditional features of their gender, these traits have little to do with your gender. You must possess both positive masculine and feminine traits if you are to grow into a well-rounded human being. You will notice that every chakra possesses characteristics from both gender-related groupings when you examine its various facets. The root chakra is one illustration of this. Feeling steadfast and confident in your work could be considered a masculine trait while feeling a connection to Mother Earth's loving energies might be seen as a feminine trait. Our goal here is to balance all aspects of ourselves. As you explore your mind-body connection with yoga and getting into your body, it is good to be aware of the types of openings you may encounter in this process.

Types of Opening

Pain-filled types of openings can cause nausea, dizziness, irritability, and physical plateaus. If this happens it is best to pause, back off, and take a break. You can recognize openings for what they are. They are an opportunity to focus inward and ask what the message is. Then you can work on that chakra with whatever techniques speak to you. Read on for options below.

Ecstatic openings may feel like a huge sigh of relief as you open the tight parts of your body and stuck emotions. It is said that as the heart chakra opens, you might experience a surge of the subtle life-force energy moving in and out of the heart. It might create a feeling of immense joy, compassion, and bliss.

Delve into the elements of each chakra by trying yoga poses that explore the part of your body associated with a specific chakra, such as grounding in tree pose for the root chakra, for example (Judith 2015). A direct way to balance your chakras is to create alignment in your physical body while in a meditative state. Your body reflects your imbalances to help you discover how each chakra is functioning. When you align your subtle and physical bodies, you create a more balanced, stable, solid base. In turn, this will enable you to be more sensitive to the energetic qualities of the chakras.

As you work with each of the following seven body chakras, I invite you to try breathing techniques for homeostasis, to surround yourself with or wear the associated chakra color to use them consciously and integrate them into your life (Segal 2010, 290). You can use meditation, visualization, mudra, and even foods specific for each chakra to deal with the associated issues, working from the root or bottom up. Try saying, humming, singing, or chanting the resonant sounds and seed mantras. Note that you can use the seed, or Bija, mantra as a stimulating sound. In addition, you might layer in another technique (Judith 2015, 323) by using the resonant sounds for clearing the chakras then the seed sounds for stimulating them. When in doubt, Judith suggests using the resonant mantra for clearing your chakra first. Then use the corresponding seed mantra for stimulating the chakra second. Clear then stimulate is the general order of operation.

First Energy Center:
Root/Muladhara Chakra

BASIC ELEMENTS

Resonant (Clearing) Sound: OH as in *road*

Seed/Bija (Stimulating) Mantra: LAM

Keynote: C

Color: Red-color therapy to bring passion, heat, power,
   movement, and action into your life. Draws money,
   opportunity, and prosperity into your life.

Element: Earth

Location: Base of spine and pelvic floor

Body Parts: Sexual organs, reproductive system, hips,
   knees, and joints. It extends from your legs to your feet.

Root Chakra: "I Am"

This is the first chakra and the seat of your kundalini, or life-force energy. It lies dormant until activated (by meditation, breathwork, and yoga) and is channeled upward through your chakras for enlightenment. Your root energy center, aka *muladhara* in Sanskrit, translates to root of existence. The emotional characteristics of your root are survival, safety, and feeling secure. It deals with survival and your most basic means of food, shelter, money, namely all the things that preserve you. In the context of trauma healing, your root is important because bringing it into balance enables you to feel supported and safe in your own body. This safety feeling is the groundwork (pun intended) for healing trauma, which you will see emphasized throughout this book. The root chakra focus is on presence and feeling stable. Being calm, centered, and connected to earth, nature, and all beings is the goal.

Your root chakra is also your roots and where you came from. This includes your tribal instincts and family ties, and it links you to your family of origin. It is here you can experience your foundation, grounding, extending your roots, and surrendering to gravity. This is the digestive area of your body that encompasses elimination for getting rid of waste after the nutrients have been absorbed. Similar to how you would prune the dead parts off a plant, you can rid yourself of the non-serving programming you've outgrown.

Even if you have a roof over your head, you might still struggle in this area because of the stress of modern life. Maybe you never really feel fully grounded, present, or able to relax. Technology has exacerbated this issue with constant distraction, the addictive quality of social media, and a frenzied pace of 24-7 connectivity. In *The Social Dilemma* documentary, research shows exposure of the internet causes us to have 50 percent more life experience than the generations before us. Tragically, it is taking a toll with increased anxiety and higher suicide rates in teens and preteens.

This underscores the value of tech hygiene tips, including taking social media breaks, being mindful of what you allow in via your feeds, and taking a news fast. I love nature for getting grounded and connecting to the cycles of the earth. Spend time in the quiet solitude of a sunset, walk in the woods, or watch white fluffy clouds float across a big blue sky. Taking care of yourself is significant because you are important. Love is your divine birthright, and you have the right to be here. Working with your root chakra will get you connected to the larger tapestry of life. Like we say in yoga, you've got to ground to grow, root down so that you can rise tall to your full potential, radiant soul!

Root Chakra In Balance When your root is clear and balanced, you are more likely to feel a strong sense of security and groundedness that allows you to try new things, take risks, and enjoy your life. You gain energy and self-confidence rather than arrogance or fear. You take care of yourself, practice self-regulation, have connection to earth and others, and get your basic needs met. As a result, you are more ready for what life brings. You will know your root chakra is balanced when you feel supported and safe in your own body, which brings healing on all levels. By working with your root chakra, you will branch out from your solid roots to try new things and take risks.

Root Chakra Out of Balance When your root is out of balance, you may feel anger, fear, insecurity, and the need to manipulate or control things in your life in order to feel safe. It is being stuck in a fight for survival. Have you heard of those who see red with anger? We could say they are experiencing a root chakra out of balance. Without the tether of your roots, you may feel low energy and spacey. Other evidence of root chakra issues could include

- problems in the legs, feet, rectum, tailbone, and immune system

- issues with the reproductive parts and prostate gland

- degenerative arthritis, knee pain, sciatica, eating disorders, and constipation

- stress about money and financial security
- lack of safety and trust in your body, maybe with overconcern for how it looks

Areas of Opening in Your Root Chakra There are areas of opening you might experience that give you information about where to focus your attention for healing.

FRONT BODY OPENINGS

- pelvis and upper thighs can hold issues of trust, fear of intimacy, and holding on

KNEES CAN HOLD:

- conflict with authority
- fear of commitment
- inflexibility or stubbornness
- not wanting to move forward

ANKLES CAN HOLD:

- early anger
- fear of the world, like the world is not a safe place
- fear of being alive

FEET CAN HOLD:

- our belief systems
- cramps may indicate questioning our belief systems or feeling criticized for our choices

How Trauma May Present in the Root Chakra As you know, life-threatening traumas at any age disrupt your ability to trust that life is safe enough and that you have the capacity to take care of and protect yourself. Examples of things done for self-preservation and security might be binge behaviors. These could include binge buying, excessive screen time, or binge eating or drinking. This may even include stubborn tendencies and hoarding for fear of not enough. These may result from energy that is stuck in the first chakra from fear. Trauma divides you from your body. Early abuse may cause you to question your fundamental right to be here. Rather than being a source of safety and support, family may be a source of struggle and pain. Maybe there are multiple things at once. As you heal from trauma, you can treasure each regained piece of physical awareness. You may sense your determination to survive as you battle old patterns of despair. I find it helpful to focus on progress instead of perfection. Remember, healing is a journey.

ROOT CHAKRA STORY
From Struggle to Balance

In 2001, after leaving an abusive relationship, moving across the country, starting a new life and relationship, getting married, the events of 9/11, and leaving an unfulfilling corporate career, I started struggling with an eating disorder. These three root chakra challenges were survival, purpose in life, and money worries. Alan Finger, a master teacher and the creator of Yoga Works, Be Yoga, and Yoga Zone, affirms that bulimia and obsessive eating are symptoms of a root chakra imbalance. This is what I experienced.

Despite my initial attraction to yoga, anxiety and my desire to find alignment with my soul's mission resulted in a destructive cycle of bulimia. Finger verified the connection for me. If there was a theme to my recovery, it would be all about finding the balance in nourishing my body and soul. Meditation and mindfulness, coupled with mindful eating, became crucial in curbing my compulsive behavior. Navigating the physical and emotional challenges, I found equilibrium by restructuring my diet, experimenting with fasting, veganism, and vegetarianism before settling into intuitive eating (Tribole 2003).

Intuitive eating is a simple idea recommended to me from a family education program on disordered eating, and it is a way to make peace with all types of food. Unlike traditional diets that restrict or ban certain foods, intuitive eating requires you to stop looking at food as good or bad. Instead, you learn to listen to your body and eat what feels right for you. You might think this means you just eat whatever you want, anytime you want. That's not the case. Experts say intuitive eating means tapping into your body's natural ability to tell you when you're hungry or satisfied. It's about practicing a pause and checking in for satiety clues. When you eat intuitively, you also let go of the idea that you need to lose or gain weight so you can look a certain way. The idea is to help you focus on foods that work best for your overall physical and mental health. For me and many others, this is an ongoing process.

Old cravings come back sometimes, but recognizing them and talking about them with my support system—aka my husband and my therapist (separate people)—has helped me maintain my recovery. Participating in a weekend intensive yoga program for eating disorders called *Eat, Breathe, Thrive* with Chelsea Roth was a game changer. I went with an old friend and this allowed for a profound release of fear, shame, guilt, and humiliation while also providing useful tools for advancement. When I come out to myself and others, it helps me to take responsibility for my actions and to talk about it, which helps to lessen the embarrassment.

Since then, my work with mental health, my commitment to self-awareness, and my connection with my root chakra's intuitive nature have all helped. Yoga has helped me by diminishing my anxiety and building my awareness. Taking care of my plants, going on daily hikes with my dog, and practicing grounding help me discover self-care in nature and maintain my equilibrium. Rejuvenating my root chakra by using nature as a space for self-care is something I do every day and is one of my favorite practices.

My compass has been teaching yoga since 2001. It reinforces and reminds me like the repetition of a mantra, by encouraging self-acceptance and positive aspirations. I appreciate all of my yoga students for continuing to inspire me to practice over the years. You have saved my life. Learn what you teach, and teach what you know, right? By doing this, I think every one of us can contribute to the positive ripple effect in the collective awareness.

Root Chakra Affirmations

Using these root chakra affirmations can help you to become more energetic, have stronger will power, and build endurance. They can help you feel a greater connection with nature, a sense of security, and more stability with your finances, mental health, wellness, and spirituality.

- I am taken care of and safe.

- I am financially secure.

- I am worthy and happy to be alive.

- I am grounded, strong, and secure.

- I am trusting the universe to provide.

- I am finding the balance between what my body needs versus what it craves.

- I am at home in my own body.

Associated Yogic Technique: Root Lock, aka Mula Bandha

A bandha is a yogic term for an internal lock. This yoga technique associated with the root chakra is called *mula bandha*. It means root lock, like the root of a plant. It is also known as the creation bond. In it you lift your pelvic floor, like a Kegel or as if to stop urination mid-stream. It tones your pelvic floor and draws energy up from the base of your spine. This effects all systems of the body, especially internal energy. Using it unites the upward and downward pranic energy of the body channels. It is said you lose energy throughout the day, but this can help activate an upward pull of energy to retain it. The Sanskrit word for this upward pull is *apana*.

Yoga Pose to Explore the Root Chakra

The goddess squat is a yoga pose to explore the root chakra, and it works the legs, ankles, and base of the spine. This posture encourages grounding down to create an equality of opposition in growing tall and expanding outward from your roots in the earth, the way a tree's roots expand as wide beneath the ground as the branches reach outward and up toward the sun. It opens your hips and the pelvic bowl to assist with elimination.

Please note that for all recommended yoga poses throughout this book, each pose should be vetted for your own health conditions. Bear in mind that what is fine for one may be a risk for another. As an example, from the mentioned note that goddess pose is contraindicated for those with knee or ankle injuries, limited hip flexibility, or those who experience discomfort in the hips, severe lower back problems, and balance issues. In which case, the pose should be avoided or modified by sitting on the edge of a chair or on a block(s) with your back at the wall. You might also work with an experienced yoga teacher or other trusted health care provider.

Other Healing Options for Your Root Chakra

- Marching, walking meditation, and dancing, all to feel your feet on the ground, especially "earthing."

- Watching the sun rise and set to attune to the cycles of nature.

- Gazing at the moon at night to help you sleep.

- Eating red foods in their natural form, such as tomatoes, apples, strawberries, and raspberries.

- Red color therapy: Wear it or surround yourself with it for energy, heat, vitality, and power. Red represents fire, growth, excitement, stimulation, passion, and courage.

- Aromatherapy has powerful healing properties. Try essential oils, candles, or incense such as sandalwood, cedarwood, patchouli, clove, and ginger.

- Shake it out!

- Foot rolling. I use a tennis ball.

Root Chakra Journal Prompts

- Does my life feel out of control?

- What can I do to ensure my basic physiological and safety needs are always met?

- Do I suffer from being over- or underweight, from disordered eating, or anorexia nervosa?

- Do I have ongoing issues with my parents, children, or other family members?

- What does it mean to me to be grounded?

- How can I cultivate the feeling of being grounded in my life?

· · · · · · · · ·

*Do you have other ideas? Write your
own responses in your journal.*

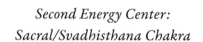

Second Energy Center:
Sacral/Svadhisthana Chakra

BASIC ELEMENTS

Resonant (Clearing) Sound: OOO as in *pool*

Seed/Bija (Stimulating) Mantra: VAM

Keynote: D

Color: Orange color therapy for healing unhealthy emotions. Use it for improving immunity and vitality, sexual and creative energy. It symbolizes warmth, prosperity, and determination.

Element: Water

Location: Center of the abdomen and sacrum

Body Parts: Sexual organs, reproductive system, hips, inner thighs, knees, and joints

Sacral Chakra: "I Feel"

The sacral chakra is located in your lower abdomen between your belly button and your pubic bone in your pelvis, which is near your sacrum and where your emotions, sexuality, and creativity are housed. It pertains to your physical, emotional, and creative fulfillment. This chakra is often described as the first rung up your ladder of consciousness. *Svadhisthana* in Sanskrit translates to "one's own place," and is all about working with your emotions for self-discovery. The element water correlated to finding a state of flow, surrender, trust, and allowance. Work with it to open to fun, play, and flexibility. Use it to go with the flow, like water, and to direct your flow of prana, or life-force energy.

This energy center focuses on how much you are willing to feel your feelings, a hot topic in therapy. Yes, even the challenging ones. We can take a clue from the Buddha's teaching of working with our minds and embracing our fear so that it loses its power. It's like learning to face the monster in your dreams. It pertains to your emotional expression and core beliefs in life. It also informs how you handle new experiences.

Balance in the sacral chakra brings you a sense of joy and fulfillment. The area is also concerned with the relationship with yourself and others. The emotional characteristics here are pleasure, abundance, having enough, and feeling that you are enough. It's about how you digest your life experiences. It helps you find a balance between what your body needs versus what it finds pleasurable.

Sacral Chakra In Balance When your sacral chakra is spinning strong, you are confident in who you are and know that you matter. There is joy and fulfillment. You can express yourself creatively, and you are flexible. When balanced, the second chakra enables you to accept and solve your life challenges in a creative manner. It helps you understand and incorporate your sexuality responsibly, and it helps you to fully feel and express your emotions. When clear, you feel empowered to take creative risks and to be outgoing. Balancing your sacral chakra helps you embrace your sexuality as the most powerful kind of creative energy. After all, it leads to the creation of life.

Sacral Chakra Out of Balance Conversely, the negative emotions that may emanate from an imbalance may manifest as sexual and reproductive health issues. This chakra helps you work with scarcity or poverty consciousness, which often present as money issues and the feeling that you do not have enough. You might fret that you are somehow not enough. It could present as relationship problems or feeling stuck creatively, like there is no spark or inspiration. You might feel stifled, question your worth, or be rigid and judgmental of yourself. Other issues may present as:

- urinary problems or kidney dysfunctions

- hip, pelvic, and low back pain

- inability to express your emotions or desires

- constant fear of betrayal

Areas of Opening in Your Sacral Chakra

FRONT BODY

- Stomach indicates fear of intimacy.

- The genitals and lower intestine can hold anger or guilt, often toward the opposite sex.

BACK BODY

- Lower back can indicate support, conflicts with authority, and money issues, and emotional lack of support.

- Sacrum presents conflict with authority or in being one!

How Trauma Presents in the Sacral Chakra Sexual abuse interferes with the vitality and creativity that makes life interesting. Feelings of guilt or being emotionally and sexually out of control could present as imbalances in the second chakra. Self-gratification behaviors can present as addictions and emotional dependency on others and may result from life energy being processed through guilt. You are afraid to feel your feelings and attempt to numb and anesthetize yourself with addictive behaviors. Sexual abuse causes this chakra to shut down or get locked open. You may question your right to want intimacy or be afraid of it. You may question your right to allow your desires and ideas to develop in quiet darkness until your own sense of timing says they are ripe and ready to be born. As you heal, you will learn patience with your deep rhythms.

SACRAL CHAKRA STORY
Coming Home to My Body

I've come to see that attempting to numb my feelings with the mindset that I like to work hard and play hard wasn't good for me. Activities such as overworking, constant stimulation, alcohol, or overindulgence just made me feel more worn out and alienated. They also invited in the unwanted visitors of anxiety and melancholy. The encouraging thing is that those suppressed emotions linked to the sacral energy region actually worked as a catalyst for change by pushing me to listen closer to my body's signals. The sacral chakra, which is strong in creativity, inspires me to express who I am and pursue my interests.

This is consistent with Joseph Campbell's theory that pursuing your passions and following your bliss will help you find your life's purpose. Did you know that your stomach is a storehouse of intelligence, particularly in the sacral region? Being aware of your emotions is essential since emotional blocks can negatively impact your physical health. That's what I've observed in myself, at least. Here are some accessible techniques to help you sense and process your emotions. Ask yourself how am I feeling? Practice some meditation for clarity and accept your body's feelings without passing judgment. It all comes down to striking a balance, allowing feelings to surface, and becoming more receptive to joy and play. Similar to how you could surf a wave.

Sacral Chakra Affirmations

Using these affirmations improve your creativity and encourage a healthy attitude about your feelings, sexuality, and body. They could increase your acceptance of others and help you to be compassionate to your flaws. They've helped me to feel more vibrant, optimistic, and playful. Try these on for size:

- I am safe in my sexuality and finding pleasure.
- I am comfortable in my body.
- I am joyful and in touch with my feelings.
- I am solving life's challenges in a creative way.
- I am fully feeling, trusting, and expressing my feelings and emotions.
- I am living a pleasurable life.
- I am allowing my creativity to flow through me freely.

Yoga Pose to Open the Sacral Chakra

Try the hip opener of happy baby pose to draw on your root chakra, open your leg channels, and move energy up your spine to your sacrum. In this pose, you are encouraged to access your own place of sensation as well as the feelings, desires, longings, and urges that rise up from your root to your core. The water element of the sacral chakra encourages you to let your emotions and creativity flow. It might even mean your tears flow, and that is okay.

Other Healing Options for Your Sacral Chakra

- Engage in expressive arts such as writing, art, music, and other creative therapies (which we will delve into in chapter 8).

- Orange color therapy: Wear it or surround yourself with it for healing unhealthy emotions by bringing them to the surface for healing. Use it to improve immunity, vitality, and to awaken sexual and creative energy.

- Orange foods in their natural forms such as carrots, oranges, pumpkin, apricots, sweet potatoes, and cantaloupes.

- Aromatherapy can restore feelings of sensuality and creativity with essential oils, burning incense, or candles with eucalyptus, chamomile, spearmint, rose, or clarity sage.

- Try Hula-Hooping.

Associated Yogic Technique:
Abdominal Lock/Uddiyana Bandha

Uddiyana bandha helps energy rise up through the center of your core. It is also known as the upward abdominal lock, as it involves the pulling in and lifting of the abdominal muscles. This causes the belly to become concave as the navel is drawn back toward your spine. This internal lock or bandha lifts energy, as it also intensifies upward energy from mula bandha in your root chakra.

Benefits of abdominal lock include:

- strengthening the abdominal muscles and diaphragm

- massaging the abdominal viscera (internal organs), solar plexus, heart, and lungs

- increasing your gastric fire to improve digestion, assimilation, and elimination, and purifying your digestive tract of toxins

- stimulating blood circulation in the abdomen and blood flow to the brain

Yoga Pose: Abdominal Lock, or Uddiyana Bandha

Step 1: On your next inhalation, expand your rib cage in all directions.

Step 2: Exhale and feel that energy moving up higher, upward through your core as you deeply draw your belly muscles in and up toward the spine until the belly hollows out.

Step 3: Keep length in your spine and hold the lock for five breaths while maintaining a connection to the energy flow within the central channel, which moves up with each breath.

Step 4: Release the internal lock, inhale, and take two normal breaths.

Step 5: Notice the effect of using the abdominal lock.

Sacral Chakra Journal Prompts

- How would embodying my sexuality, bringing forth my true desires, and being creative make me feel?

- Do I become addicted easily?

- Do I have difficulty sustaining relationships?

- What do I want from my life?

- Where can I be the most creative and energetic in my life?

• • • • • • • • •

Do you have other ideas? Write your own responses in your journal.

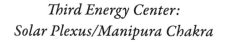

Third Energy Center:
Solar Plexus/Manipura Chakra

BASIC ELEMENTS

Resonant (Clearing) Sound: AH as in *father*

Seed/Bija (Stimulating) Mantra: RAM

Keynote: E

Color: Yellow color therapy brings bright, sunny,
joyful, fun, and abundant energy. It supports your
intellect and boosts memory and self-esteem.

Element: Fire

Location: Solar plexus

Body Parts: Solar plexus, muscles, skin, digestion, and liver

Manipura Chakra: "I Do"

Your third energy center, the solar plexus, translates in Sanskrit to "filled with jewels." The jewels are the qualities of this chakra as the seat of your desire for power, control, freedom, and autonomy. It is related to your will-power and your personal power. Work with it to strengthen your assertiveness and boundaries. Your solar plexus is the powerhouse of your chakras that stokes the fire in your belly and builds up your energy.

You can then channel this energy in many different ways. It can go to your intention, your physical digestion, and to igniting the necessary spiritual combustion to burn through blockages in your path. It can light a fire under your butt when you are sluggish. It helps you extend your will into the world. Its function is to give you vitality and the momentum to move forward and realize your desires. Remember, you are a unique expression of the Divine and you have an important mission that only you can share with the world.

It also represents your ability to be at ease, especially in the muddy water. That is, to feel okay in the trying times, to do your best (which will be different when you are healthy as opposed to sick). To be supportive and accepting of yourself and others. To help you change yourself and your situation. No mud, no lotus! I love this Disney quote from the movie *Mulan*: "The flower that blooms in adversity is the rarest and most beautiful of all."

Likewise, your solar plexus chakra challenges you to be a warrior who seeks to be genuine in every aspect of your life. Self-control confers safety. In turn, you gain more freedom, control, and autonomy. Its ultimate aim is to help you achieve mastery over yourself and your life. This journey requires awareness, dedication, and years of practice. Mastery involves turning your intentions into reality and consciously shaping your experiences. By channeling your energy into purposeful intention, you tap into your personal power. This demands effort and discipline.

Solar Plexus Chakra In Balance When healthy, this energy center helps you to feel confident in yourself. It opens your consciousness to the will of your higher intelligence and to peace and abundance. Your creativity and work will manifest more easily. You will feel increased self-respect and self-compassion. It helps you practice self-care. This can manifest as self-compassion that is nourishing, like self-soothing. It can also be self-care that is fierce, like holding boundaries or asking for what you want depending on the situation. You can work with this chakra to become the director and creator of your life.

Solar Plexus Chakra Out of Balance The negative emotions here are feelings of not having enough, or poverty consciousness, plus relationship problems, money issues, and feeling creatively stuck or having a creative block. It can also present as:

- digestive problems

- chronic fatigue

- pancreas and gallbladder issues

- an unrelenting inner critic

- constant fear of rejection

Areas of Opening in the Solar Plexus Chakra
FRONT BODY

- holds fear, guilt, and resentment

- fear of being fully alive

- connects with loss and grief

- storehouse for emotions

BACK BODY/MIDDLE BACK

- guilt and trust issues

- will not receive until helpless

How Trauma May Present in the Solar Plexus Chakra Issues of powerlessness, control, or low self-esteem indicate imbalances in the third chakra. Behaviors that reflect uncertainty about your personal power, such as poor follow through, passivity, or the need to be domineering, may result from your energy being processed through an underlying feeling of shame. Abuse and trauma teach you about helplessness and power over others, rather than strength and power from within. As you heal, you learn to take back your power and take action on your own behalf.

SOLAR PLEXUS CHAKRA STORY

Getting Your Mojo Back

Seeing Meg (not her real name) slide meekly with her head down to the back of my yoga class, I smiled encouragingly, as I always do with my students. Her downcast eyes and introverted body language gave off a depressed vibe. She seemed to be trying to make herself invisible. She didn't engage with the others' laughter or conversation. Yet I was happy she was taking time for herself in being there. I tried to draw her out.

In chakra language, her body language was evidence that the fire of her solar plexus was low. We've all been at low points in our lives. The way we use this third chakra is by cultivating our ability to change ourselves and our life situations. It is associated with the part of our consciousness having to do with power, control, and freedom. It also represents our ability to be at ease, to be supportive, and to be accepting of ourselves and others.

When the manipura fire needs stoking, it may present as the following type of issues: never finishing school, losing custody of children, breaking promises to self and others, always wanting to have a certain profession but never doing it. When I first approached Meg about modifying a pose to better suit her, her reaction was to shrink back apologetically, as if she was not worth the attention. I waited then tried again a couple classes later. This time her eyes lit up when I encouraged her practice.

In time, she started emerging from her shell. I learned she had been in an abusive relationship, so I never pushed her, but I suggested that she honor herself. Often, the focus was on her being in control of her body and practice, something I shared given my own experience with leaving a dysfunctional relationship. She deepened her practice and kept coming until our time together stretched into a year.

Meg told me yoga was helping her feel more powerful in her life, just as it had done for me. She said her therapist suggested yoga so she could learn to be more at home in her body. "At first, I just wanted to run away," she said. "In time, I felt more present to the sensations in my body, ones I previously couldn't feel because I was numb. It has helped my healing process. I feel stronger and like I've got my mojo back."

Over time, Meg transformed herself into a confident woman. She took part in a yoga teacher training program and became comfortable enough to share her insights with others. She was empowered and even eventually found a healthy relationship that made her happy. Examples of a strong third chakra would be the empowering things Meg and I did in leaving unhealthy relationships and finding yoga and therapy that supported our healing. More ideas might be things you have always wanted to do, such as enrolling in college, starting your own business, adopting a child, getting a new job, or joining a support group. May you find a renewed zest for life like Meg and I did. May you, dear reader, be led to the empowerment of having your manipura chakra in balance.

Solar Plexus Affirmations

These can help you to develop your talents and become confident, and assertive with healthy, compassionate boundaries. You'll feel like you know yourself better and trust in yourself.

- I am powerful and strong.

- I am working with ease and flow.

- I am honoring myself.

- I am easily manifesting my creativity and work.

- I am confident and comfortable with myself.

- I am my authentic self.

- I am making decisions with confidence and conviction.

- I am stoking the fire within me to burn through all blocks and fears.

- I am motivated to pursue my true purpose.

- I am allowed to move past things and people who no longer bring positivity into my life.

- I am willing to believe that things will always work out, even when they don't feel like it.

- Everything is unfolding in perfect timing.

- I trust. I believe. I receive.

Associated Yogic Technique:
Skull Shining Breath, or Kapalabhati Breathing

- Breath is rapid, rhythmic, and continuous.

- Inhales and exhales are through the nose.

- On the exhale, air is expelled through the nose by pressing the navel back toward the spine. On the inhale, the belly relaxes and the diaphragm flattens down.

- The focus is on the exhale and the action should be forceful but not agitating. The vacuum created by the exhale will naturally lead to an inhale. This is called a passive inhale.

BENEFITS OF SKULL SHINING BREATH

- releases toxins

- balances the sympathetic and parasympathetic nervous systems

- expands lung capacity and stamina

- energizes blood flow and circulation

- delivers oxygen to the brain, resulting in improved focus and a natural state of calm awareness

- strengthens the immune system

Yoga Pose to Heal the Solar Plexus Chakra

Plank pose taps into the fire element to activate your core with abdominal strengthening and good alignment through engagement of your shoulders, arms, hands, legs, and feet. These articulations together are foundational for a strong practice and are especially good for igniting a fire in your belly. The elements of plank work together in balancing your will with surrendering it in a genuine way as you relax the muscles that are not supporting you, such as your brows, scalp, jaw, and tongue. Here you harness energy with intention as you become the creative director of your pose and your life.

Other Healing Options for Your Solar Plexus Chakra

Try strong physical activities that evoke your courage, personal power, and accomplishment, such as interval training, hiking, surfing, or martial arts. Whatever it is that turns you on, do more of it!

- Color Therapy: Wear or surround yourself with yellow for this chakra. It is bright, sunny, abundant, fertile, and refreshing. It is known as the color of intellect and is useful for mental stimulation, self-expression, and creativity.

- Try yellow foods in their natural forms, including bananas, lemons, corn, star fruit, ginger root, pineapple, potatoes, and yellow squash.

- Aromatherapy: Use essential oils or burn incense or candles with saffron, musk, sandalwood, ginger, and cinnamon.

- Try belly dancing.

Solar Plexus Chakra Journal Prompts

- Where do I feel confident or a lack of confidence in my life?

- Do I have trouble making decisions?

- Do I engage in self-destructive behavior?

- Do I feel powerful in my body, mind, and life?

- Do I feel I have a choice in creating my ideal life?

- How would it feel to be confident, powerful, and know that I am creating my life?

. . . .

Do you have other ideas? Write your own responses in your journal.

Fourth Energy Center:
Heart/Anahata Chakra

BASIC ELEMENTS

Resonant (Clearing) Sound: AY as in *pray*

Seed/Bija (Stimulating) Mantra: YAM

Keynote: F

Color: Green color therapy helps to overcome fear, calm the body, and release frustration and anger. Useful to mend heartbreak, replenish energy, relax, and heal.

Element: Air

Location: Center of the chest, the heart

Body parts: Shoulders, mid-back, circulatory system, lungs, and chest. It affects the arms and hands.

Heart Chakra: "I Love"

Your fourth chakra is *anahata*, which translates in Sanskrit to unbroken, unstruck, or unhurt. The implication of its name is that under all of the grief and pain of living on Earth, there lies a spiritual place of purity and equilibrium where no hurt exists. To me, this means that well-being is your birthright and true nature. Your heart is where you process emotions. As we've learned, you have to feel it to heal it.

Your heart is the place through which energy flows to sustain you. This energy center is the joining point between higher and lower chakras. This chakra integrates complementary forces, bringing together the spiritual aspirations of the higher chakras and the earthly ones of lower chakras. This chakra is encapsulated in the phrase "I love" because here is where you can experience perceptions of love, trust, and compassion for yourself and others.

The goal here is to embody love and healing, to increase compassion, and bring balance. The best way to receive love is to give love. It governs how you relate to yourself and others, and how you handle relationships. Let your focus here be on helping yourself and those around you. It is to forgive old grudges and to let go of the past. In this way, you can mend your heartbreak and let down any shields you've erected around your heart for protection so you can let the light of divine love in. Then you free yourself of the residue of pain and suffering. I like to visualize divine love surrounding me as a shield that allows in higher, healing energies and acts as a barrier to lower energies. Here we can tap into divine love from source for vitality, prana, and healing of our past, present, and future.

Heart Chakra In Balance This is the center of love, empathy, and all the relationships in your life, especially your relationship with yourself. When it is stable, you have a clear balance between giving and receiving in your life. That might mean you no longer keep giving until exhausted but find harmony between what you give and what you allow yourself to receive.

Your relationships are nurturing and supportive. You have good boundaries with other people. You learn to be loved and to feel worthy of love. You feel joy, gratitude, love, and compassion for yourself and those around you. It will also be relatively easy for you to forgive. You feel connected to others and understand unconditional love. Here you can accept others without judging them. You also experience a lightness of being that is nourished by the inspiration and wisdom of your higher chakras and strengthened by your lower chakras.

Heart Chakra Out of Balance When the heart chakra is out of balance, you may withdraw from relationships to protect yourself, give too much, have poor boundaries, and resent your relationships. You may feel lonely and isolated. Psychologically you may have erected walls around your heart to protect yourself, but that can also keep out your good. You might have dysfunctional relationships with issues of jealousy, criticizing, fear of rejection, codependence, and clinginess. You may be over-loving to the point of suffocation, experience bitterness, and be in constant fear of being alone. You may also experience:

- asthma, allergies, bronchitis, and immune disorders
- upper back and shoulder problems
- arm and wrist pain
- lung and heart problems
- allergies and respiratory issues
- adrenal fatigue and high cortisol levels

Areas of Opening

FRONT BODY

- chest and heart-suppressed or unexpressed anger from an early age
- lack of emotional support

- anger is the "container for sadness"

- deep grieving may be held here

BACK BODY

- shoulders and upper back issues

- responsibility, burdens, and obligations

- reacting with our most negative
  core beliefs about ourselves

- trust issues

How Trauma May Present in the Heart Chakra Child and partner abuse mix your natural wellspring of love with pain and shame. As you heal, you learn that love does not have to hurt and you regain compassion for yourself as well as others. Over time, tightly closed hearts can open again. Wide-open hearts can learn self-protection. Rather than looking for the one right way, you weave a middle way between extremes. Since the heart chakra's basic concerns are love, compassion, and acceptance, trust issues of overwhelming rejection and betrayal take a toll on the human heart and intimate relationships. There could be a tendency toward isolation, emotional coldness, emotional reactivity, difficulty with forgiveness, fear of abandonment, or being loved.

HEART CHAKRA STORY

Increasing Your Life Force for Healing

Breath is life. Breath is vital to your heart chakra, as well as a tool for navigating life because it can be used as a guide or to regulate your nervous system. The heart is the most important organ in the human body, second only to the brain. It is in charge of distributing nutrients and oxygen throughout your body. Life is over if it stops pumping blood. The energy surrounding your heart is crucial because of its significance and value. Breath and your heart chakra merge in ayurveda, the age-old Science of Life. It is said that physical manifestations of lung deficiencies, such as asthma, allergies, coughing, bronchitis, or other respiratory/pulmonary issues, can be made worse by an imbalance in your heart chakra.

To be clear, these, along with many more, are legitimate medical problems. Of course! This is not meant to imply that someone is fabricating symptoms. Not at all. It is meant to refocus your attention on raising knowledge of complimentary techniques that can be added to alternative modalities. Plus, research shows that these actual medical disorders can also be treated energetically and consciously but this should not be used in place of medical attention.

If you have breathing issues, you are all too aware that respiratory problems and shortness of breath can be frightening and feel like impending doom. It has happened to me during severe colds. This triggers your excite response or sympathetic nervous system. Naturally, being able to inhale deeply makes it simpler to feel more at ease and tranquil. The air element of the heart chakra revolves around breathing.

My friend Frank told me he was prone to pneumonia. Although athletic, he was very familiar with the kind of dread that comes with breathing issues. When breathing became a major problem during one episode, he discovered that diaphragmatic breathing prevented the problem from evolving into pneumonia. He demonstrated for me how, similar to what we do in yoga class, he would put his hands under his ribs and inflate them. This case study may serve as a composite in support of this pranayama and a testament of what myself, Frank, and others with breathing issues have found to be helpful in dealing with it.

Daily deep breathing exercises may also assist in clearing any blocked emotions and feelings, as well as increase your life-force energy, plus oxygenate your cells and support all the systems of your body. Calm is restored when the prana in your heart chakra moves. Aim for complete circulation of the breath down to your tailbone. Many only get fresh oxygen up to the base of the chest's heart chakra, where the diaphragm instantly blocks it. Chest breathing is the term for this shorter breath, which is more likely to cause a physiological stress reaction. Breathing solely into your chest thus prevents oxygen from freely flowing throughout your body, which leads to an imbalance in many bodily systems, including the other chakras. Deep breathing does the opposite.

Yogic texts cite that conscious deep breathing, known as pranayama or breath extension, also disperses and integrates spiritual understanding of love, compassion, and connection to everything you encounter. Air, like love, is within and all around us. You can embody this element by keeping your heart center open and your love free-flowing. The anahata chakra color of green (and can include pink) represents transformation and love. I call it expansive, healing energy. If you are visual, you may want to see a beautiful green hue entering your heart with your in-breath using the diaphragmatic breath technique to help your lungs fill more efficiently and exhale slowly.

IN PRACTICE
Diaphragmatic Breathing

Your diaphragm is a dome-shaped organ below your ribs that sits between your abdomen and chest. It helps you breathe. In diaphragmatic breathing, you learn how to breathe from your belly, the region around your diaphragm, rather than just from your chest. This breathing technique helps to strengthen your diaphragm, slow your breathing, and fully meet your body's oxygen needs. There are various forms of diaphragmatic breathing but here is a basic one to improve your respiration:

Step 1: Lie down on a flat surface with a pillow under your head and one beneath your knees to help keep your body in a comfortable position.

Step 2: Place one hand on the middle of your upper chest. Place the other hand on your stomach, just beneath the rib cage.

Step 3: To inhale, slowly breathe in through your nose, drawing the breath down toward the stomach and down to your tailbone. The stomach should push upward against the hand (as air enters the lungs the diaphragm moves down and contracts to fill the bottom of your lungs). Your chest remains still. Feel your belly rise and feel fresh oxygen flow throughout your torso. Pause for a brief moment at the top of your inhale.

Step 4: To exhale, tighten the abdominal muscles and let the stomach fall downward (as the diaphragm moves up and expands). Gently release the breath back up through your spinal chakras while exhaling through the nostrils. Again, the chest should remain still so you can practice isolating your diaphragm.

It is suggested you practice this breathing exercise for five to ten minutes at a time, around three to four times each day. Once you become comfortable with it, you may start to practice the exercise while seated or standing. Try to keep your shoulders, head, and neck relaxed. If anxiety or issues arise, take a break or, if needed, consult your physician. It might take some time to get used to your new breathing pattern, but stick with it for better breathing, the calming effect, and to stave off any respiratory issues.

Plus, you and your chakras will feel the benefits almost immediately. Remember your breath is your constant companion, so utilize it anytime you need a pause. In those moments, take a deep breath in and breathe out with a huge sigh of relief.

IN PRACTICE
Yoga Pose to Balance the Heart Chakra

Start in kneeling, or hero's pose, with your hands together in front of your heart in a prayer position known as anjali mudra. You can intend this practice to be a divine offering, which is the translation of anjali.

Try alternating camel and child's poses to focus on taking down your defenses and opening your heart chakra. Notice how the backbend of camel opens your chest and shoulders, enabling you to expand your breath. Then tune in to how you feel as you are opening your back body in the forward fold of child's pose. Here you have a pose followed by its counter pose. All the while you can tune in to the air element for equilibrium with a breath-guided movement.

Heart Chakra Affirmations

These heart chakra affirmations help you to be more loving and gentler with yourself and more welcoming to others. You'll feel more empathy, wisdom, interconnectedness, friendliness, and enjoy more emotional balance.

- I am open to give and receive unconditional love to myself and others.

- I am forgiving myself and others.

- I am radiating love like a bonfire.

- I am connected to all that is.

- I am welcoming love with an open heart.

- I am worthy of love and I receive more of it every day.

- I am breathing in vitality and love.

- My heart is grateful and my mind is at peace.

- I am kind, generous, and compassionate.

- I am compassionate and peaceful.

- I honor my heart. I honor my loving energy. I honor who I am.

Other Healing Options for Your Heart Chakra

- Aromatherapy for the heart chakra: Use essential oil, or burn candles or incense with scents of rose, lavender, orange, and jasmine.

- Color therapy: Wear or surround yourself with green to relax, meditate, heal, and replenish your energy. Green helps calm your body, release frustration and fear, and supports harmony in any situation. It is known to mend a broken heart, give hope, and helps in centering.

- Eat green food in its natural forms, such as lettuce, peas, broccoli, cucumbers, green beans, and green apples.

- Try swimming the breast stroke.

- Practice heart-opening techniques like hugging.

In Practice
Open-Heart Meditation for Challenging Emotions

This meditation gives you the opportunity to connect with your heart and relax into whatever it may hold. I've found that the highest states I have experienced to date are directly correlated to the level of openness I am able to achieve. I find that making my intention to be open is key and works wonders.

Step 1: Once in a comfortable position, begin by deepening your breath and feel how the in breath expands your lungs and helps to relax your body and mind.

Step 2: Bring your attention to the center of your chest as you tune in to your heart. Much like getting a splinter, the pain of challenging emotions is relieved by removing them. Do this by first allowing them to come into your awareness.

Like a splinter, this emotion may be painful to remove, but think of the eventual relief that follows when it is removed.

Imagine opening your heart and feeling your emotions come up. Be brave and let them wash over you. Use compassion to stay with them as if they were a crying baby you are comforting.

Step 3: As you attend to these emotions with awareness and self-compassion, like how you cradle and rock a baby, these emotions will appreciate your attention. They are comforted and will settle down. As the pain of the emotional splinter is removed, there is a release of charged emotions. Watch them subside.

Invite the fear to transform into love.

Does this emotion have a message for you?

Step 4: Thank the emotions for their message or lesson.

Be creative with the visualization and use it any way that works for you.

Heart Chakra Journal Prompts

- How are my relationships with myself and others? How are they balanced or unbalanced?

- How do I show myself and others love?

- Am I overly emotional or emotionally shut down?

- How would it feel to find balance in my relationships, showing love to myself and others while freely giving and accepting love?

- Do I have trouble finding meaning in my life?

. . . .

Do you have other ideas? Write your
own responses in your journal.

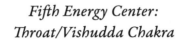

Fifth Energy Center:
Throat/Vishudda Chakra

BASIC ELEMENTS

Resonant (Clearing) Sound: EEE as in *speak*

Seed/Bija (Stimulating) Mantra: HAM

Keynote: G

Color: Sky blue in color therapy is for tranquility,
serenity, and peace by soothing your mind. Helps with
purification, truth, and connection with the Divine.

Element: Space, ether

Location: Throat

Body Parts: Shoulders, neck, throat, mouth,
ears, tongue, thyroid, arms, and hands

Throat Chakra: "I Speak"

Your fifth chakra is located at the base of your throat and is your instrument of expression and communication of all that is happening in your consciousness. It is the mouthpiece for your heart and is all about speaking your truth and being true to yourself. Its emotional characteristics are love and joy. It helps you to embrace your originality, unique voice, and individual experience in the world. *Vishudda* translates in Sanskrit as "to purify," as it is associated with cleansing and connecting to the power of truth and honesty. It pertains to finding a healthy internal dialogue that supports you. Use it to strike a balance between speaking and listening. It is your means of seeking, communicating, and sharing your truth. It includes your social skills, personal integrity, and honor.

Your throat chakra is responsible for the flow of hormones in your body and the function of all matters of your throat and head. This chakra is related to the element of sound. Sound is propagated into the air, and its vibration can be felt in your whole body. The throat chakra works closely with your sacral chakra, which governs creativity. It is the throat chakra that allows you to express your creative ideas, rather than stifling them for fear of others' opinions.

Throat Chakra In Balance When open and balanced, this chakra allows you to communicate truthfully and to express your feelings as well as your creativity. You will be better able to receive and to experience abundance and grace. You hear your intuition and connect to your higher wisdom and guidance. It helps you be articulate, honest, and truthful yet firm. The truth brings strength. When in balance, you will:

- have a clear, resonant voice

- be a good listener

- attract abundance and be open to receive

- listen to your intuition

- connect with higher wisdom and guidance

- clean up your internal dialogue

- improve your social skills, personal integrity, and healing

Throat Chakra Out of Balance The negative emotions associated with a closed throat chakra are sadness, loneliness, and anger, sometimes from old issues. You may also experience:

- thyroid issues

- sore throats

- ear infections

- neck and shoulder pain

- issues expressing yourself

- constant fear of being out of control

Areas of Opening

FRONT BODY

- tight jaw houses our conditioned response to not expressing what is true for us (old issues)

- throat holds unexpressed emotion often from the past

BACK BODY

- neck holds stubbornness

- only seeing things from one perspective

- having to be right

- being right versus being at peace

How Trauma May Present in the Throat Chakra Being yelled at, lied to, and overly criticized disrupts the capacity to recognize truth and to speak forthrightly. In these cases, there are tendencies to be shy or fear speaking up. The fear and shame you may have experienced during traumatic life events can energetically "strangle" your voice. It may leave you feeling incapable or unworthy of that expression. Chakra healing can help you regain the ability and desire to express yourself with love.

The Issues Are in the Tissues

The year was 2001 and I was undergoing yoga teacher training at the Medical Healing Arts Center in Doylestown, Pennsylvania. In taking turns with another trainee, I was playing the role of student while she was adjusting me. There in the kneeling backbend of camel pose, I had a yogic throat chakra opening. It was a challenging type of opening rather than a euphoric one. Note that both are possible in your own practice!

I was attempting the articulations she was instructing as follows: "With your knees hip-width apart, hug your thighs together to internally rotate them toward each other. Next, take a breath and arch your back even higher," she said while placing her hands beneath my shoulder blades to support me to go deeper in a backbend. All of a sudden, it hit! As my chest opened, I felt queasy and lightheaded, like I was reeling. I let out a weak, "I have to come out." I quickly pulled my hands from my heels and came down to my hands and knees. "I think I'm going to be sick," I said, waving her away. I was confused as to what was happening and didn't realize for a while what it meant. It happened a few times in subsequent tries but dissipated in time.

If this happens to you while practicing yoga, please remember to stop, back off, and take a break. That's what I learned from the opening. That and it is good to try and recognize these openings for what they are: yogic openings. Your body is releasing trapped energy. Try settling into a sense of curiosity and stillness. Although it could be difficult, it will work best if you use it as a chance to go inward and ask your body, "Is there a message?" After that, you can use the methods described next to work on that chakra. If the voice piece of your heart is your throat, then mine was requesting regular attention and care. This message resurfaced over the years.

I sometimes felt stuck or a sense of being strangled in my throat. Throughout my life, a lot of the physical signs of blockage have consistently appeared. For example, I frequently harbor stress in my jaw and neck, often noticeable when I drink coffee or when I am under stress. Interestingly, as an adult, I had laryngitis, sore throats, and a raspy voice for years. There was then a thyroid problem. All right, message received already!

There were undoubtedly unresolved, unspoken emotions from my history to investigate. I have previously experienced fifth chakra problems that needed mending. I was a highly sensitive child who had speech therapy in kindergarten to learn to say the "TH" sound. I was quite shy in grade school and often afraid to speak up. I eventually had enough of feeling invisible. I decided to act as if I was bold even though I didn't feel it. I learned to apply the adage "fake it until you make it" while I was in the eighth grade. When I faced my fear, I still felt it, but this act made me feel more confident. I promised myself that I would act as though I owned the place whenever I walked into a room or a party. There were wildly varying degrees of success, as you might imagine.

Fast-forward many years of acting until one day I had an epiphany. It dawned on me that I wasn't acting anymore! So exciting. I don't remember the exact moment, but I had learned to open up at school and in social situations. I gained such joy at being able to let my True Self emerge. It was indescribable and refreshing. I learned that boldness has a genius. Since it is said that anything that takes you away from the life you desire is a chakra block, the change made a big difference. I was so happy to be known, to feel like I was a part of things, and to see the change in how people reacted to me. My heart leapt with pride when someone would say they didn't see me as shy. "Not anymore," I'd say.

My throat chakra continued to need work. I still noticed my tendency to oscillate between bravado and crippling insecurity. An internal battle raged on. I was recalibrating, and discovering my True Self was somewhere in between. Then vocal nodules formed, which I worked to heal with herbal tea, speech therapy, Reiki, pranayama, and meditation. This was followed by a diagnosis of thyroid cancer that led me to explore all manner of throat chakra healing through surgery, meditation, sound healing, acupuncture, chiropractic, aromatherapy, color therapy, and regular therapy.

As a writer, narrative therapy, or the writing about past issues and trauma, was key to processing them for me. I've always kept journals and made books out of paper folded in half and stapled up the side when I was a child. It's who I am. My first book was all about learning to be true to myself. It took time and wasn't easy, but I found remission. Each time I speak my truth, a victory is won and I gain momentum. In 2024, I auditioned for and was miraculously accepted into a competitive barbershop chorus. I am now learning to use my voice to work on my throat chakra on another level. I can feel my voice getting stronger. I also love the creativity of this form of self-expression.

Speak your truth. Dear reader, uplift yourself for any and all progress you make on the path to being true to yourself and speaking that truth with kindness to others. The yogic principle of satya/truth has worked for me. It means being truth and acting out your truth in word, thought, and deed. It means telling your truth faster and not letting things fester. It's all about clear communication so you say what you mean and mean what you say. It helps me strive to follow actions in my truth and to avoid my peacekeeper tendency to try to please and placate others. I understand more deeply the importance of putting my own truth and needs first so that all others in my life will be taken care of out of that. The gift of self-care!

Throat Chakra Affirmations

- I am truthfully expressing my feelings and creativity with love.

- I am honestly attracting the grace and abundance I deserve.

- I am clear and powerful with my voice.

- I am honest and authentic in my speech and actions.

- I am happy and free to be me!

- I am hearing and speaking my truth.

- I am sharing my experiences and wisdom, and I know when it is time to listen.

- I am listening to my body and feelings to know what my truth is.

- I am the truth. (Another way of saying this is with the mantra *sat nam*.)

- I mean what I say and say what I mean.

IN PRACTICE
Yoga to Heal the Throat Chakra

Strike the shoulder stand pose, known as the mother of all asana, to utilize the chin lock and stretch your neck. This detoxifying inversion activates your thyroid for a metabolism boost and increased energy flow. It brings a fresh blood supply to the brain and rests the heart. This chakra activates the element of sound and air as it refines your communication through purification. Modify with your tailbone on a bolster, lying on your back.

IN PRACTICE
Chin Lock, or Jalandhara Bandha

Throat lock is a powerful stretch for the neck, an area that often holds tension and gets knotted up from looking at screens all day. Physiologically, practicing the throat lock is thought to be beneficial for promoting thyroid health.

Step 1: Place your hands on your knees with the palms facing upward. Inhale so your lungs are about two-thirds full and then retain your breath.

Step 2: Drop your chin down and draw it back closer to your chest, making a double chin. At the same time, lift your sternum toward your chin.

Step 3: As your chin drops toward your sternum with breath exhaled, swallow. This will help to activate this bandha. Relax your shoulders away from your ears and enjoy the stillness.

Step 4: Hold as long 10 seconds or as is comfortable and then lift your chin up and inhale deeply before releasing the breath. Notice how you feel and what the effect is, if any.

Other Healing Options for Your Throat Chakra

- Color therapy: Wear or surround yourself with sky blue for a sense of tranquility, serenity, and peace to help soothe your mind. This color can be used to calm and sooth your mind and nerves or even purify your aura. It can lead you to your truth and your connection with the Divine. Mentally immersing yourself in shades of blue helps protect you from dense energy and to get centered. It is the color of cooling, detoxifying, and clearing.

- Aromatherapy: Use essential oil or burn incense or candles with frankincense, sage, peppermint, and eucalyptus.

- Do throat and voice exercises like singing, chanting, mantra recitation, or humming.

- Try gargling or breathing exercises that use throat and mouth techniques.

Throat Chakra Journal Prompts

- Do I dominate conversations or keep overly quiet?

- Do I live in a way that is true to my core beliefs and values?

- How do I express myself?

- How would it feel to be speaking my truth and fully expressing myself?

. . . .

Do you have other ideas? Write your own responses in your journal.

. . . . . .

Sixth Energy Center:
The Third Eye/Ajna Chakra

BASIC ELEMENTS

Resonant (Clearing) Sound: MMM as in *OM*

Seed/Bija (Stimulating) Mantra: AUM or KSHAM

Keynote: A

Color: Indigo blue can be used as color therapy
to enhance intuition, purification, protection,
manifestation, and concentration.

Element: Inner sound combining all the elements:
earth, air, water, and fire

Location: Behind your eyebrow center, several inches
behind your brow

Body Parts: Eyes, forehead, temples, facial nerves and
pineal gland

Third Eye: "I See"

Ajna chakra translates in Sanskrit as "to perceive or command," and it is the sixth energy center in your body's system. Your consciousness expands from this chakra. It is often seen as the gateway to the inner realms and spaces of higher consciousness. It relates to how you connect your outside world to your inner dialogue. Having strong third eye energy allows you to use your powerful intuition for spiritual growth and a more generous attitude toward life.

One of your third eye chakra's main functions is to balance your everyday activities. It also governs your internal guidance system. Its purpose is self-trust, perspective, and clarity. Its properties are radiance, beauty, stillness, single-pointed focus, and steadiness in core inner light. It enables you to develop your intuition for illumination, luminescence, and psychic senses. Some may think of it as a sixth sense. You may even experience clairvoyance as you tune in.

Your third eye helps you with your spiritual growth and your inner vision or visualization ability. When this chakra is balanced, you look beyond your issues to see a more complete, "enlightened" picture of reality with an expanded consciousness. Its purpose is the enlightenment you achieve through meditation. It is home to your spirit and the part of consciousness that influences your actions. It brings balance in your everyday activities. This enables you to view the world from a higher perspective or vantage point, and see the big picture. Ajna governs the part of your life that your actual eyes cannot see. This is your intuition and spiritual growth.

Your third eye chakra is also your instinct, which senses things like opportunities or danger. It helps you read people and situations beyond minute visual and body language cues. If you were Spider-Man, it would be your "spider sense." It can help you become more aware of the motivations behind your own or others' actions. It is associated with your gut feeling and seeing below the surface of a situation. It relates to how you connect with the outside world through your inner dialogue.

I agree with Anodea Judith that it is the pineal gland, not the pituitary gland, that is associated with the third eye. The pineal gland is located deeper in the center of your head, where melatonin and serotonin for sleep are produced. This gland is light sensitive and involved in producing visions, even those of mystical significance, which are the visions associated with the third eye (Judith 2015).

Third Eye Chakra In Balance The sixth chakra governs your internal guidance system, much like the GPS in your car. When it is flowing free, you feel focused and determined. It also enables you to be more open to receiving advice, guidance, and instruction from others, your environment, or Source. It is about finding clarity, wisdom, and vision. This can also be everyday enlightenment from any and all sources that teach you about yourself. You might feel supported by something higher than yourself. It gives you a strong gut instinct and relates to your imagination. It helps with memory and the abilities of recalling dreams and being able to think symbolically. It also helps your ability to visualize concepts, ideas, and dreams.

Third Eye Chakra Out of Balance When this chakra is imbalanced, you may feel lost or as if you do not trust your path or purpose. It can dull your memory or cause you to mistrust your inner voice or cause indecisiveness. A block here may present as difficulties imagining the future or being stuck in the past. It could include insomnia, confusion, amnesia, denial, cynicism, and delusion. Excessive energy here can lead to difficulty concentrating. A deficiency here could cause a dull memory and distrust of your inner voice leading to indecisiveness. Other possible issues associated with the third eye out of balance are:

- nightmares

- headaches and dizziness

- blurred vision and eye strain

- sinus issues

- moodiness and stubbornness

Areas of Opening

BACK BODY

- headaches may be expressed or unexpressed anger in having "no choice"

- feeling like no matter what you do, it won't make a difference

FRONT BODY

- Head often holds anger and denial. Feeling like you don't want to deal with or see issues. It also pertains to surviving with resentment and suppressed anger.

How Trauma May Present in the Third Eye Chakra

Through traumatic experiences, your spiritual self can be damaged. As a result, you may feel disconnected from others, from deity, or from the universe. Working with the ajna energy can help you reestablish your sense of connectedness. Feeling supported by a higher power (whatever name you choose) can help you draw strength to cope in challenging times and figure out the best way forward. You've probably had divination experiences where you just knew something, which would have emanated from your chakra command center. I find that the more I trust my intuitive knowing, the stronger it gets.

Through your eyes you perceive the world, and with your consciousness you assign its meaning. Even more so, your internal guidance is fired up when you really see with clarity. That is, when you perceive and grasp the underlying truth of reality. What I am going to say next may raise the freak factor for some. If so, substitute in the word *intuition*. However you think of it, the ajna chakra encompasses the "clairs." This term is for that which is known through the mind beyond the five senses. They are forms of the sixth sense. It does not necessarily mean seeing dead people. I don't.

Claircognizance is knowing something as fact without knowing how, why, or where it came from. Clairvoyance is the ability to see beyond the range of ordinary perception, such as auras. Clairaudience is the ability to hear beyond the range of ordinary perception. Together, these examples are forms of extra sensory perception (ESP), which is sensing things with the mind, outside the known senses. I am open to messages from the universe that I may get through the words of a song, conversations from people that turn out to be exactly what I needed to hear, a book that comes to me, my inner voice, and signs that are answers to my questions.

Whatever your perspective on the clairs, psychology and common sense echo a similar sentiment. That your intuition and feelings have important messages and guidance that can enable you to march to the beat of your own drummer rather than blindly follow the crowd. The third eye helps you practice discernment, find your next steps, and activate your bullshit meter, as I call it. It enables you to tune in to your gut to sense for danger, a trap, or some form of deceit. It's like working a muscle because you gain strength by using it.

THIRD EYE CHAKRA STORY
Follow Intuition to Strengthen It

True story: When I met my husband-to-be at work, we were introduced and chatted. I then turned around, walked back into my office, and blurted out the following cringy statement to a colleague, "If we got married, our names would be Jack and Jackie Jackson." Weird. I was mortified that those words just slipped out before I could stop them. I now know this was my intuition and my sixth chakra at play. Then, I had no clue as to where such an idea came from. I was an independent human flying solo and happy to do so. I was not looking for marriage and never talked about it before. But now we're married and yes, I changed my name. Suffice to say, people remember us due to that fact. It's not even surprising when I think back because as soon as I met Jack, I felt as if I already knew him for a lifetime or in another one. It was intuitive, a no-brainer. I just knew it. Sure, that sounds like something a yoga teacher would say. Maybe cliché. I get that. For the record, that was before I was a yoga teacher.

You can use visualization to fire up your manifestation power through this energy center by honing your intuitive skills. Never underestimate the power of your imagination to create what you want! Research and commonsense support this. After all, "Imagination is more important than knowledge," as Einstein said. When you feel you've lost your way or your groove in your relationship or job, that your creative juices seem to have run dry, or that which once was easy now seems impossible, these are signals your third eye center needs some work. Have faith: there are ways to fire it up and clear out congestion. Meditation is your go-to for tuning into intuition and guidance. Try one of the many meditation apps, such as Insight Timer. Did you know that meditation can be expressive, awareness-based, or focus-based? Find your style to recharge, get clarity, and tap into your intuition.

Meditation Types Expressive-based meditation could be painting, dance, playing an instrument, or making a quilt. Anything you do for the sheer love of it. It is those moments when you are so engrossed that you lose track of time. It's those moments of total absorption. This is a type of meditation. For me dancing is sheer joy. And then there is yoga, reading, nature, and writing. Awareness-based meditations are mindfulness practices, like the breath-counting technique, for example. It would also be about noticing the temperature of the air as it moves in and out of your nostrils or being aware of the sounds around you and observing them in relationship to yourself. It's all about using your five senses. Focus-based meditation could be the use of a mantra, a prayer, or a sacred sound in any language that speaks to you or is meaningful for you. The object of your focus can vary but the point is to give your mind something to lean on to distract it from its endless chatter.

Third Eye Affirmations

- I am insightful as I pay attention to direction from within.
- I always know what to do in any given situation.
- I am seeing clearly and my inner eye reflects my inner light.
- I am highly intuitive and guided by my internal guidance system.
- I am connected with my higher self.
- I am confident in my ability to make my life work.
- I am worthy of the life I want.

Yoga Pose to Balance the Third Eye Chakra

For this chakra, try pigeon pose, which is used to invoke the element of light for insight and guidance. In the forward folding variation of the pose, resting the forehead brings the focus to the eyebrow center for centering, imagination, turning inward, and visualization. The hip-opener requires engagement to keep your hips level while striving for length in the spine and ribs. Simultaneously, you bring relaxation to your shoulders as you reach with an equality of opposition beyond your extremities.

Associated Yogic Technique: Gaze Points, or Drishti

Drishti is a Sanskrit word that means "focused gaze or gaze point." It is a means for developing concentrated attention. It relates to the fifth limb of yoga (pratyahara) concerning sense withdrawal, or turning inward for direction. It is also connected to the sixth limb of yoga known as dharana, or concentration. The practice of Drishti is a gazing technique that develops concentration and teaches you to see the world as it really is. The idea is that a steady gaze creates a steady mind for clarity.

In each yoga pose, there is a gaze point to keep your mind from wandering off. When you get caught up in the outer appearance of things, your life-force energy flows out of you as you scan the stimulating sights. Allowing the eyes to wander creates distractions that lead you further away from yoga or being present. To counteract these habits, control and focusing your attention are fundamental principles in yoga practice. When you control and direct your focus, first of the eyes and then of your attention, you are gaining the benefits of drishti.

To use a gazing point while in a yoga pose, simply select the point where your eyes are naturally directed by the alignment of the posture. If you reach up then look up. The use of gaze points in yoga postures is to be developed slowly over time. First, you can develop and focus on the alignment of the asana, then the breath, and then finally the drishti. In meditation, you can gaze upward behind your closed eyelids toward the eyebrow center. This is a calm point. I've had my yoga students comment that I look up as I teach yoga classes and it's true. It helps me concentrate.

Other Healing Options for Your Third Eye Chakra

- Enjoy sound healing (more to come in the following chapter),

- Listen to uplifting, beautiful music.

- Try toning as a form of vocalizing on your exhale.

- Practice creative visualization.

- Do tai chi.

- Make a vision board.

- Use a guided meditation like Yoga Nidra, or psychic sleep.

- Try aromatherapy, using essential oil or burning candles or incense with palo santo, nutmeg, and chamomile.

- Color therapy: Wear or surround yourself with indigo to stimulate your intuition, to inspire you, to activate your wisdom, and to increase your manifestation and concentration abilities. It can help release stress and bring clarity and direction in life for healing.

Enjoy your exploration of the chakra at the eyebrow center. Notice what it is like to use it for guidance. By doing this, you learn to trust yourself. It is invaluable.

Third Eye Chakra Journal Prompts

- In what ways do I trust or mistrust myself?

- Am I able to tune in to my inner guidance system through my emotions and thoughts for direction?

- How would it feel to be truly trusting of myself and this guidance?

- In what ways do I see things that others don't?

· · · · · · · ·

Do you have other ideas? Write your
own responses in your journal.

Seventh Energy Center:
Crown/Sahasrara Chakra

BASIC ELEMENTS

Resonant (Clearing) Sound: NG as in *sing*

Seed/Bija (Stimulating) Mantra: OM or silence

Keynote: B

Color: Violet color therapy is for regenerating
your nervous system; aiding insomnia, mental
disorders, physical illness; an activating intuition;
opening creativity and psychic awareness.

Element: Inner light

Location: Crown of head

Body Parts: Head, brain, the nervous system in
general, and the pituitary gland (master gland)

The Crown Chakra: "I Know"

Located at the top of your head, *sahasrara* is all about enlightenment, higher purpose, and consciousness. It is your source of divine energy, self-realization, and a gateway to higher dimensions. *Sahasrara* translates to "thousand petaled" in Sanskrit and is represented by a thousand-petaled lotus. It is your spiritual connection to yourself, your higher self, others, cosmic energy, the universe, and to spirit or something greater than yourself. It sounds like a lot but put it together and you have unity consciousness.

With it you gain enlightenment and awareness of a divine presence, God, Energy, Source, Creator, or whatever you want to call that presence. It also plays a role in your life's purpose. It is the source of divine energy, self-realization, and a gateway to your higher self and higher dimensions. It helps you feel that you are here for a reason and that you are learning from your life choices. This instead of feeling like things just happen to you randomly. Maybe you think of things happening for you, not to you. It's all about your soul's journey, your higher purpose, and consciousness. Its elements are consciousness and thought. It governs the principles of omnipresence, in Sanskrit this is called *sat, chit, ananda*, or truth, consciousness, and bliss. These are your true nature. Its purpose is awareness and unity with the Divine. It is samadhi or enlightenment, and we've all experienced it a little at times. It feels like silence and union with Source. It is the end goal of yoga found through the eight-limb path.

Crown Chakra In Balance It is said that this chakra is linked to every other chakra (and therefore every organ in your system) and so it affects all of your organs along with your brain and nervous system. When this connection is clear, you have an unshakable trust in your inner guidance. You experience oneness with your higher consciousness, God, and unity with all beings. Your crown is where you surrender to divine will. When your crown chakra is clear, you can experience inner light, light, and higher intelligence. You feel tapped into higher wisdom beyond the human condition.

Your balanced crown chakra brings the realization that everything is connected on a fundamental level. This is the part of you that forgives with more ease, judges less, and finds kindness in spaces where previously you could not. This connection helps you feel compassion and a depth of love for everything and everyone. Sound intimidating? With practice, this chakra becomes stronger and can help you build a deeper connection with the Divine one breath, or one petal opening, at a time. It also signifies a shift in perspective. It is not about how much darkness there has been in your world, or the larger world. It becomes more about how you show up in that darkness as a point of light.

Crown Chakra Out of Balance When this connection is lost or out of balance, you may feel insecure, frustrated, restless, and small. You may experience symptoms of anxiety, depression, or a lack of joy and happiness in your life. This is feeling as though you are disconnected from your source and your strength often characterized by:

- rigid thoughts and attitudes

- analysis paralysis, a type of overthinking resulting in an inability to make a decision

- constant fear of alienation

- feeling abandoned and alone

How Trauma May Present in the Crown Chakra Through traumatic experiences, your spiritual self may become damaged. You may feel disconnected from others, from deity, or from the universe. Getting better by working on the crown chakra can help you reestablish your sense of connectedness. I imagine that coming to earth is like being dropped in a jungle with a two-way radio to Source. When you have connection to Source, you know how to proceed. Without it, you feel lonely and lost. Feeling more connected to a higher power gives you energy to draw from and strength to cope with adversity.

· · · · · ·

Connect with Source for Strength

Not lovable. Not good enough. Separate and alone. Stupid. These are some of the negative core beliefs that are rather common, perhaps subconsciously, to the human condition. They relate to the crown chakra, which holds the realization of yourself as a divine being, connected with Source. I distinctly remember one afternoon as a child, lying on the couch in the living room of our family home, crying and ruminating on my own *not lovable* scenario. My mind was caught in a negative loop, and I found myself naming all of the people who hated me.

I was so young that the list was relegated to the neighbors and my family members. You know, the only people I knew. I was listing people with my fingers. Kevin hates me. Colleen hates me. Norman hates me. Mom hates me. Dad hates me. Jill hates me. Mrs. and Mr. Boelle both hate me. Oh, the drama! I was really having a go at it. The moment stuck with me all these years because I caught myself in the act of doing it! Yep, even way back then. Although I have no idea what set me off that particular day, I noticed that there was a space between my strong, sad feelings, and emotionality.

There was another part of me that was able to watch and notice what I was doing. It struck me that my mind was playing a trick on me. I was able to watch my mind. This disrupted my tantrum. Sometimes I still catch myself in a similar pattern and think back to that day lying on a brown-patterned couch by the fireplace in the living room with the super high ceiling feeling sorry for myself and then being able to observe my thinking from another vantage point.

There is a connection between your brain function and your crown chakra when you realize you don't have to believe everything your mind says. You create space to choose more positive, reality-based, and enlightened thoughts. Neurologists call this creating a new habit or developing new neural pathways in your brain. Brain function is part of the crown chakra, and it deals with your thoughts. But where do your negative core messages come from? Maybe they are from the pressures of a stressful, fast-paced, modern life or from parents who never learned to love themselves.

Maybe it is based on your experience of unresolved trauma and deeply rooted, negative core beliefs developed in childhood that have been reinforced throughout your life from society, religion, school, family, friends, and the media. Only you can discover your truth. Through traumatic experiences or just by living life on earth, there comes a point in all our lives when we feel disconnected from our true selves, from others, from deity, and from the Universe. Regardless of what our beliefs are or where they came from, they are a result of being separated from self/Spirit/Source. Just as the mind gets disconnected from the body in trauma.

Another symptom of trauma being held in sahasrara chakra could be lack of empathy. But overall, having a blocked crown chakra is often the result of being conditioned to believe that you are a detached and isolated being who is defined by the ego. This is the opposite of seeing yourself as connected or in touch with your higher self. The anecdote is a healthy crown chakra or the experience of unity consciousness, or oneness. Recovering can help you reestablish your sense of connectedness as a way to heal your crown chakra.

What helped me was the awareness of how my self-defeating thoughts were hurting, not helping me. When I find myself in the same unlovable loop or another negative spiral, I remember the insight of that day way back in my childhood. *Oh, I see what is happening,* I tell myself. *Stop.* Then I imagine closing the door to the negativity of my thinking. Feeling union with a higher self through this type of recognition can help you draw strength to cope with the ups and downs of life. It can also be an *ah-ha!* moment, seeing the light, or when you find that game-changer solution to a problem.

It is associated with being plugged into your creativity through the field of potentiality. Quantum physics refers to this as tuning into the binding energy of the Universe. Others may call it God force. Connecting with a divine source is enlightenment or *samadhi* in Sanskrit. Because of the constant unfolding nature of this chakra, it is called the thousand-petal lotus. It is said that enlightenment is the lotus opening petal by petal, or breath by breath. Often, I've found these moments of inspiration come from the still small voice within, as the Quakers call it. For many, it is accessible through meditative and spiritual practices, spiritual songs, hymns, chanting, prayer, or certain kinds of group spiritual practices. Do you have another practice that works for you?

The mantra for the crown mantra is OM, or silence. Notice that silence of your mind only happens when you are totally present. Only then do you have access to greater understanding through the information and wisdom around you. Can you see that this is how you access higher intelligence? Much depends on your willingness and ability to focus and see clearly. This state is yoga and also the goal of the practice, which is to quiet the mind. In these moments, you can experience yourself as the observer or the seer. You can call it witness awareness. On a deeper spiritual level, you become aware that you are a part of the larger whole and that you are connected to the Universe, like a grain of sand is to the beach; you are a separate part of a larger whole. Like individual waves that make up the ocean, you rise from it at birth and resolve back into it at death.

To me this is ultimate reality and the essence of the namaste salutation. It means the divine light within me recognizes and salutes the same divine light within you. When we are in this place, we are the same. I like to say "at the source, we are all the same." If we all share the light within all, then we all contain a spark of the Divine through this energy center.

Crown Chakra Affirmations

- I live in gratitude, joy, light, peace, and acceptance.
- I am connected with all beings.
- I am in touch with my higher intelligence.
- I am surrendering to divine will as I stand in my personal power.
- I am composed of the same fabric that encompasses the entire universe.
- I see the divine light within all beings, whether they are aware of it or not.

- I am open to the abundance and greatness the Universe offers.

- I am trusting in the support of the Universe.

Associated Yogic Technique: Service, or Seva

Seva means "selfless" and is helping others. It describes nonrecognition and nonreward for your actions. You do not expect to receive compensation, recognition, or even appreciation from what you offer. Instead, you offer help without strings attached. When you serve others, your actions resonate with the unifying principle of the crown chakra. Selfless service can be performed in small acts, such as holding the door for someone or picking up a random piece of litter in your neighborhood. Seva can also be performed through more dramatic and recurring gestures, such as anonymously donating funds to a cause you care about or making meals for a friend who has a long-term illness. Plus bringing happiness to others brings it to yourself. This is the spiritual truth of all being one. The law of one.

Yoga Pose to Open the Crown Chakra

The yoga pose to open the crown chakra is the rabbit pose. This posture features your head touching or reaching toward the earth. This creates a sense of reaching out from within from this kneeling position that invites maximum stretch between the vertebrae. As the crown chakra touches the earth, it brings the focus to the element of consciousness or thought. This awareness is used to draw inward and upward in meditation, concentration, and enlightenment. As with all inversions, rabbit invites stillness and a new perspective.

Other Healing Options for Your Crown Chakra

- light therapy

- eye exercises or lying quietly with an eye pillow

- brain-training exercises

- all types of meditation and use of mantra for quiet

- silent retreats or times of the day

- Aromatherapy: Use essential oils or burn candles or incense with myrrh, camphor, and frankincense.

- Color therapy: Wear or surround yourself with white. White includes the entire spectrum of color and heals your whole body. It is great for purification and clearing toxicity for clarity and understanding. Use it for balance, peace, comfort, and to dissipate negative thoughts and feelings. Did you know that combining white with another color is beneficial to another part of your body that needs healing?

Crown Chakra Journal Prompts

- In what ways do I feel connected with or disconnected from others?

- Do I believe there is something higher than myself?

- How would it feel to be at one with others, as though they are a part of me?

- How would believing in something greater than myself make me feel?

- Can I tap into the power of the Universe that surrounds me?

· · · · · · · · ·

*Do you have other ideas? Write your
own responses in your journal.*

· · · · · · · · ·

4

Reiki: Raise Your Energy with Hands-On Healing

The most beautiful thing we can experience is the mysterious. It is the source of all art and science.

· · · · · ·

SCIENTIST AND GENIUS ALBERT EINSTEIN

If you are ready to mix the imaginative with the experimental, try delving into the many forms of energy healing. Some are modern methods while others have ancient roots but all methods aim to provide a balance of energy flow throughout your mind, body, and soul. They open doors to connect your thoughts, feelings, spiritual being, and physical sensations. This plethora of approaches can be used either by physically touching your body or non-physically working with your body's energy. In science we call it *energy*, in religion we call it *spirit*, and on the streets we call it *vibes*. All I am saying is, you can learn to trust it and work with it. Even with the variety of styles that fall under the topic of energy healing, such as shamanic healing, acupuncture, Qigong, and theta healing, for example, I am only sharing the ones I've directly experienced. Note that emotional freedom technique (EFT) is another that will be explored in chapter 8. While energy healing is an alternative healing method, a growing number of hospitals and wellness enterprises have begun to use forms of it as a core treatment model thanks to evolving research and acceptance.

Medical Reiki

For the breast cancer patients undergoing surgery at the New York-Presbyterian/Columbia University Medical Center in New York City, Reiki, or hands-on energy healing, is offered as a complementary service to those facing the fear of going under the knife. Having a Reiki Master who goes into the operating room with patients is a prime example of how complementary healing modalities can come together with allopathic medicine to holistically support patients who are fighting for their lives. For me, a holistic approach means drawing from all available resources. The intense suffering endured by those in medical treatment for their disease is often scary, traumatic, depressing, and even life-threatening in itself. With these escalating and harrowing illnesses, medical Reiki comes forward as a part of conventional medicine, so that it might become available to all who might want their doctors to add it to their treatment plan.

Medical Reiki Defined

Medical Reiki is the specialized practice of performing Reiki in the operating room, or other appropriate hospital or outpatient environments, in compliance with gold standards. It was developed by Raven Keyes, an internationally recognized Reiki master teacher and author of three books on the subject who recently passed. Keyes spent years working in the operating room with top surgeons, including Dr. Mehmet Oz and Dr. Sheldon Marc Feldman, Chief of Breast Surgery and Breast Surgical Oncology and Director of Breast Cancer Services at Montefiore, respectively. Keyes has shared her knowledge with many in the United States and abroad and trained hundreds of Reiki Masters in this practice (Keyes 2024).

Feldman explained his rationale for incorporating Reiki into his breast cancer surgeries. "We're [the medical team] all so busy during an operation with our specific tasks that we sometimes forget there is a patient there. When Raven [as their former resident Reiki Master] is in the operating room administering Reiki, there is someone present to take care of the patient, and every one of us is reminded why we chose our professions in the first place: we get to remember that first and foremost, we are all there as healers" (Keyes 2012).

How Reiki Can Help Medical Procedures

Medical Reiki began in the year 2000 when Oz first invited Keyes into his operating room to administer Reiki during an open-heart surgery. During the subsequent years, Keyes continued with her Reiki practice of assisting patients during surgery, almost exclusively with Feldman. Feldman noticed that when Reiki was administered during surgery, the patients seemed to do much better. There was less bleeding, the surgeries went more smoothly, almost no pain was present a day or two after surgery, and the patient seemed to heal faster. In the foreword to Keyes' book *The Healing Power of Reiki*, Oz noted that on the surface, bringing an energy practitioner to the operating room seems to attack the foundation of modern medicine, a field that seeks to measure objective benefits from every treatment (Keyes 2012). Although difficult for the medical community at large to accept, an energy worker and a surgeon may be able to assist one another to ensure the full recovery of the patient. Oz said, "Organized medicine must help shoulder the responsibility to study these challenging, new theories of healing" [referring to Reiki and other energy healing modalities].

How Reiki Heals

The word *Reiki* is the Japanese name for "universal life force energy," which is the life-giving energy present in everyone. The best way to understand Reiki is to view it as your experienced sense of being alive, your essence, or your life force. Reiki therapy is a gentle touch therapy that involves the placing of the therapist's or patient's hands on or above various locations on the patient's body to promote relaxation and a sense of calm. At the master level, it can be performed at a distance. As a form of alternative touch therapy, it is commonly referred to as energy healing. Reiki emerged in Japan in the late 1800s and involves the transfer of universal energy from the practitioner's palms to their patients to help the body heal by removing blocks in the body's energy field, aligning and balancing the body's energy centers, and supporting the body in finding homeostasis.

Practitioners say energy can stagnate in the body where there has been physical injury or possibly emotional pain. In time, these energy blocks can cause illness. Energy medicine aims to help the flow of energy and remove blocks in a similar way to acupuncture or acupressure, improving the flow of energy around the body with the goal of enabling relaxation, speeding up healing, reducing pain, and other symptoms of illness.

Is Reiki Really an Energy?

Some Reiki practitioners say that the life-force energy enters through the crown of the practitioner, moves down to the heart, and then along each arm and out the hands to the receiver. They think of Reiki as an energy that moves through the practitioner to the receiver. From an Eastern perspective on healing this description makes sense as a possibility as to what is actually happening when in the practice of Reiki. However, instead of thinking of Reiki as an energy, you may be more comfortable thinking of it simply as a practice that reconnects you with your natural intelligence and healing ability. In this way, a Reiki attunement would be the transfer of a special piece of information passed on from teacher to student. This piece of information may be a powerful reminder of the incredible inner wisdom you already possess and can be enabled to access.

It's that same creative life force and intelligence that heals your wounds without your effort, that which tells seeds to grow into trees, that creates galaxies, and all of life. It's always there and it's everywhere. When a practitioner places their hands on or near you, you are given an opportunity to respond to this information. Each person will respond uniquely, depending on what is possible at the time. Most practitioners feel twitches, tingling, heat, and other interesting sensations in their hands while practicing Reiki. Is this the feeling of life-force energy moving through the hands?

Some feel it to be more like the receiver's etheric body or bioenergy rearranging in response to the reminder of your natural capacity for self-healing. It's like the practitioner establishes the connection to this information and then rebalancing begins to happen naturally. As the Reiki Master said in my first attunement, the energy goes where it is needed. When I went to see Keyes, she said she considers herself as the practitioner to be like a hollow bone and that the Reiki energy flows through her to her clients and patients.

Benefits of Reiki

It is proven that Reiki is not harmful to you in any way and it is safe to use in conjunction with chemotherapy, radiation, and medications used in the medical treatment of cancer. It's important to note that Reiki is used in health care as a complement but never as a substitute for your regular medical treatment and medications. Reiki supports your natural healing abilities.

Reiki can be helpful in:

- promoting relaxation

- reducing stress and anxiety

- increasing energy levels and reducing fatigue

- promoting an increased sense of positive well-being

Reiki Principles

Five principles form the foundation of the Reiki philosophy. These ideas offer direction for balancing and healing with Reiki energy. Reiki principles can be repeated throughout the day to help direct your thoughts and actions. I would also contend that this fosters spiritual and personal development and aids in leading a healthier, more contented existence.

1. **Just for today, I will not be angry.** This idea intends to aid in the discharge of this energy. In order to attract peace into your life, it urges you to recognize your anger and let it go.

2. **Just for today, I will not worry.** When you're carrying around anxious energy or worrying about the future, it can make you feel bad. However, if you're able to let go of this energy, you could find it simpler to focus on the now and lessen your anxiety about the future.

3. **Just for today, I will be grateful for all my blessings.** This is a reminder to express gratitude for all that you have. By slowing down and recognizing the good in your life, it may help you foster more positive energy.

Qualities of All Reiki

You may hear of different traditions of Reiki with names like the already mentioned medical, as well as karuna or kundalini, and this could be confusing. Whatever the name, these guidelines can be used to help discern what is a Reiki technique and what is not. If a healing technique has these four qualities, then it can be considered to be a type of Reiki:

1. The ability to do Reiki comes from receiving an attunement, rather than developing the ability over time through the use of meditation or other exercises. Did you know that a Reiki attunement is almost always something you pay for and that there are varying degrees of attunement? In the Usui tradition where I trained, the levels are Reiki I, Reiki II, and the Master Reiki Level. Some Reiki schools offer four levels. If you are interested, please note that there can be a substantial time and money commitment.

2. All Reiki techniques are part of a lineage. This means that the technique has been passed on from teacher to student through an attunement process starting with the one who first channeled the technique.

3. Reiki does not require that one guides the energy with the mind, as it is guided by the higher power and knows where to go and how to act all on its own.

4. Because of this, Reiki can do no harm.

4. **Just for today, I will expand my consciousness.** In Reiki, actively practicing mindfulness is key to balancing your energy. This principle encourages you to recognize how you can be more conscious about appreciating the present moment.

5. **Just for today, I will be kind to all living beings.** This principle focuses on how being kind to others lets you receive positive energy in return. It includes being gentle with yourself, which is essential for spiritual health.

History of Reiki

Reiki has been practiced for countless years in various forms. The Usui tradition, which was created in 1922 by a Japanese Buddhist named Mikao Usui, is one well-known variation of Reiki. During his lifetime, Usui reportedly taught the Reiki technique to 2,000 people. Through Hawaii in the 1940s, the technique expanded to the United States, and later, in the 1980s, it reached Europe. It is also known as hands-on healing or palm healing. The popularity of Reiki is rising, and many of us who get it find it effective. There are currently 68,900,000 results for the word in a Google search.

Reiki and Holistic Healing Modalities in the Hospital

This age-old technique is employed by the Integrative Health and Well-being department at NewYork-Presbyterian to help with pain management and stress reduction. Manna Lu-Wong, an integrative nurse and Reiki practitioner/master teacher in the hospital system, says on the website that she needs only one minute to convince skeptics of the therapeutic effects of Reiki. She says people just need to feel it. The sensation of the warm, subtle vibrations has a calming effect, and most times patients feel relaxed after the session. And once they feel it, she says they realize it is real.

Lu-Wong is also among a group of practitioners at the Integrative Health and Wellbeing program at NewYork-Presbyterian, in collaboration with Weill Cornell Medicine, who are using a range of holistic healing techniques to manage pain, decrease anxiety, and promote health and wellbeing. They offer complementary practices, such as yoga and acupuncture, in addition to Reiki, that augment but don't replace medical care (Columbia Presbyterian 2017).

Reiki Research

Lu-Wong also is exploring the tangible benefits of Reiki, most notably in a 2015 pilot program she conducted at NewYork-Presbyterian Lower Manhattan Hospital to determine whether a method of relaxation can produce immediate and prolonged declines in perceived anxiety, stress, and pain in radiation oncology patients. Twenty-four NewYork-Presbyterian patients ages forty to seventy-nine undergoing radiation therapy during cancer treatment participated in the study. After their radiation session, they underwent thirty minutes of relaxation exercises, which consisted of Reiki, therapeutic touch, sound therapy, music therapy, and aromatherapy. Blood pressure, heart rate, and pain level were recorded before and immediately after the intervention.

Interestingly, the data showed a consistent pattern in decreased blood pressure, heart rate, anxiety, and pain scores among radiation oncology patients. Lu-Wong felt this clearly shows evidence of the benefits of complementary and alternative medicine. We now have 1.2 million people in the United States who have sampled Reiki or a comparable therapy at least once the year prior, with 900 institutions and health-care systems in the United States that now use Reiki as a supplemental therapy. It's fair to say Reiki and preventative care is gaining popularity and momentum (Cleveland Clinic 2021). One study evaluated the effects of Reiki on patients recovering from a heart attack (Burg et al. 2010, 995–6). It found that Reiki had a larger impact on patients' overall emotional state than not using it and showed an increase in heart-rate variability within three days, which shows they had a significant drop in stress. There are bountiful uses of Reiki, and it can help anyone at any age. People use Reiki for everything from self-practice (which follows), chronic pain, stress, anxiety, or simply to promote overall health, and well-being (Cronkelton 2022).

Since becoming a Reiki practitioner in 2003 while pregnant with my first son and then reaching the master level as the COVID shutdown hit on March 16, 2020, I use it on a daily basis for myself, my family, friends, the greater family, my dog, my yoga students, for the greater good, and in my yoga classes, workshops, and retreats. Like Einstein said, "Energy is everything." Working intentionally with energy through Reiki has created a fundamental shift in my perspective that has made a difference on many levels from the physical to the psychological, spiritual, and mental. Sound interesting? If you want to try energy healing on yourself, you can try it now.

Experiencing Your Own Reiki Energy

Although you must receive attunements by a Reiki Master teacher in order to transmit it to others officially, you can channel love and light with the power of your prayer, intention, imagination, awareness, breath, and spiritual guides or higher power as a self-healing practice. Experiment with the presence of the energy in your own hands just by rubbing your palms together, pulling them apart and tuning into the energy created between them. Whether you call it Chi, Reiki, Therapeutic Touch, Hands of Light, or Healing Hands, there is a historical and universal application of touch for healing worldwide and throughout history. Energy healing has been used for centuries in various forms. Now you can use it for yourself. While you can read about Reiki in a book and learn hand positions, until attuned or connected as a channel to Reiki, some say you cannot truly practice it, especially if you want to practice with others in an official capacity. That said, I invite you to try this Reiki self-practice with or without having received Reiki from a practitioner. Let it be an experiential practice and a testament to the healing power of touch and intention.

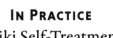

IN PRACTICE
Reiki Self-Treatment

Be creative and feel free to customize the following practice to meet your unique needs. Interestingly, the Cleveland Clinic prescribes Reiki self-treatment as an aftercare protocol once patients have had a Reiki session by a Reiki Master at their hospital. The idea is that self-treatments can help you to continue to receive Reiki on a daily basis if you perform it on yourself at home. Reiki self-treatments can help anyone to receive the benefits of healing touch on a daily basis. This practice includes the standard Reiki hand postures and ideas, and so it is universal.

Reiki self-treatment can be done whether you feel healthy or not. Approach your Reiki self-treatments as special times you set aside as self-care to invoke peace and calm. Maybe start with a twenty-minute session first thing in the morning and then another twenty-minute one at the end of the day. Customize this practice to suit your preferences. These treatments can be performed for longer stretches of time if you would like, maybe for thirty to sixty minutes. Adjust the time of day to best fit your schedule.

These self-treatments can be performed while sitting in a chair or lying on your back on a sofa, a bed, or the floor. Perform your self-treatments alone unless you need someone present in the room for your care and safety. I like to kick off my shoes, cover up with a blanket, and use an eye pillow. Often, I listen to sound healing music in the background. I find it really helps to keep my focus and attention on my breath and body as I perform the various hand positions. You may love relaxing instrumental music during your self-treatments.

To perform a Reiki self-treatment, follow the hand position instructions in the order in which they are described on the following pages. Feel free to make any adjustments you believe will help support you. For example, in a twenty-minute self-treatment, perform each hand position for about two minutes. No need to worry about the exact amount of time. If you feel you want to stay in certain hand positions for a longer time than others, go with that. You are in charge. Find what works for you. With practice, you will memorize the hand positions. Don't worry about doing the hand positions perfectly. Just relax and do the best you can. That will be good enough. Finally, feel free to place your hands in other places on your body that need relaxation and healing. Maybe do a pain rating scale of one (the least stress) to ten (the most stress) before and after the Reiki treatment as your own scientific experiment.

Opening Your Reiki Session

Hand Position One Start by gently placing your hands together in a prayer position in the middle of your chest, just below your chin. Close your eyes. Notice and make mental note of any special places in your body or mind that need special attention in your session. Scale any pain or anxiety from one to ten with one being the least anxious or painful and ten being the most pain or stress imaginable.

- Intend for your Reiki self-treatment to be performed for the highest and greatest good and to invite your body's innate healing energy to activate.

- Keep your hands in this position for a moment or two while focusing your attention on your in-breaths and out-breaths. Breathe slowly and deeply to promote relaxation of your body and mind.

Hand Position Two Gently place both hands on top of the head. Focus your attention on your hands as they rest there. Allow this hand position to relax the skin, muscles, and flow down to the bones of your head from the outside in.

Hand Position Three Put both hands over your eyes. Focus your attention on the light pressure over your eyes. Feel the temperature of your hands where they rest. Avoid placing your hands over your nose so your breath can move easily. Allow this hand position to relax the muscles and skin in your forehead, face, and eyes. Imagine expansive healing energy moving inward for each hand position and body part in the sequence going forward.

Hand Position Four Place your right hand over your throat and the left hand over your heart. Focus your attention on your throat and heart. Avoid too much pressure with your hand over your throat to stay comfortable. Allow this hand position to relax the muscles in your neck, throat, and upper chest area inward.

Hand Position Five Put your hands just below the breast line. The middle fingers should be touching each other over your diaphragm. Focus your attention on the area under your chest. Allow this hand position to relax the muscles in the center of your chest and rib areas and flow inward.

Hand Position Six Move your hands one hand-width down from your breast line, gently placing them over the upper stomach (the solar plexus area). Focus your attention on this area of the body. Allow this hand position to relax the muscles in this area.

Hand Position Seven Situate your hands over the stomach and navel area. Focus your attention on this area of the body. Allow this hand position to relax the muscles here. Invite in a sense of softening and release.

Hand Position Eight Gently place both hands on the shoulder muscles. Focus your attention on this area of the body and allow this hand position to relax the muscles from the outside to the inside.

Hand Position Nine Place your hands above the waistline, on the kidney area. Focus your attention on this area of the body and allow this hand position to relax the muscles all the way down to a cellular level.

Hand Position Ten Set your hands on either the tops of your feet or the soles of your feet. You can do this by crossing your left leg over your right knee to reach your left foot. Cross your right leg over your left knee to reach your right foot. Avoid strain and just do the best you can.

Once complete, congratulate yourself for practicing this form of self-love! Take time to tune in to the results of this practice. If you did the pain rating scale of one to ten before your Reiki treatment, ask yourself what the number is now. Did it go down? Notice however you feel, allowing the distinction between any labels like good, bad, or indifferent to dissolve. Prepare to move into the remainder of your day or waking state. Whatever your approach, the important part is your effort and presence in the process.

Reiki Attunements

Unlike other healing arts, Reiki is passed from master to student through a Reiki attunement ritual that allows you to connect to the universal Reiki source by opening your energetic pathways. Attunement means to harmonize, unify, or blend and allows you to become a vessel of Reiki and move Reiki energy for yourself and others. Many think of an attunement as an energetic opening that allows the Reiki energy to flow freely through your body to impact your health and that of others.

It was unusual but my friend and colleague at OPLM, Heather Ross, a family recovery coach, received all the Reiki attunements at once, which she feels might explain how intense it was.

"I had a vision and could see how every event from my childhood played out in my adulthood. I saw how it affected my mothering in how I interacted and reacted as a mother. It was painful, but I could see the impact of generational trauma and there was a healing," said Ross. She said she was amazed to see her impact on another person and how connected we all really are. The whole thing went back and forth from her childhood to motherhood and lasted for a long time, like thirty minutes, but Ross made a choice to stay with it though it was hard.

"It showed me how much power I had and gave me clarity. It showed me the importance of healing pain for ourselves and others and how we can hurt others because of our pain," said Ross.

Other side effects of a Reiki attunement can be a rush of energy around your body; a shift in consciousness, such as gratitude or love for all beings; and crying, the release of stuck emotions. It is also said that the opening of an attunement has the effect of enhancing other energetic healings and channeling pathways. Some students report that receiving an attunement causes increased intuitive awareness. I have found each of these to be true.

Dr. Feldman's Personal Story

Dr. Feldman has expressed his continued support for further research to prove the value of Reiki so that in the future all patients will be able to receive Reiki as part of their treatment protocol. Feldman shared the story of his beloved sister, Fern, who succumbed to breast cancer when she was only in her thirties with three small children. This event impacted the course of his life and profession. Witnessing his sister's illness and cancer treatments often left Feldman and the whole family traumatized before her eventual death. This led Feldman to become a breast cancer surgeon. Fern had taught him the importance of finding a better way for women enduring breast cancer treatments. Even though currently under-researched, Feldman sees Reiki as an option to create that better way forward (Keyes 2012).

Power of Touch

If Reiki still sounds too woo-woo, there are alternatives. Consider the cutting-edge research that proves everyday forms of touch can bring you to emotional balance and better health. And we've all felt it. A pat on the back or a caress of the arm are everyday, incidental gestures that we usually take for granted, yet they are far more profound than we usually realize. After years spent immersed in the science of touch, Dacher Keltner, the executive editor of *Greater Good* magazine that focuses on science-based research at Berkeley, explains how compassion is literally at our fingertips. He says it is because touch is our fundamental language of compassion and a primary means for spreading it (Keltner 2010).

A flurry of studies in recent years have revealed amazing advantages of touch for both physical and emotional well-being. This research confirms what most intuitively already know: that touch is actually essential for human connection, communication, and health. And really, who hasn't felt better with a hug? It's how we show love and encouragement to our children and pets. It brings us comfort in the challenges of life.

Power of Touch: Amma the Hugging Saint

Have you heard of the saint who gives hugs? Amma, aka Mother, has been on Oprah, toured around the world, and has literally touched thousands of people. Her goal? To use the power of a hug to change the world. Followers of this famed Indian Hindu spiritual teacher and humanitarian congregate to experience the enveloping power of her embrace. Amma also oversees Embracing the World®, a global network of nonprofits with operations in more than forty nations (Mata Amritanandamayi 2019). When I was on the receiving end of her hug, I almost felt like crying because her presence emanated a pure compassion that was touching. The point is that touch is universally healing, and we've all felt the effects as another form of healing touch.

Energy Healing: Attachment Cord-Cutting Technique

Do you want to go where your energy is reciprocated, celebrated, and appreciated? Of course! Are you ready to be rid of exhausting influences? Who isn't? Here is an energy healing technique for creating the conditions for both of these things. In the context of spirituality and energy healing, you may hear the terms *etheric cords* or *attachments*. Simply described, they are energetic, mental, or emotional connections to people, things, or places that either give you energy or drain it from you.

These invisible bonds that tie you can be healthy or unhealthy, such as addiction. Healthy attachments, such as the bond between a mother and a child, and the later attachment cords are typically fear-based cords, or unfavorable ties you create with someone or something out of need or fear. Knowing about these types of attachments and learning how to cut them has been freeing for me. Whatever your belief system, you could think of it as a psychological release. You can also have attachments to past things, places, and events. It seems most of us tend to focus on attachments to individuals.

This ritual does not imply abandonment, ditching, or detachment from someone when you cut these attachment cords. These bonds could form between members of your family, friends, coworkers, an ex, or other acquaintances. For instance, you may have a friend who is kindhearted but in great need. Whenever you are with them, you notice a decrease in energy since they are unintentionally draining you of it. Cutting the cord of attachment does not mean leaving your friend. Instead, it means cutting the unfavorable bond that has grown. In essence, you are building a stronger, healthier bond! Another example is an attachment with an ex. You have parted ways but the other person is not moving on, is bothering you, or is harassing you. Do cord-cutting with such people to help with these types of issues. Professional healers, doctors, and teacher types tend to form these types of attachment cords more than others.

Ways to Clear an Unhealthy Attachment Cord

When should an attachment be cleared? It should be done if you experience a strong psychic connection to someone who is draining your energy, you want to stop bad habits or addictions, or you feel pulled back into unpleasant relationships. Before you try an attachment cord cutting rite, start by taking the following preventative actions to avoid repeating old patterns that do not serve. Then your cord-cutting will be more effective.

Forget and Forgive Intuitively, unforgivingness is the main cause of recurrent unhelpful attachment. You will unintentionally become attached to the person or thing that you don't want if you have any feelings or thoughts of blame, hatred, or retaliation. That is enough justification to drop it! When I forgive, I feel free. I once spoke with a woman who had the capacity to speak to and pardon the murderer of her husband. She was liberated from the burden of resentment and bitterness as a result of not being connected to a murderer.

Drop the Drama Living in and enjoying drama is the second most frequent reason for nonserving attachments. Dramatic energy is a chaotic energy that cannot offer harmony or tranquility.

No Gossip Although it may sound like drama, this is mainly about the advantages of avoiding falsehoods or lies about the people close to you, as well as about yourself.

Action and Intention Perform as needed. It only takes a clear intention to accomplish this. All nonserving etheric links can be severed.

Avoid Depleting People and Environments It goes without saying that you will be putting yourself in a position for potential attachment if you surround yourself with people and things that are not in your higher benefit or that drain you. Go where your energy is reciprocated, celebrated, and appreciated. Also, pay attention to the areas you frequent. Top locations to be cautious of as energy drains include public transit, workplaces (as if they can always be avoided!), offices, pubs, and clubs. Only surround yourself with people who improve your energy. This might be seen as letting in only what strengthens your character and adds to your personal power.

Conserve Your Energy It is imperative to make an effort to quit thinking and talking about a certain person if you have a nonserving relationship with them. Since thinking and communication are energy, this could make it more challenging to break harmful thought habits.

Don't Pursue, Follow Up on, or Stalk As clear as it may seem, if you are actively looking for someone and monitoring them, it is impossible to cut off nonserving ties with them. It won't work if your behavior conflicts with your aim to end nonserving attachments. It's possible that doing so will make it stronger. In order for the action and the intention to be effective for you, they must be coordinated. You probably already guessed that!

IN PRACTICE
The Cord-Cutting Ritual

If you already have a meditation practice, you may want to include a nonserving, attachment cord cutting visualization into it as needed. Or let this be a stand-alone practice. You can use this visualization anywhere and you do not necessarily need to be meditating.

Step 1: Begin by relaxing your body. Breathe in deeply and breathe out slowly three to five times.

Step 2: Close your eyes and call upon your divine intelligence/ angel/higher self (or whatever loving Source you call on for help). Ask them to guide you through this process.

Step 3: Feel the presence of your Source/angels/guides and recite the following prayer: "Dear Archangel Michael (known for cord cutting and clearing), I call upon you to help me heal, let go, and cut any attachments and cords that are no longer serving my higher purpose. I ask that all cords that are attached and that are not aligned with love be cut. Help me to release them on all levels past, present, future, in all dimensions, and for all time."

Step 4: Option to close your eyes and visualize the attachments in the form of cords, chains, or ropes, as some people do. Imagine a beautiful, blue, laser-like forcefield starting at the crown of your head moving down and around your whole body to your feet and back up, severing these cords. Use your senses to feel, watch, and experience them being released until you feel lighter. Tune in to the areas where the cords may have attached. Is there sensation in these areas? If nothing obvious crops up, trust that the work is done.

Step 5: Visualize a color you associate most with healing, such as sparkling white, sky blue, or emerald green. See it flowing down from the Source to the crown of your head. This is a powerful, healing light flowing into the areas where the cords once were. It cascades through them and completely encompasses your entire body and surrounds you like a blanket of light and rejuvenation.

Step 6: See the areas where the cords were cut, now clean and clear. They are healed and sealed with bright, white light, like a spiritual caulking.

Step 7: You may need to repeat this prayer two to three times a day. That's okay, keep doing it as much as you need to.

Step 8: Say, "Surround me with your blue cloak of protection to shield me from future attachments. Thank you."

After the ritual is over, you might like to do some sort of energetic clearing of the room and yourself. You can smudge (use aromatics or burn incense/candles) your surroundings, diffuse some oils, or take a warm salt bath.

Divine Help: Angelic Reiki

Years ago, I was sure I didn't believe in angels. I struggled with including them here for fear of shooting my credibility. If you are open and the following helps you, go with it. If not, skip ahead. Maybe like me, you dismiss such notions of invisible winged beings reaching down through another realm to be a part of your daily life. That is until I opened to the high, uplifting energy I sensed whenever I read about them, was introduced to their teachings, or tried meditations that included them.

In reading Keyes's book *The Healing Light of Angels: Transforming Your Past, Present & Future with Divine Energy*, I again had the same experience (and others) which led to me definitively changing my mind. I stayed open, did the meditations, and it helped me through some dark times. This connection has become a source of strength for me. For those with a spiritual orientation, Reiki can be used in creative collaboration with divine help. Talk with angels (or your version of a higher power, spirit guides, the Universe, or your higher self). If you are amiable to this, call it what you will.

This special addition to a Reiki session can add another layer to your energy healing toolbox. In order to reach out, you need only ask for assistance. For example, "Archangel Raphael, please assist me with the greatest possible healing for the highest possible good. Thank you." The angelic frequency is said to be a vibration with a sound measurement of 888 hertz (Hz) and when I listen to it, I like how it makes me feel. As I sit here typing it plays on my Google speaker. I also play it at night while I sleep. The recording I love sounds like the shifting sands you hear when swimming beneath ocean waves.

Archangels: Their Meanings and Use in Reiki

These archangels and the meanings of their names are drawn from various sources including my Master Reiki Manual (which in itself draws from a variety of spiritual and religious texts) and Doreen Virtue's *Archangels and Ascended Masters* book as well as what experientially works for me. I find it interesting to note that angels are known to be genderless, so the pronouns reflect this.

Archangel Chamuel whose name translates to "One who seeks God." Love, passion, heart mending, and relationships are all aided by Chamuel. When you're lost, ask for help finding goods and navigating around. The message is to let Chamuel guide you through the difficulties of life and ensure that your trip is successful. It gives them joy to replace pain's energy with calm.

Archangel Gabriel whose name translates to "God is my strength" or "Hero of God." Gabriel facilitates writing, communication, children, childbirth, adoption, purification, and defining your future course of action. From actors to writers to dancers, musicians, models, reporters, vocalists, teachers, and spiritual leaders, Gabriel supports people whose lives are devoted to the arts. The message is, permit Gabriel to pave the way for you who follow the call of your heart to play, perform, or create on a larger scale.

Archangel Jophiel whose name translates to "God's Beauty." Archangel of wisdom, insight, and judgment, Jophiel can be called upon for support in creative endeavors, lovely contemplation, connecting with one's source through the crown center, and organizing space. Jophiel offers inspiration, helps people avoid making the same mistakes twice, and helps them discover *joie de vivre*, or the love of life! The message is that worry never helped anything, so why turn to it during times of need? Rather, create in order to reflect the Creator.

Archangel Michael whose name implies "One like God." Michael is revered as a ferocious, fiery fighter, the spiritual bouncer, and the patron saint of law enforcement. Michael offers courage, protection, guidance, and a strong commitment to one's convictions. Ask Michael to help you with all areas of your life's motivation and purpose, as well as to help you let go of attachments and expel negative energy. Fear not for what tomorrow may bring is the message. Let the truth shine boldly and with optimism in your thinking. The light, the force, and the knowledge of the Divine surround and direct you.

Archangel Raphael whose name implies healing by God. Raphael is the patron of all types of healers and physicians who aid in the healing of humans and animals as well as the release of addictions and cravings. Raphael assists in releasing spirits from individuals and locations that have lower energy. Raphael, who is regarded as the patron of travelers, can be consulted for guidance on both inward spiritual journeys and safe travel. Raphael's message, linked to manifestation and the development of the third eye, or intuition, is that "Every morning is a new day of renewal." Make a connection with the flow of all the positive energy around you. Let go of the past, embrace the present, and anticipate the future.

IN PRACTICE
Clearing and Shielding Energy Techniques

If you are an empath or prone to be like a sponge absorbing and carrying everyone else's junk, it is essential to shield and clear your energy field daily. It is time to release anything that is not yours to carry and take care of your own energy. This way you can fulfill your purpose and share your healing gifts with others, the earth, and animals in your full power. The following two techniques were taught to me by Raven Keyes after her Reiki session with a loved one. She suggested using them frequently, which I do. The results I've noticed are feeling lighter, brighter, and more at ease.

Clearing

Step 1: Stand tall with your arms out wide, palms down.

Step 2: Right away you will feel the earth connection.

Step 3: Once you do, raise and circle your arms up and cross them overhead, down and out to their respective sides with arms back out.

Step 4: Declare your intention of clearing your energy field with authority and confidence. Say aloud or to yourself with authority, "I am now cleared of anything that doesn't serve me."

Shielding

The shielding is to be done right after the clearing exercise above.

Step 1: Take the same standing tall position with your arms out and palms down.

Step 2: Once you feel the earth's energy with your hands, reverse the arm movement as follows: Arms come down to your sides and cross in front of your hips, circling up overhead, around, and pressing together like a prayer in front of your heart.

Step 3: Say with firm determination, confidence, and strength, "I am shielded in divine white light. I decree it, and so it is."

IN PRACTICE
Breath Sweep to Clear Your Energy

When using the breath sweep technique, use your breath and your imagination to dive in. It is applied to situations you don't want to be tied to or to cleanse the energy of other people. I like it just prior to receiving Reiki. I believe it was created by Angie Webster. It's also a great way to start the day and wind down at the end. It is especially helpful if you have recently gone through an unpleasant, traumatic, or disorienting experience.

Imagine your aura encircling you for six feet all the way around, permeating every surface in the vicinity. Imagine that the energy you possess is being swept away by your breath, leaving only your own energy remaining. It is possible to call your own energy back to you by employing visualization and breathing techniques.

Step 1: Begin with your hands on your belly to feel your belly muscles relaxing. Take a full breath in and feel your belly expand like a balloon. Release it, inviting your belly to contract back in toward the spine.

Step 2: Shut your eyes and sense your body's vitality. Pay attention to how you are feeling and any areas of your body that seem tight or tense. Take note of any feelings or energy you might be storing.

Step 3: As you inhale again, visualize the breath rising from your feet (6 feet down), going up your body, and ending at the top of your head (6 feet). As you release the breath, watch it move back down your body until it emerges from your feet.

Step 4: Imagine as you take your next in breath, the air enters your body from the back (from 6 feet behind) and travels forward through you, exiting your body through the front (6 feet). Exhale, imagine your breath enters your body from the front (6 feet) through you and exits from the back (6 feet).

Step 5: Inhale, imagine your breath enters your body (6 feet from your left) through your left fingers, traveling up your arm, through the length of your body and exiting your body through your right arm and fingers. Exhale, visualizing your breath enters (6 feet from the right) through your right arm and fingertips, through your body, and out your left arm and fingertips.

Step 6: Request all the energy that is not yours to be released to the earth and the universe so that it might be repurposed for the greater good.

Step 7: Request the restoration of all your dispersed energy to you, as well as energy from others to be returned back to them.

Step 8: Take one final inhale to clear your energy field, sweeping away any debris. As you exhale, see it floating away.

You may also find this breath sweeping technique useful prior to meditation, on days when your mind is feeling overactive, or when you are struggling to settle down. If I could sum up this chapter in a few sentences, I'd say focus on how you direct your energy with purpose. As best as you can, avoid using your energy to worry. Use your energy to believe, create, love, grow, glow, manifest, and heal.

5

Change Your Brain with EMDR, CBT, and DBT

The goal of EMDR treatment is to rapidly
metabolize the dysfunctional residue from the
past and transform it into something useful.

. . . . . .

PSYCHOLOGIST AND CREATOR OF EMDR FRANCINE SHAPIRO

While researching this book, I had the privilege of learning from several leading experts in the field of trauma healing. A clear theme emerged from those interactions: eye movement desensitization and reprocessing (EMDR) therapy consistently stood out to them as one of the most effective, evidence-based treatments for trauma. Its power lies in its ability to directly and efficiently rewire the traumatized brain.

I first encountered this perspective from licensed clinical social worker Bonnie Rumilly. It was reinforced during Bessel van der Kolk's trauma healing retreat at the Kripalu Center and echoed again by Dr. Sheila Salama. All three—highly experienced and deeply engaged in trauma work—share their insights in this chapter, helping to explain why EMDR is widely regarded as a gold standard in trauma therapy.

At the same time, you'll also discover the importance of a multifaceted approach. Treatments such as trauma-informed cognitive behavioral therapy (CBT) and dialectical behavior therapy (DBT), which are also discussed in this chapter, add valuable tools to the healing process. Later in the book, modalities like somatic experiencing (SE) and a range of other mind-body practices illustrate the benefits of a holistic approach. Healing is never one-size-fits-all—there are many paths, and each person's journey is uniquely their own.

Eye Movement Desensitization and Reprocessing (EMDR) Therapy

If you want a way to manage and move on from trauma, EMDR is a highly effective way to directly change or reprocess trauma memories in your brain without the re-traumatization of overly talking about it. And it can be used in conjunction with other treatments for a broader range of support tools. The latter of which can be done on your own, and we will delve deeper into them later in the chapter. All are from psychology and can be combined with the complementary practices of various mindfulness and yoga therapeutic techniques to add to your recovery tool belt. The goal? To retrain your mind and change your brain itself.

How EMDR Works

It is kind of amazing that EMDR works directly in reconfiguring the neuroplasticity of your brain. This, along with the overlapping stress reduction and lifestyle management techniques of yoga therapy, gives you more options for finding relief from symptoms of trauma and building resiliency to combat it. We return to our friend Rumilly, the trauma specialist from chapter 1. Interestingly, it is EMDR that Rumilly has found to be the most effective therapy, over all the others, to reprocess trauma and other disturbing life experiences. And this goes for helping her clients heal from the events at Sandy Hook and 9/11 and for her first-responder clientele.

The Broken Glass of Trauma Memories

Traumatic memories, unlike standard ones, are altered like shattered glass because the overpowering experience sets off something like a fire alarm in the amygdala. It's like your amygdala gets hijacked. This is the memory-storing region of the brain that becomes inhibited as a result of the activation. This causes the memory to be dispersed randomly. The order of things happened inconsistently. If you have experienced trauma, you may remember the event happening, but not all of the details, such as the time or location where it took place. You may remember just a sensation or one small piece of information. Maybe you cannot remember the face or last name of the perpetrator where it was previously known to you.

Bilateral Stimulation (BLS) in EMDR

Created by the American psychologist and educator Francine Shapiro, EMDR is a unique therapy that uses a set protocol and a technique known as bilateral stimulation (BLS). There are a variety of BLS options. These include sounds or tones from a headset; visual movements in which your eyes follow a moving object back and forth across the perceptual field; or kinesthetic or tapping cues, which require tracking respectively by the ears, eyes, or your body. If you are not familiar this may take a moment to absorb. BLS helps to activate both sides of your brain, which helps your brain to process the memory until it can be stored "properly" or in a more organized fashion. The EMDR procedure converts your memories and creates new, more orderly neural pathways in your brain. Literally, this is the ability of your brain to form and reorganize synaptic connections.

This trauma can be in response to learning, an experience, or even following an injury. As the memories are processed or recovered, symptoms subside as the memories are rearranged or rewired. This helps your brain to heal itself, which it wants to do. This is its natural inclination because your brain, as well as your whole being, seeks wholeness. Well-being is your birthright. It really is. The first step in the eight-phase protocol is for the therapist to gather your history to pinpoint what the impactful traumatic memories are. For example, if you are experiencing nightmares, which is a common symptom of PTSD, EMDR will help you process the traumatic memories in order to get to a place where nightmares subside and you are able to successfully sleep again. You can say that you are not changing the memories of what happened, you are changing how it lives within you. This is a very important point. It is the main point and a theme you will see resurface as a pattern in all types of trauma work.

EMDR and Rapid Eye Movement (REM) Sleep

Are you wondering how the heck this actually works? The point of the eye movements in EMDR is to mimic your rapid eye movement (REM) sleep cycle, the most restorative time during sleep. This sleep cycle is where your cellular regeneration occurs. It is also where short-term memories get transferred to long-term memories in your hippocampus. This is the brain region that manages learning and memory. EMDR allows for an unconscious memory, core belief, fear, body memory, or whatever was stored in the memory network to come to the surface in conscious memory for healing and redefining.

In essence, EMDR helps to shift the processing of traumatic memories from the emotionally charged amygdala to the more rational and integrative hippocampus, allowing for a healthier and more integrated understanding of the traumatic experience. Cool, huh?

Other Applications for BLS

A remarkable yet nuanced point for me in conversing with Rumilly was her feeling that EMDR is not just for extreme trauma situations. It can even help with self-esteem and negative feelings about self that interfere with personal growth by alleviating symptoms. This is what makes it so useful and such a successful therapy modality in her practice. There are days when Rumilly said she uses BLS on herself, as she displayed her BLS device, with two small paddles to hold in each hand that physically tap your hands from side to side as you hold them. Sometimes she uses it to avoid secondhand trauma, the indirect trauma experience that comes with her line of work.

EMDR Case Study One

Sheila Salama is a psychiatrist who offers EMDR, brain spotting (another form of EMDR), somatic experiencing (a type of bodywork covered in chapter 6), the emotional freedom technique in chapter 8, Qigong (mind-body-spirit exercises), yoga (chapter 2), and other non-pharmacological modalities in her practice. I met Salama at a local trauma healing talk she gave. Working extensively with veterans coping with war trauma and survivors of early childhood abuse, Salama says that the reprocessing in EMDR ultimately changes people's feelings about themselves.

"It is not just the release of the trauma but the way the reprocessing neutralizes the trauma memories. The result is that clients feel that, if they had to do it over again, they know they did the right thing and they feel better," said Salama. Salama explained that the right and left sides of the brain see things differently. The bilateral stimulation connects the right and left brain so that both parts can communicate and the result is that the brain is changed in the process. The outcomes are impressive in some pretty tough cases.

In one such case, Salama had a seven-year-old client who was traumatized by being sexually assaulted by his own father. The boy suffered with various symptoms including horrific nightmares. Salama worked with the boy using eye movement to change the ending of the nightmares. She told him he didn't have to talk about it but encouraged him to pretend to play a movie (aka the movie technique, which is used therapeutically to soften the experience in one's mind). He was to go back in the movie and have the incident disrupted. He was told he could do whatever he wanted with his father to change the ending. He chose karate moves. Over time, by repeating the EMDR process over multiple sessions, and following the protocol, the boy was empowered to release the feeling of victimhood. Eventually the boy got stronger, was released from treatment, and moved on. Salama would check in with him from time to time. As an adult, he said he felt sorry for his dad because his dad missed out on knowing him. Salama felt this was a healthy perspective for someone who lived through sexual abuse from a parent. Such is the restorative power of EMDR.

EMDR Case Study Two

The more I learn about trauma, the more I want to work on my own. EMDR was the modality I picked based on Rumilly's success with the method and my own research. I chose a practitioner and met the clinician with a list of about seven traumatic memories I wanted to work through. I had ruminated on these issues for years. They seemed to haunt me in that they hung out in the dark recesses of my mind, waiting for a trigger to resurface. I never really got over them. Intellectually, I knew they were not my fault but deep down they took up too much headspace and ended up depleting me.

Initially, I had four sessions. Each time I found that my response to EMDR was like an unraveling of events. Each traumatic memory I explored somehow jumped across the years to one from my childhood. In my mind, it was like following the memories backward along the neural pathways and seeing them connect with each other in haphazard patterns. Each window had a different picture of my life and it went so fast that I couldn't focus clearly on one. It was more like a moving target going back in time.

After those sessions, I looked back and realized I really had done the best I could, and I no longer felt the need to blame myself. Each time I went, it helped me deal with fear, betrayal, and anger that sprang up. It gave me a greater sense of being in control, like I was finally going to get past these issues. Enough of that old crap already! I'm done with victim mentality and wallowing in darkness. My traumatic memories became far more workable and were laid to rest. They seemed to shrink in size and magnitude. Eventually, they were not nearly as noticeable or recurrent in my awareness as before. I don't mean to sugar coat these sessions. They are not easy. It is a process. Often, when I did EMDR therapy I shed tears and felt shaky and vulnerable the rest of the day but a little better. Every day after I felt a little improvement and the traumas faded more as time went on.

If you decide to try EMDR, it is best to schedule a light day afterward because it is tiring. My therapist said it was the equivalent of three hours of talk therapy. It helps to take time to breathe consciously and drink extra water right after. Years later, if I recall the original trauma list I took into my first EMDR session, I see that those events now exist like shadows in the past. I am not reliving them and they haven't come up in the same way since. I can tell that EMDR changed how the memories live in my body because I feel more at ease with them.

As I progress with the work, old programming continues to come up for excavation. I remind myself not to worry, that this is normal. It helps to see it as an opportunity to shift my perspective that what is coming up is there to be released. I am peeling back layers of the old paradigms that no longer serve me. I am recalibrating and getting lighter each time old, dysfunctional memories or patterns drop away. I say these last two points as an affirmation. Below are EMDR resources you can use anytime you want to be kind to yourself. They, like the other practices throughout this book, are not relegated to therapy. Let the goal be to incorporate the self-care strategies that work for you into your everyday life, where they are most needed.

In Practice
Butterfly Hug Calming Technique

You can calm or soothe yourself with a butterfly hug whenever you feel angry, sad, or hurt. Butterfly hug was calming for me in my EMDR sessions, and EMDR practitioners place a lot of importance on self-soothing techniques in therapy sessions.

Step 1: Cross your thumbs and open your fingers in the shape of a butterfly and hold them under your collar bones. Or cross your wrists and hold your shoulders if that is more comfortable.

Step 2: Take a moment to breathe deep and close your eyes. Hold here if you like.

Step 3: Begin tapping your hands on your body ten times. Then pause and take another deep breath. Continue tapping until you feel more relaxed.

Step 4: To try bilateral stimulation (BLS, from page 177), alternate tapping with your right hand under your right collar bone, then your left hand under your left collar bone ten times. Then pause and take a deep breath. Continue until you feel relaxed.

If it's not too busy, feel free to combine the butterfly hug with the calm breath technique or the safe space meditation.

IN PRACTICE
Eagle/Garuda Mudra in Yoga

Eagle, aka *garuda mudra*, is the same hand posture as butterfly hug with the thumbs and hands crossed, palms open under the collar bones. *Garuda mudra* translates to "gesture of the eagle." *Mudra* is Sanskrit for "seal" and is a type of symbolic hand or finger gesture used to control the flow of energy in your body. If the fingers or hands were wires, holding the thumbs is like closing a circuit so the energy can be strong and directed. Eagle mudra is meant to clear your mind and bring it back into the present. It is used to bring airflow and balance to both sides of your body while increasing blood circulation. Using eagle mudra with intention has proved to be beneficial for my students, especially when used with the calming breath technique.

It does not matter whether you call it a hug or a mudra; there are benefits to hugging yourself. (You will find another form of this called self-containment in chapter 6 on somatic healing). Did you know that criticism and negative self-talk are often associated with anxiety? You can offset that with a hug.

One of the biggest benefits of hugging yourself for anxiety is that it encourages you to treat yourself with a lot of compassion. Let the butterfly hug be a reminder that it is good to have high standards and it is also important to view yourself with loving eyes. Intuitively, you can feel how berating yourself only makes your spirit sink versus how self-acceptance helps it rise. This method of self-soothing allows you to develop a sense of compassion and self-care. You can also try it alone or combine it with the following calm breath technique or calm/safe place sanctuary meditation that follows.

IN PRACTICE
EMDR Calm Breath Technique

I invite you to try calm breath. Prepare by sitting up straight and comfortable in a place where you will not be disturbed.

Step 1: Inhale for a count of three.

Step 2: Exhale for a count of six.

Notice that in this ratio the exhale is twice as long as the inhale on purpose since this is optimal for calm. The longer exhale downregulates your central nervous system and is a way to comfort, soothe, and settle yourself. If you need to shorten or simplify, start with inhaling for two counts and exhaling four and work up to more. The important part is the focus on extending the exhale regardless of the count.

IN PRACTICE
EMDR Calm/Safe Space Sanctuary Meditation

Similarly, the calm or safe place sanctuary meditation is all about creating an emotional retreat in meditation, for self-soothing or if you were in session with an EMDR practitioner. This is an internal place you can go to recover stability when feeling stressed. It is also backed up by the yoga sutras as part of the concept of dharana, or concentration, which involves teaching your mind to focus on one point or image. "Concentration is binding thought in one place," says Patanjali, author of the ancient *Yoga Sutras*. The goal is to still your mind and gently push away excess thoughts by fixing your mind on some object such as a candle flame, a flower, a mantra (sacred sound for quieting the mind), or in this case, a safe place. You will know your mind is concentrating when there is no sense of time passing.

Sure, a form of this type of meditation can be used in therapy, but anyone at any time is welcome to use it. I have found it helpful for falling asleep at night or in dealing with anxiety. One of my safe spaces is in the ocean where I can hear the shifting sands. It comes from a memory of snorkeling in Costa Rica. It was incredibly beautiful, swimming with schools of fish over coral reefs beneath the waves, when suddenly a little brown octopus shot out from under a rock and glided along the bottom with me trailing behind in wonder until it disappeared. This imagery was awesome in the true sense of the word because it was so beautiful and filled me with deep peace and wonder. Ready to create your own sanctuary within?

Step 1: Start by getting comfortable in a quiet place where you won't be disturbed and take a minute to focus on your breath.

Step 2: Close your eyes, soften or lower your gaze, and become aware of any tension in your body. Let go of that tension with each out-breath.

Step 3: Imagine a place where you can feel calm, peaceful, and safe. That place may be a beach or a mountain. It may be a place you've been to before, somewhere you've dreamed about going to, somewhere you've seen a picture of, or just a peaceful space you can create in your mind's eye.

Step 4: Look around you in that place. Notice the colors and shapes. What else do you notice?

Step 5: Now notice the sounds that are around you or perhaps the silence. Tune in to sounds far away and those nearer to you. Those that are more noticeable and those that are more subtle.

Step 6: Observe any smells you notice there.

Step 7: Focus on any skin sensations. Notice the earth beneath you or whatever is supporting you in that place, the temperature, any movement of air, or anything else you can touch.

Step 8: Notice the pleasant physical sensations in your body while you enjoy this safe place.

Step 9: While you are in your peaceful and safe place, you might choose to give it a name, such as *heaven*. Maybe personalize it, such as *Jackie's heaven*. Whether one word or a phrase, you can use it to bring that image back any time you need to.

Step 10: You can choose to linger there a while, just enjoying the peacefulness and serenity.

Step 11: Remember you can leave whenever you want to, just by opening your eyes and being aware of where you are now. You can also return by closing your eyes.

Step 12: Finally, bring yourself back to alertness in the present moment.

Congrats on cultivating your well-being with this practice. You are retraining your brain! Please keep in mind that your effort and presence are the most important part of practice, no matter what does or does not happen. Be aware there may be times when you end up "stewing in your own crap" so to speak. That is, when you experience monkey mind. It's natural. Come out as needed. This is an experiential practice.

IN PRACTICE

Reducing Anxiety with the EMDR Light Stream Grounding Technique

The light stream grounding technique is a soothing approach used in EMDR to reduce negative affect, such as emotions that feel challenging, including sadness, fear, or shame (Wolf 2011). It is a favorite in the support groups I facilitate, which have nothing to do with EMDR but everything to do with self-care. It was adapted as follows:

- I invite you to become mindful of what you are experiencing and feeling at that moment. Ask yourself what emotions am I feeling right now and where do I feel it in my body?

- Imagine that those feelings are an object. The goal is to take the first thing that comes to mind after recognizing the emotions and location. Mentally ask yourself these questions about the object:

    » "If it had a shape, what shape would it be?"

    » "If it had a size, what size would it be?"

    » "If it had a color, what color would it be?"

    » "If it had a temperature, what temperature would it be? Hot or cold?"

    » "If it had a texture, what texture would it be?"

    » "If it had a sound, what kind of sound would it make? High or low pitch?"

- Moving into a direct imagery exercise:

  » Pick a color that you most associate with healing.

  » Imagine that there is a stream of bright light in this color that is coming from the center of the universe. This is a magic light, because the more you need it, the more of it is available to you.

  » Allow this beautiful light to flow into your head and focus it down on the object. Let the light vibrate and resonate like a laser beam in and around this object.

  » Allow yourself to just notice what happens to the object.

  » Remember that the more light or energy that you need, the more becomes available to you. Allow yourself to feel the light enter your mind and allow the healing light again to vibrate and resonate in and around the object and notice what happens to the object.

  » When you notice that the object is gone or feel that it is contained, let the energy from the light flow into the rest of your body.

  » Feel it to reach the tips of your fingers and the tips of your toes.

  » Allow yourself to be engulfed, surrounded, and filled by the energy. Count to three and open your eyes.

  » You should notice that those feelings are now reduced or completely gone.

Congratulations, you did it! There is no right or wrong way to do this. Use the space below to expand on any insights you felt.

Mindfulness Journaling

Write how you feel and ask what the object or feeling's message was from the light stream meditation.

Multipronged Approaches to Trauma

Rumilly corroborates her experience with what we already know about trauma. It is different for everyone and there is not an equation for how it is classified or treated. She finds a multipronged approach, or a combination of treatments, to be essential in supporting her clients for best outcomes.

Rumilly gave an example of how you could combine different strategies in dealing with your anxiety or trauma symptoms: "Clients could use EMDR with their therapist and then employ other coping skills like cognitive behavioral therapy (CBT) in order to manage symptoms and heal. You may use CBT when you are at home or at work to manage intrusive thoughts, changing your negative thought, or going into a mental calm place, which is taught in early stages of EMDR therapy."

Rumilly felt that CBT is a very specific tool for addressing symptoms. After all, CBT is a form of psychotherapy for treating problems and boosting happiness by modifying dysfunctional emotions, behaviors, and thoughts. CBT teaches you self-regulation techniques and helps you change unhelpful or negative thought patterns. Rumilly stated she has success with CBT for anyone but especially those who suffer from obsessive compulsive disorder (OCD), a pattern of unreasonable thoughts and fears (obsessions) that leads to repetitive behaviors (compulsions). OCD isn't the only use for CBT; engage it whenever you experience your mind in an unhelpful loop. Rumilly helps those on a path of negative thinking to use CBT as a tool with one mode called the Stop Sign Technique. In it, you close your eyes and visualize yourself at a fork in the road with a stop sign at the end. You can focus on the stop sign, see it, and choose your direction to break the negative thought.

And there are additional practices I use after my EMDR sessions. Just recently we worked on a multiprong approach called the cognitive triangle.

It consists of how thoughts lead to feelings which become physical action. Knowing that you are hardwired to the negative as a survival mechanism, you can give yourself some grace or slack. It takes a lot of effort to be positive. Another CBT approach is practicing a pause, which we explore in this chapter. Both create space or breathing room to respond rather than react.

The idea being that, typically, when you react to a situation it comes out of a place of emotionality but when you respond to something, it comes more from a place of skill. Reacting is instant and filled with adrenaline, whereas responding takes time and comes from an inner place of calm and mindfulness. Pausing also works for emphasis in speaking, thinking, and acting in order to slow things down. You can use it to give yourself and others a moment to absorb information. Other CBT-inspired options might take the forms of grounding techniques, breathing exercises, or creating space by stepping away from challenging people or situations.

Cognitive Behavioral Therapy (CBT) Defined

CBT as an intervention is strong for addressing and changing cognitive distortions and behaviors, improving emotional regulation, and developing special coping mechanisms geared at overcoming immediate obstacles. It is really about bringing your awareness to specific thoughts in order to change harmful or negative thinking patterns. Say you're dealing with depression after a breakup. In checking the reality of your thoughts for accuracy in CBT you might ask yourself will I really die if my love breaks up with me? (Thought). Probably not. That is unless I am standing unawares in front of a speeding bus. (Reality check). This is a cheeky example of how you would fact find using CBT.

Trauma-Focused Cognitive Behavioral Therapy (TF-CBT)

Trauma-focused cognitive behavioral therapy (TF-CBT) still focuses on flawed thinking, effective coping, and interpersonal skills. It also aids healing by processing your traumatic memories and helping you learn skills for stress management. It is sometimes focused on children, teens, and their parents with things like positive parenting, behavior management, and effective communication. But it's useful for all ages.

TF-CBT combines elements drawn from these multiple approaches and theories:

Behavioral Therapy to identify and help change potentially self-destructive or unhealthy behaviors. It's based on the idea that all behaviors are learned and that behaviors can be changed.

Family Therapy examines patterns of interactions among family members to identify and alleviate problems.

Attachment Theory emphasizes the importance of the parent-child relationship and aims to build or rebuild a trusting, supportive relationship that will help prevent or treat anxiety or depression.

Interpersonal Neurobiology (IPNB) based on continuous brain growth shaped by relationships with the foundation to heal trauma is stimulating the brain with powerful and positive persuasion through meditation, awareness, and creating new neural pathways (*Psychology Today* 2018).

CBT vs. Dialectical Behavior Therapy (DBT)

As a subfield of CBT, I want to include dialectical behavior therapy (DBT) as part of the multiprong approach. DBT can help you change your behavior patterns, as opposed to trying to think or talk through the issues you are struggling with in CBT. The idea behind DBT is that pain cannot be avoided nor should it be. It may be hard but it is nature's way of signaling that something is wrong. Rather than sitting in the hell of what is wrong, the goal of DBT is simple: to help you get the hell out of it! No need to pitch a tent there. What makes DBT unique is its emphasis on learning how to tolerate and accept distress as a means of dealing with it.

DBT was designed by Dr. Marsha Linehan to treat a broad range of complicated symptoms and concerns, even subclinical, or what was previously thought to be "untreatable" cases. In DBT, you are taught an array of skills to cope with unhealthy thoughts and behaviors that involve a targeted approach that embodies:

Mindfulness Moment-to-moment awareness without judgment in order to accept unpleasant events and to stay present.

Distress Tolerance To learn to accept emotionally stressful, internal events.

Emotional Regulation To manage strong emotions such as fear, anxiety, and panic with less sensitivity.

Interpersonal Effectiveness To gain skills that develop more effective, consistent relationships (Chapman 2006, 62–8).

The Breakdown of DBT

The *D* means "dialectical." A dialectic is a blend, synthesis, or integration of opposites or contrasts using strategies to help you get unstuck from extreme positions.

DBT focused on validation and embracing yourself and reality as it is. It's the idea that reality is made up of opposites. In the trauma field, it is known that if you experience too much focus on change it could leave you feeling misunderstood and that your suffering is unjustified. When you have heightened emotional sensitivity, feeling a sense of acceptance and transformation can bring you more balance.

The *B* stands for "behavioral." A behavioral approach targets behavior that relates to your goals in order to figure out how to solve your problems.

Dialectical Thinking

Instead of black-and-white thinking, in DBT you can practice finding where two opposites can coexist. This requires you to hold two emotions at once. It is all about the importance of the word *and* versus *but*. The latter negates everything that comes after it. Here are examples to consider.

- I can understand why you feel this way *AND* I feel different about it.

- I accept things as they are *AND* I want to make changes.

- I am doing my best *AND* I want to do even better.

Post-Traumatic Growth Question Answered

As you move forward in your healing process, you might consider post-traumatic growth (PTG) as a goal down the road. Maybe it is something you want to work toward. PTG answers the question "How did you move forward and grow as a result of what happened to you?" Please remember, you are not what happened to you. You are not your diagnosis either. You are what you choose to become. You may turn to clinical advocacy. For example, if you lose a child to sudden infant death syndrome (SIDS), you may find empowerment and healing in helping others prevent such a loss. For me, advocacy on the mental health network has been a lifeline in my own journey.

What is the spark that happens? There is a reprioritization of what's important. Often this shift in preferences becomes a catalyst for change, as you do what you feel is important, such as using your experience to help others. Rumilly cited another client who'd had multiple miscarriages that left them with no physical evidence to show for their losses but they were left carrying the burden every day. She finds EMDR useful when a person finds they are having traumatic symptoms and also carrying a negative belief about themselves as a result of the trauma, such as self-blame. They may think they caused the trauma to happen to them or they failed in some way. EMDR is useful for letting go of that belief once the memories are reprocessed.

- I am spending time with you *AND* I want to make time to be alone.

- I am doing enough *AND* I can set new goals.

The point is that these seemingly opposing things are not mutually exclusive and they can be combined. The rub is that you can learn to hold space for both and that they can exist at the same time.

Who Would Benefit from DBT?

If you struggle with complex symptoms of anxiety and depression, emotional regulation, and self-harm in some combination, then DBT may work for you. Its goal is to reduce harmful behaviors and improve your overall life experience. This therapy is effective for treating a wide range of disorders including PTSD, depression, emotional dysregulation, anger management, suicidal ideation, substance misuse, and eating disorders.

DBT Treats the Untreatable

There is a wealth of evidence supporting the effectiveness of DBT. In the first randomized controlled trial of DBT, Linehan and her colleagues found that DBT resulted in significant improvements for chronically suicidal and self-injuring women with borderline personality disorder. I hope it is encouraging to discover that there is evidence proving these issues are more responsive to DBT than was ever previously known. That's good news to know these issues can be healed. Always there is hope.

DBT Takeaway

DBT makes a smart assumption that problematic or maladaptive behaviors evolve as a way to cope with a situation or attempt to solve a problem. While these behaviors might work in the short term to provide temporary relief, they often are not effective in the long term. This is a key concept worth repeating! According to trauma expert Dr. Gabor Maté, "It is impossible to understand addiction without asking what relief the addict finds, or hopes to find, in the drug or the addictive behavior. There is a purpose to all behavior and feelings. We just need to look a little deeper to find it."

The maladaptive coping strategy of addiction (substance use disorder, a mental disorder that affects a person's brain and behavior, leading to their inability to control their use of substances) can be replaced with any other compulsive behavior, such as workaholism, cutting, excessive screen time, gambling, or an eating disorder, to see the universality of this concept in recovery and treatment of all sorts. Once you identify what you gain from a maladaptive behavior, you can work to find a healthier substitute. For example, if drinking helps you feel happy and relaxed, you can substitute it with exercise, meditation, playing with a pet, or reading a book to activate your pleasure pathways and get your dopamine levels up naturally (Cleveland Clinic 2022).

The Healing Journey

When given love and opportunity, you can heal. Remember healing isn't linear. I've noticed my healing comes in waves. It also moves like an upward spiral instead of a circle. For example, sometimes I see old issues resurfacing and it feels like I'm circling back through them. Instead of getting exasperated because it feels like I've been working on them *forever*, I find it helpful to see them moving like an upward spiral. Each time they come around, I have a higher vantage point. I can see how far I've come. I can choose not to fall into unhelpful patterns.

Healing also doesn't mean the damage doesn't exist. It means that it doesn't need to control you. One of the most amazing decisions I think you can make is to finally let go of what is hurting your heart and soul and find what helps you instead. In other words, you are responsible for how long you let what hurt you continue to haunt you.

You are unique, and healing trauma is an experiential practice. It is messy because we are human, and that's okay. There is likely to be some trial and error, so I say draw from all available options! The complementary practices of yoga techniques are meant to be combined in such a way as to enhance your work in healing trauma through therapy, but they are not a substitute for professional therapy in a clinical setting. Instead, yoga and mental health care professional practices can come together to empower you to manage your moods and find relief from stress. Together they offer an integrative, holistic approach to healing.

Remember, if you are a survivor that is amazing in itself. You are still here. Keep going! Even when it is hard. You may be about to turn a corner. Maybe you are closer to freedom than you think. Someone out there could benefit from what you have to offer. You are important and you are here with a purpose. The world needs you. Where there is breath there is hope. Maybe you can see your hope as the transition from the way things were to where you want them to be. Let your hope be stronger than your fear. Maybe you can see it like Rumi, who said, "Our wound is where the light can enter us." Look for the telltale signs that you are healing from your past. They include prioritizing self-care, forgiving yourself for what you did in survival mode, and being drawn to help other people. It is true. The final stage of healing is using what happened to you to help other people.

6

Somatic Experiencing: Bodywork for Calming Your Nervous System

The single most important issue for traumatized people is to find a sense of safety in their own bodies.

TRAUMA EXPERT BESSEL VAN DER KOLK

A pounding heart, an upset stomach, panic attacks, nightmares, and fatigue. These are some of the many ways your body manifests trauma, anxiety, and fear. What your voice cannot say, your body does. When words fail, your body speaks its own language. Sometimes it's a secret language, but you can learn to tune in to its messages. As such, van der Kolk has said it is ineffective to just talk about trauma too much. Sure, it is important to an extent. It is good to put words to and name the trauma experience but somatics (bodywork) needs to be used as well.

Van der Kolk asks how could traumatized people's minds possibly be healed if they found the bodies that encased those minds so intolerable? Often, he says he finds it unfortunate that most psychiatrists pay no attention whatsoever to sensate experiences (your body's sensations). He said they simply do not agree that it matters (Interlandi 2014). Talk therapy need not be pitted against bodywork. Not at all. The two complement each other. If you've yet to hear of the term, *somatics* describes any practice that uses the mind-body connection to help survey your internal self and listen to signals your body sends about areas of pain, discomfort, or imbalance. These practices allow you to access more information about the ways you hold on to your experiences in your body. In talk therapy or psychotherapy, van der Kolk feels there is often a single focus on the verbal processing of thoughts, feelings, and experiences. But this can be seen as only half the equation. This said, I've come to think of talk therapy as a stand-alone intervention, without addressing the physical component of trauma, to be like tearing open scabs that are trying to heal. Who wants to keep starting the healing process over or risk deepening their existing scars? Psychotherapy alone runs the risk of retraumatization.

Somatic Experiencing®

Enter somatic experiencing (SE), a body-oriented therapy that is shifting the paradigm from simply talking about trauma to feeling it in your body. *Somatic* literally means "being in the body" and offers a more holistic approach for processing (there's that word again) and releasing the pent-up energy of trauma. Its basic premise is to unearth the mental issues that are held in your body's tissues. I often repeat this, as it is also the goal of yoga practice, as you heard in the yoga chapter and maybe in a yoga class. Catchy and true. Likewise, SE therapy is aimed at relieving the symptoms of post-traumatic stress (PTS), post-traumatic stress disorder (PTSD), and other mental and physical trauma-related health problems by supporting you to be present and work through the issues. Why would you want to do that hard work? So that you can ultimately be free of the stressors.

Created in his forty-five years of clinical practice, trauma therapist Dr. Peter A. Levine does this by focusing on the perceived body sensations, or somatic experiences, in sessions with his clients. This body-oriented approach resulted from Levine's multidisciplinary study of stress physiology, psychology, ethology (the study of animal behavior), biology, neuroscience, and Indigenous healing practices, together with successful clinical application. The idea is to release traumatic shock, which Levine has found to be effective in transforming PTS/PTSD. This also works for the wounds of emotional and early developmental attachment trauma, or childhood relationship bonding issues.

SE Synopsis: Feel It to Heal It

SE works to counter the tendency of your higher brain (that's the thinking, remembering, and reasoning part that carries out your purposeful movements) to disrupt the process of your body's attempts to heal. You tell yourself not to shake, cry, tremor, yawn, or do all the things your body naturally knows how to do in order to heal itself. But there is no way around it. You've got to feel it to heal it. Your body is elegantly designed to heal, but you interfere with it. Instead, you stay too busy or you drink, smoke, pop a pill, eat, or reach for some other distraction such as screen time or shopping.

Why? Because you are very uncomfortable with the physical signs of release. This is not finger-pointing; everyone does it. Have you ever felt your body shake after a scary incident? I have, and it terrified me more than the trauma until I learned that this is the body's way of releasing pent up trauma, anxiety, and fear. As a culture, we have suppressed our natural healing abilities in these ways. SE is all about re-accessing the body's natural healing ability. Yes, it totally sucks to feel terrible feelings, but the only way out is to go through them. If you find yourself in hell, keep going! The trick is to move through it instead of getting stuck there. Likewise, the goal of SE is to get to the other side.

The SE Approach

SE offers a framework to assess where you got "stuck" in the fight, flight, freeze, or fawn responses and offers you the clinical tools to resolve these stuck or fixated physiological states. The goal is to provide effective skills that can be appropriate for use in a variety of healing professions such as mental health, medicine, physical and occupational therapies, bodywork, addiction treatment, first response, education, and others. SE addresses the underlying cause of trauma symptoms by assisting the completion of what are called self-protective motor responses. Once this is done, the trapped survival energy in the body is released. Like the victim of an attack who was never able to defensively put up their arms, palms out, and shout, "NO!" to stop their attacker. That act with the hands is the self-protective motor response.

You are gently encouraged to gradually increase your tolerance for challenging bodily sensations and repressed emotions throughout therapy up until the point where you are professionally encouraged to express yourself in the manner you didn't get to do back when you experienced the trauma. Once that is done, the trapped energy can be expelled, or you could say it is liberated, from your body. Then you are free!

The Science of SE

Heart rate, digestion, and respiration are all things regulated by your autonomic nervous system (ANS), along with automatic body functions such as blood pressure and body temperature. Levine argues that the symptoms commonly associated with trauma (flashbacks and a heightened startle reflex) are the result of trauma-induced disruptions in the ANS. The goal of treatment is to help your ANS to re-regulate itself and get back on track.

In their definition of trauma, practitioners include both one-time traumas and developmental traumas, such as neglect or abandonment. Either way, the focus is on helping you gain awareness of emotions and physical reactions. In the early parts of SE therapy, you are encouraged to do this by increasing your emotional and sensory awareness then progressing to awareness of physical tension in the body. This is done with mindfulness and present-moment awareness. SE practitioners argue that trauma causes chronic tension because the body's fight or flight system was not able to fully react to the trauma. The goal is to experience the trauma in small bits and learn to release it safely.

Waking the Tiger: Nature's Lesson

Beginning in the 1970s, Levine's explorations into how animals deal with threat led to the development of his SE method. The clinical methodology is based on the following question: Why is it that animals in the wild are not traumatized by routine threats to their lives? As humans, we easily get overstimulated and frequently experience the traumatic symptoms of hyperarousal/overstimulation, hypoarousal/shutdown, and dysregulation. If you haven't heard of this last term, it is the inability to successfully manage emotions, handle conflict, and develop a tolerance for uncomfortable experiences.

How do animals heal their own fear and stress? They shake it off! It's not just a Taylor Swift song. Animals literally shake out their survival energy, just like how a wet dog shakes water off. If the animal can run and get to safety, it will then proceed to expel the energy in this way. The idea is to act with the lower brain, often known as the reptile brain, which is primarily concerned with basic biological processes, in order to access the body's memories. Levine claims that this is the hormonal peak of the unresolved trauma of being overwhelmed. The instinctive, self-protective reaction is finished. When the pent up energy is clear Levine calls this "awakening the tiger" (Levine 2015).

This is because the release often has a dramatic impact on his client's lives. Levine has seen the dissolution of symptoms and clients who then showed a renewed, sustained vigor in living. Because of this, he says the tiger is a symbol of our aliveness, our innate nature waiting to be unleashed. If trauma work sounds too dark for you, imagine the relief, freedom, and lightness on the other side it!

Stored Memories

It makes sense that neutral or fond memories, such as milk and cookies, are stored differently than the trauma of that sixth-grade bully type of memories. Pleasant memories are stored as "declarative or explicit memory." It means they can be recalled and simply stated. The facts, data, and events are clear, clean, sequential, and orderly. An example would be remembering where you were when you first learned to ride your bike, your first dog's name, or your sister's wedding.

Clean Up Your Story!

The point of SE is to get all the pieces together into one story and put the story together into a cohesive narrative. The treatment is used to calm your nervous system down enough to create a neat story for storage. Other therapy goals are to build resilience, to do lots of grounding, and to utilize tools such as breathing techniques.

Here is a real-life example: A man who survived a life-threatening car accident was never able to turn the car wheel to avoid the collision that traumatized him. Through the SE approach, he was guided to eventually complete the physical action (turn the car wheel) once it was identified as the incomplete action needed to release the pent-up trauma. This was done at the pivotal point in therapy where he was able to process the trauma to the place where he reenacted the moment, physically made that movement, and "saved" himself. That moment was a game changer in the man's treatment, which helped him relieve his trauma symptoms and get back to normal life (Crane-Godreau 2015, 93).

Titration: Slow and Steady Modifications

The key here is to do this trauma work in *increments*. It's all about small microdoses, as we've established. Levine borrowed the term *titration* from chemistry, which relates to medication, meaning to tweak the dosage until the benefit to liability ratio is optimized. In the same way, trauma must be approached very slowly, "drop by drop," so as to avoid unnecessary distress, flooding, overwhelm, and potential retraumatization. In other words, you definitely don't want to be freaked out.

In SE therapy, the slowness, pacing, and moving of attention away from the object of pain and back again is the only way the nervous system can process what's happening and move toward health and integration. Please note this next part, as it is key. "The trick is not to deny, but not to get swept away with the intense emotions associated with trauma," Levine suggests. Amen. Feeling these emotions as physical sensations in the body while releasing these sensations incrementally is an important way to safely free stored energy associated with trauma.

Everyday Titration (Adjustments)

Titration can also be used to describe how you can go about your daily life. When you can intentionally titrate or modify your behavior in response to a situation, you perform better than someone who always operates at their baseline or natural level. You probably do it with intellectual rigor, as an example. When connecting with a young child, as opposed to an adult, you speak more simply. But to be highly successful, you can also adjust in less obvious circumstances. In a situation of conversing with someone you assess as having superior reasoning skills, you use all your brain power, but when interacting with someone you believe is a weaker thinker, you scale back to the level you think is best. You would then monitor the person's reaction and adjust as needed. You learn to press down or ease up on your brain power pedal.

Learning Our Limits

Working within and discovering your limitations is the point of it all. Being with your experience as it is allows you to discover your limits. To stay with an experience continuously is definitely not a good idea if it feels overwhelming. Finding an external resource for calm, like nature or someone to encourage us, becomes more crucial at this time than continuing to be present with the experience. In SE therapy, like in life, this knowledge is crucial.

Say I am struggling with the grief of a sick loved one and I decide to go out and try to be social with friends who may say something triggering. Knowing DBT, I can make an exit strategy in advance. I tell myself, if I start to feel upset, I will excuse myself to the restroom for composure and then say I got a call and need to leave. Sometimes the act of connecting and being social is a good distraction for me, so I go with a plan. This type of planning ahead comes from DBT. Called *coping ahead*, it is all about making a plan for yourself for dealing with a stressful situation that you will encounter in the future. Having a plan cuts down the anxiety.

Resourcing

Resourcing is the practice of inviting your mind/body to attune to sensations of safety or goodness, however small they may be. I think of it as self-soothing, and you may already have your own way of doing it. In SE therapy, it is the process of attending to a felt sense of *okayness*. This begins the process of teaching your nervous system that it can experience stress and then come back to a state of calm. Resourcing is simply moving your attention away from the strong sensation to a pleasant or neutral area in your body.

It could also be something pleasant or neutral that is external to your body or to an image, a message, or a memory that gives you a sense of ease and safety. Maybe it is repeating the word *peace* or *OM*. Resourcing is what you turn to for comfort. Is there a friend you can reach out to? Do you have a pet, a favorite tea, or a favorite song? Maybe you visualize your safe place at the beach, for example. Throughout my life, I found comfort in sleeping with feather pillows. This type of security blanket is a small thing I've always found assuring. As a child, I remember hugging my pillow and feeling it was like the comfort of my mom. This is a shout out to Donna Brubaker. Love you, Mom!

How Resourcing Works

Resourcing aids the sympathetic nervous system in helping the body relax. In a deep way, you can realize that what you are is larger, like the ocean, and the pain is just waves on the surface. These are all ways of touching the pain and letting go, of titrating between big emotions and resources to offset them. Grieving is another example of how this method can support you. If you've ever lost someone close to you, due to separation or death, you know firsthand how completely overwhelming the emotions and sensations can be.

As sadness, anxiety, anger, and other emotions arise, you may put a hand on your heart, take some deep breaths, feel the waves of intense emotion roll over you. This gesture and awareness are compassion in action, knowing how much you can handle and when to shift your attention. This is a form of self-love. It is said that resourcing is essential in working with trauma to ground yourself in resources/comfort before navigating the traumatic terrain. SE focuses on developing and expanding the resource-repertoire of clients in the safety of the therapy.

What I have found helpful when I am consciously feeling my feelings and letting them come up is that there may come a point when I need to cry a little, like when I am sharing my pain with my sister. I try to stay with it and let it come and go like weather patterns across the sky. Instead of plunging all the way into a pool of sadness, I bring myself to the present moment and notice the sensations of my five senses. I can extend my exhale into a sigh of relief. I may shift my attention to a fluffy cloud; a magenta flower; or the elephant mobile of Ganesh, the remover of obstacles floating above my desk. I may say a prayer. You can pick anything pleasing or something you are grateful for in the moment. When I notice the contrast of what I don't want, I can choose the next best thought to replace it and really delve into the appreciation of it. This helps me to raise my energy back up.

Using the Law of Attraction can bring you more of the essence of what you already have as you concentrate on the positive aspects of it, even if they make up a limited part of your experience. By focusing more of your thoughts on the things you actually want, it can support you in turning what may become a downward spiral into an upward spiral. Try using an affirmation like "I can turn a downward into an upward spiral by shifting to good feeling thoughts."

Besides focusing on your desires instead of your fears, you can mindfully look for the positives by cultivating good feeling thoughts called glimmers. The term *glimmer* came to me from a meme on an OPLM chat from an unknown author. It said a glimmer is the opposite of a trigger. Glimmers are the moments of your day that make you feel joy, happiness, peace, or gratitude. Once you train your brain to be on the lookout for glimmers, these tiny moments will appear more and more. Whatever term you give these shimmering flashes, look for evidence of them to lift your mood.

Grounding

By strengthening your sense of being inside your body and anchoring to the ground or earth, you can become more fully and completely grounded. In order to provide support, grounding involves bringing awareness to your bodily sensations. Keep in mind, the thing that disappears in traumatic conditions when your body is overloaded and abandoned is your body awareness (Kelloway 2023). Grounding examples would be lying in a hammock, putting your shoes or bare feet on the earth (aka earthing), taking a bath, or taking in and appreciating the greenery of woods and blue sky. It could involve thinking of someone, a place, or a memory that brings calm, peacefulness, or joy. Many grounding exercises help deepen your connection to anything that is supporting the weight of your body. Grounding is a powerful tool in the trauma-healing tool kit because it generally reduces states of activation, sometimes quickly and significantly.

The experience of down-regulation that you feel in nature may be surprising, since grounding is so very simple. I always liked to hike and be outside, but in college I spent stretches camping in the wilds of West Virginia and couldn't help but notice the remarkable calming effect it had on me. Prior to that, I never considered myself an anxious person, but the difference seemed to imply otherwise. This deeper connection I forged with nature was a profound shift. I call this soothing sensation and connection with nature *infinity energy*. For me, it is embodied in the pace of how flower petals open and close and the slow, almost imperceptible movement of clouds across the sky on a calm day.

Try Grounding

When grounding by connecting your bare feet to the earth or objects that support your body, you may tune in to the following kinds of feelings in the body. This can be indoors or outside. Try asking yourself:

- What does it feel like to be physically supported?
- What is the feeling of having a definite physical location like?
- What is it like to feel the solidity and stability of the physical objects that are supporting your body?

Outdoor Grounding

When you're outside, you can easily ground yourself by allowing the bottoms of your bare feet, palms of your hands, or entire body to touch the earth. In cold weather, hands on a tree, or tree hugging, is another option. Walk in the grass, lie in the sand, or swim in the sea. I remember Emilio, a surfing instructor in Santa Cruz, saying that the ocean is an awesome, living being and we should submerge ourselves in it to experience our connection and its power. Despite the cold of the Pacific, my son and I took a thrilling plunge with that notion in mind. These are all easy ways to naturally reconnect.

Other Man-Made and Year-Round Grounding Product Ideas

Walking barefoot outside and having direct contact with the earth are great but most of us spend the majority of our time either indoors or wearing rubber-soled shoes, so we rarely spend time having physical contact with the earth. There are other options for products you can use to make grounding more accessible.

You can buy grounding mats, blankets, and sheets that allow for an earth connection when indoors and re-create that equilibrium of the earth's electron charge (Sullivan 2023). These products are said to stimulate the effect of connecting to the earth to improve your mood, sleep, and pain or inflammation. They claim to create an electrical connection between your body and the earth by replicating the physical connectivity you would make by walking barefoot on the ground. The connection allows electrons to flow from the earth into your body to create a neutral electrical charge.

The mats usually connect via a wire to the ground port of an electrical outlet, which is the kind I have on my bed. The mats may be placed on the floor, on a desk, or on a bed so the user can put their bare feet, hands, or body on the mat and conduct the earth's energy. Likewise, there are socks woven with conductive silver to enhance the flow of electrons rather than muffle it. Although prices vary, there are affordable options.

IN PRACTICE
SE Resources to Keep Grounded in Trying Times

Of course, SE is a therapy for trauma, yet you can use its focus on nervous system regulation in the following self-soothing exercises. These are adapted from Peter Levine's *Healing Trauma* book. Perhaps start with at least one to five minutes for each exercise.

Notice Your Current Physical Comfort Tune out of your surroundings for a moment and bring attention to your physical comfort.

- While sitting in a chair, take a moment and notice how you are feeling overall.

- Move your feet on the floor, moving and shifting until you really feel connected to the floor.

- Now feel your back and bottom on the chair, noticing how the chair supports you. (Ask yourself am I perching on the chair? If so, allow the chair to support you by sinking into it.)

- Adjust until you find your most comfortable position. Take a few moments to really enjoy the comfort of being supported by the chair and stabilized by the floor.

- Look around and notice something that feels resourceful or calming, such as the tree right outside the window, a hummingbird flying by, something artistic in your surroundings, a calming color, the floor, etc. Savor the peaceful feelings.

- What do you notice about your current level of mental and physical comfort?

Recalling a Kindness Your physiology can automatically react to a sensation of threat that is heightened by uncertainty. It can take all of your willpower to contain your rage when you're under stress, for example. You can encourage your nervous system to relax by thinking of comfort and kindness. The following are some ways that remembering how kindness in this felt sense can help calm anxiety.

- Recall a time when someone was kind to you.

- Remember everything you can about the words, touch, gestures, or actions the kind person used to soothe and comfort you or to provide you with help.

- As you recall what the kind person did, notice the sensory aspects of the memory in your body. What can you see, hear, feel on your skin, etc.? Feel it almost as if you're back there in that moment right now.

- As you notice your response, recall the emotion you felt back then and what you feel even now as you recall the experience.

- If a negative aspect of the memory arises, imagine setting it on a shelf and coming back to the sensory aspects of the compassionate memory.

- Notice what you're feeling in your body now. Is there a difference in your overall experience now?

When You Felt Most Like Yourself Use this exercise to promote ANS regulation and settling. The first half of this exercise is to help in regulating your emotions and nervous system and in maintaining your sense of balance. This can help you re-ground in the felt sensation of the present moment and bring you back to your true north.

- Consider your total experience for a moment.

- Then recall a time in the last twenty-four hours when you felt most like yourself, or the person you would hope to be more of the time. (Extend the time frame if something doesn't come to mind from the last day.)

- As you remember this event in a detailed way, almost as if it was happening again, notice what

happens in your body in this moment now.
Especially notice your five senses in the memory.

- Recall another time you most felt like yourself or
the person you'd like to be, this time within the
last several weeks.

- Again, as you remember this event in a detailed way,
almost as if it was happening again, notice what
happens in your body in this present moment.

- What do you notice now about your overall experience?

The "Voo" (Foghorn) Sound Odd as it may sound to some, this
effective method has the potential to provide a deep sense of
settling in the mind/body. Give it a shot for the first time when
you're relaxed and at ease because it can be stimulating for some
people. Be aware that since this technique calls for vocalizations,
you might choose to practice it alone (think the bathroom, a
bedroom, or try stepping outside).

- Take a moment and notice your overall experience.

- Now think of the sound a foghorn makes.

- Inhale deeply, then make a sound that resonates
throughout your entire body to mimic the foghorn.
Check to see whether you can sense the sound's vibrations
all the way in your pelvic floor. (Take note that this does
not necessarily imply that the sound must be loud. The
goal is to lower the sound's pitch as much as you can.)

- As you run out of breath on the Voo, let the next
breath come in naturally. Take your time.

- Stay with it and enjoy it if you feel at ease in your body.
Let go of this exercise for the moment and utilize another
one on the list to calm your system if you feel your

system is more stimulated (which the Voo can generate even if you previously found the activity settling).

- If you find the Voo to be settling, feel free to make it again to see if you find it even more settling. Doing the Voo more than three times in one sitting is not typically recommended.

- Check in. Is there any difference in the way you feel now compared with how you were at the beginning?

These SE exercises can help your body feel more relaxed, especially in the core. This is due in part to the fact that the soft vibrations can calm the muscles and internal organs. You can stay grounded by relaxing physically, for instance during economic, pandemic, or any type of uncertainty. This somatic focus of being more deeply in the body can help you stay grounded and regain your equilibrium in any stressful scenario.

IN PRACTICE
Journaling Prompt for Being in the Body

Trauma lives in the body as much as it does the mind. Remember, to somatize means to take what is emotional or mental and make it physical. Increasingly, you are becoming aware that you take on physically what you do not cope with mentally. The body speaks when words fail. Directions: You are invited to visualize a bright white, healing light flowing down from above, through your head, filling your body with energy and grounding you to the earth. Journal the end of the statement: *My body responds by...*

Mindfulness as a Resource

When you pay close attention to the sensations you experience during the revisiting of a traumatic event, you can gradually become less affected by them. Dr. Elizabeth Hoge, a psychiatrist at the Center for Anxiety and Traumatic Stress Disorders at Massachusetts General Hospital and an assistant professor of psychiatry at Harvard Medical School, says that mindfulness meditation makes perfect sense for treating anxiety. When you have unproductive worries, you can train yourself to experience those thoughts completely differently. "Oh, there's that thought again. I've been here before. But it's just that—a thought, and not a part of my core self,'" says Dr. Hoge. "Rather than push them away, we touch them, we acknowledge them, we may even make them welcome, and then we let them go. We exhale. Welcome back to the present moment" (Corliss 2014).

Hello, Anger, I See You!

Monk and meditation master Thich Nhat Hahn has a similar approach in dealing with challenging emotions. He suggests tuning in when you feel it and saying the following to yourself: *Hello, my little anger, I see you and I am going to take good care of you.* He says, "Just embracing your anger, just breathing in and breathing out, that is good enough. It will feel relieved right away" (Hahn 2021). He likens the anger (or another intense emotion) to a baby who's crying for its mother's comfort. When you hold it with your attention, it settles down and is eased. These methods allow us to touch or embrace what's occurring, rather than reject it. From here, we can choose how much we want to be with it and then we can let it go. The key is to feel like you are in charge. This taking back of control is a fundamental benefit of trauma-informed yoga, another form of bodywork.

Renegotiation: To Heal and Assimilate Body Memories

If you are tired of reliving trauma or talking about your story, try renegotiation to assimilate and heal your body memory. It is not necessary to discuss what happened if you don't want to in this process. Renegotiation is the incorporation and transformation of traumatic memories, experience, and energy into a more coherent story, sometimes with a sense of accomplishment that is life-fulfilling, such as with the example of the man who "saved himself" by turning the car's steering wheel as a self-protective response back in therapy, which helped release his trauma energy. The overwhelming reaction to the perceived threat to your life is what generates an unbalanced nervous system, not the traumatic incident itself.

You effectively renegotiate when you can release only the amount of stored survival energy that can be reintegrated back into your body without being overwhelmed by it. This release must be gradual and segmented. In renegotiating your trauma via SE, you can utilize pendulation. Titration and pendulation are forms of renegotiation in SE therapy.

Pendulation: The Yin and Yang of Emotions

We have established the recurring theme in recovery that says *feel your feelings*. It left me wondering how to do that without getting stuck in them. It was hard to let my rage come out when I was half afraid I'd open a Pandora's box of chaos I couldn't control. What if I couldn't wrangle it back in and it took me over the edge? In the past, it had overrun me, lingering for days and wreaking havoc on my mind space. .

To me, pendulation is another form of body awareness and an antidote to getting stuck. It is the shifting of body sensations or emotions between those of expansion and those of contraction. This back and forth is like an ebb and flow between the polarities of experience that allows them to gradually be integrated. Levine says, "This is a sort of assimilation, a blending and harmonizing of the opposite or conflicting emotions, as to bring them together. It is the holding together of these polarities that facilitates deep integration and, often, an alchemical transformation" (Levine 2015, 71).

If you feel safe enough and in a good head space, you may choose to try pendulation on your own. Please note this is not DIY trauma work and does NOT replace the support of a professional clinician. When you are feeling a low-level distress, start by noticing how you feel in your body.

- Where do you feel the distress?

- Can you tell if it is in your throat, chest, or belly?

- What does it feel like?

- Take a moment and let yourself fully experience this.

- Next, scan your body and find a place that feels neutral or calm. Maybe there is a place that is free from emotional pain or maybe there is a place where the feeling is just less intense? What does it feel like?

- Stay with that feeling for a moment, really giving yourself time to experience it.

- Lastly, continue this process, shifting your attention between these two areas of your body or "pendulating." Move slowly. Stay with the pain, allow yourself to really experience it.

- Then, shift your attention back to the part of your body where you don't feel the pain. Then shift back to the pain. Then shift back to the area of serenity.

- As you continue to pendulate or oscillate between the two states, notice how the distress changes.

- If you do it yourself, you can repeat the back-and-forth pendulum of touching what's unpleasant and returning to what's neutral or pleasant as many times as you like.

- In this way, you are not denying the truth of what you're feeling or being overtaken by it.

I think of pendulation as a way to bring balance. Like a pendulum that swings from extremes until it runs its course, slows down, loses momentum, and comes back to center. Pendulation of the nervous system is really just the natural pulsation between states of expansion and constriction, a basic principle or cycle of life. You can see it in the wings of birds opening and closing in flight, the movement of weather patterns, tides, and seasons. I think of it as another way of getting attuned to the calming, healing cycles of nature.

SE: Window of Tolerance

If you find it challenging to regulate your emotional responses in times of stress, you are not alone. It may have a lot to do with your window of tolerance, a place of optimal physiological and psychological functioning. Coined by mindfulness psychotherapist Dr. Dan Siegel, the window of tolerance is the place where you feel like you are supported and can deal with what is happening in your life. It's the zone that you are most comfortable in and in which you function at your best. You feel stress or pressure but it doesn't bother you *too* much. It's a doable state and the place to be when you are doing trauma work and therapy. That is, when you are doing hard things.

During the course of any day, you naturally flow within this window of tolerance, having moments of activity and rest. Since your window happens at a specific emotional arousal level, it naturally changes depending on you and the work. Some of us require more calm, while others need more excitement to get into the window. You tend to leave your window when you experience too much or too little stimulation or input. Signs that you are over the top in hyperarousal are when you are feeling constantly on guard, wanting to lash out at others or yourself. Other indications might be when you are experiencing feelings of anxiety or sleeplessness. Here is a technique to get you into your window of tolerance.

Containment with Safe Touch

I love this one and use it in support groups and yoga all the time. SE therapy utilizes touch because it more directly intervenes with the nervous system. Touch can include self-touch. The following use of touch is for a sense of containment and grounding.

- Take a moment and notice your overall experience.

- Take your right hand and place it just below your left armpit, holding the side of your chest.

- Place your left hand on your right bicep (or shoulder or elbow).

- Take several minutes to notice the feeling under your hands. Notice, does your body feel warm? Is the fabric of your shirt smooth or scratchy? Can you feel your heartbeat?

- Do you experience a sense of containment from your hands and arms? Is it pleasant like a hug?

- Notice how the rest of your body experiences this soothing and containing touch. Can you feel it in your limbs?

- What do you notice now about your overall experience?

Signs of being below or above your optimal zone may include feeling numb, frozen, or empty. When feeling listless, frozen, or under your window of tolerance, invite tiny movement:

- Starting at your head, gently and slowly make tiny movements of the head and neck.

- If this movement shifts into the spine, let it. Feel what happens as you allow your body to make tiny movements.

- Be curious about the arms and legs. Allow movement to expand outward from the spine into these areas of the body. Rest and notice how you feel afterward.

Finding your window of tolerance is a step in the process of managing severe stress without overtaxing your nervous system. By reassuring your body that everything is fine, the intention is to instill a sense of security. It's like you are installing a security system in your house. This allows the tension and trapped energy to come up and out from a safe place. One baby step at a time toward f-r-e-e-d-o-m.

90-Second Pause Technique

If you want to try another tool for more conscious choice, check out the 90-Second Pause to add to your repertoire. I've come to love it. Sitting at the pool with my friend Kristen, another friend dropped by in a panic, kvetching about her fear for her son on his flight. Her mind was really going in circles over it. Kristen said to her, "You forgot the 90-second pause." Kristen explained the power of the pause. I was intrigued. It comes from Dr. Jill Bolte Taylor, a Harvard brain scientist, who claims that it only takes 90 seconds to recognize an emotion and allow it to pass while you are just observing it (Stone 2019).

When under stress, it helps you realize you have the ability to stop for 90 seconds and identify your feelings as a means to avoid getting swept away by them. Think of how your brain works. The amygdala is your emotional processing center and its activity is lowered if you take a conscious pause. This form of emotion labeling helps you regain control. It aids by calming this brain region that is also associated with angry outbursts, according to MRI brain research (Stone 2019). Dr. Taylor says that when you have a reaction to something in your environment there's a 90-second chemical process that happens in your body. After that time, any remaining emotional response is just you choosing to stay in that emotional loop. This means you have a choice!

Using the 90-second pause, you can observe that emotions come and go. You can notice that they only endure for 90 seconds. It's like a storm passing. As an illustration, I notice that I am furious with my ignorant coworker. If I wait it out, what will happen to this feeling? You might see your emotions as ocean waves in that they rise, crest, and recede, all day long. There is a power in waiting for them to ebb back out when you notice they've rolled in. Relegating yourself to a 90-second time frame gives you a definite start and stop that is key to keeping control and feeling more happy and more confident for having done so.

Releasing Stuck Energy

Imagine someone has hurt or wronged you. Unfortunately, that may not be so hard to do! It can be challenging enough to get through life, or even a year, without this experience. Have you ever had the experience of your mind getting stuck in a loop and continuing to return to a story again and again? It replays what they said, how you responded, and all the reasons you have to be angry, upset, or wounded by them. No one puts Baby in a corner! You feel justified in your feelings, but you are torturing yourself. The continual replaying of the situation is maddening and exhausting. Does this common tendency sound familiar? Here is a way to work through it.

Healing and regeneration occur when you give your body attention. In this way being conscious of your body helps you remember your True Self. Most mindfulness begins with the body by drawing attention to breath.

What is more immediate than the breath? It's like telling yourself, breathe in and out, be here and now. Mindfulness of the body anchors you in the present while encouraging you to feel familiar with and even loving toward your body. If you pay attention to it, your body can show you what's going on inside.

Every tense muscle, achy joint, and short breath alerts you to the concerns and difficulties you are hiding from yourself. You have the ability to let go of both physical and mental stress by becoming more aware of your body and breathing relaxation into every aspect of it. As a yoga teacher, I am always reminding my classes that we can use the physical practice to ferret out the tension we are holding in the body and release it so we are better able to relax and have a peaceful mind. This is why yoga practice culminates with savasana, or corpse pose, for relaxation at the end. The practice prepares the body to be a more fit vehicle in which to house a more peaceful mind for meditation. It activates your parasympathetic nervous system.

In Practice
Body Scan Journaling

We know trauma lives in the body as much as it does the mind. When you somatize, you take what is emotional or mental and make it physical. Increasingly, you are becoming aware that you take on physically what you do not cope with mentally, therefore you are invited to explore progressive muscle relaxation: Sit quietly, take a few cleansing breaths, and perform a relaxation body scan. Starting at your toes, focus attention on each part of your body. Breathe relaxation into each area. Move from your toes upward, relaxing each body part until you reach the top of your head. Note how your body responds.

A Resilient Nervous System

All of these practices are meant to bring flexibility to your nervous system with the use of somatics. A resilient nervous system is one that can move back and forth from alertness and action to calm and rest, without getting stuck at either extreme. In psychology, these valuable, resourced states give you a sense of control over your life and can lead you to personal mastery, agency, and self-sufficiency. Let's delve in.

Clinical Somatics

Another type of bodywork for your repertoire is called Clinical Somatics, or neuromuscular education. It focuses on full-body patterns of posture and movement using breathwork, body scans, posture, and various forms of movement to address the underlying causes of pain. It does this by correlating muscle memory with chronic pain. Muscle memory refers to a muscle pattern that gets more strongly ingrained the more we perform a particular posture or movement. Our habits eventually become so ingrained in our memory that we no longer need to consciously consider them.

It seems the majority of recurrent injuries, joint degradation, and chronic pain are brought on by the way we use our bodies—that is, how we sit, stand, and move throughout our lives. Using muscle memory, our nervous systems actually learn how to make us perform these things as we get older. Also, consider that our nervous systems are in charge of directing how we should use our bodies. When we sit or stand motionless, our neurological system instructs us on which muscles to tense, when to relax them, and how to support our bodies.

According to the Somatic Movement Center, when performing these somatic posture and movement exercises, the idea is that you want to concentrate on your inner experience while you move and broaden your internal awareness to improve your sensory-motor awareness (Warren 2019). By engaging your nervous system in a deliberate and very gradual learning process that involves mindful motions, it helps to prevent injury to your body to relieve suffering. The movement techniques employed in Clinical Somatics teach your nervous system how to release chronic muscular tension so that you stand and move in natural, efficient ways. In particular, the focus is on the technique of pandiculation, or soft tissue stretching, which is used to retrain muscle memory and relieve pain. Clinical Somatics evolved from the use of pandiculation, which produced a 2022 study of its measurable benefits (Warren 2023).

Pandiculation: Yawn Your Tension Away

Imagine yawning can help release your tension away. Even if you've never heard of pandiculation, it is a natural process in which your nervous system awakens your sensorimotor system for maintaining balance while getting you ready to move. Like all other vertebrate animals, we humans have a tendency to pandiculate/stretch reflexively upon awakening or following extended periods of inactivity. You can see the pandicular reaction demonstrated when a baby stretches their arms and legs upon waking up, or when your dog or cat arches its back after a nap.

Although pandiculation may appear to be a stretch, it is really the contraction of dormant muscles. This is an unintentional soft tissue stretch that can be utilized to reduce pain and retrain muscle memory. The idea is to make this movement intentional. Maintaining good posture and range of motion throughout our lives requires preventing the accumulation of stress in our muscles. It is evident from the observation of pandiculating fetuses in the womb how essential the pandicular response is to the proper functioning of our musculoskeletal system and how deeply embedded it is in our neural system.

Unfortunately, our natural pandicular reaction usually isn't able to offset all the learning that happens in our nervous system as we get older and form unhealthy habits of standing and moving. The activities of our ancestors are very different from our repetitious, sedentary lifestyles. Because we move less and our movements are generally less varied than theirs, we tend to store muscle tension far more quickly than they did. For instance, in Clinical Somatics and pandiculation, the nervous system is gently retrained and muscle tension is removed by softly contracting and slowly releasing the muscles. These techniques also emphasize fluidity, similar to swimming, to gradually lull the body and mind into a deep state of relaxation.

Proprioception: You Are the Expert

Beyond our five senses of taste, touch, smell, feel, and hear, we have proprioception. It is our sense that continually provides information to our brains about the position, orientation, and movement of our body in our environment. It allows us to move quickly and freely without having to consciously think about where we are in space or in our environment. It is our body's mysterious ability to locate our limbs, even in darkness. Proprioception is a constant feedback loop within our nervous system, telling our brain what position we are in and what forces are acting upon our bodies at any given point in time. With this ability to sense our bodies in space, we will automatically modify our postures as we move. It is an awareness of the relative positioning of our own body parts and the level of effort we need during movement.

This perception of our own movement and body position in order to accomplish tasks is closely tied to kinesthetics, a sense that relies on receptors in our muscles, joints, and tendons. This sense plays an important role in our ability to control body movements and evolves through teaching and personal development of such awareness. As a result, muscles that are carrying unneeded tension automatically relax. And when we move, breathing naturally becomes a part of it. By directing our attention to internal sensations, rather than mostly our thinking or emotional experiences, we can create greater body attunement. We can do this viscerally through interoception which enables us to identify internal signals from our bodies such as thirst (from chapter 2). We also do this through our muscular-skeletal system using proprioception and kinesthesis.

We see here that SE is not a form of exposure therapy. It specifically avoids direct and intense evocation of traumatic memories, but instead approaches charged memories indirectly as a gradual process. The idea is to facilitate the generation of new corrective, interoceptive experiences that physically contrast those of trauma, which are typically overwhelm and helplessness. This is what makes it an effective approach for trauma remediation, if it speaks to you personally as something you want to explore.

Clinical Somatics and Its Roots

If you want to delve into somatics and find ways to become physically and intellectually free, meet the somatics field founder, Thomas Hanna. He was a philosopher, professor, and movement therapist who, through years of research, developed Clinical Somatic Education, also known as Hanna Somatic Education back in the 1970s. These practices were meant to reorganize connections between your brain and body. Hanna felt you can realize your power and take responsibility for your own life by using particular bodywork methods to address your postural problems. This enables you to regain control over your muscles, freeing them from constricted positions. Of course, in somatics you know this leads you to free your mind. The term *Hanna Somatic Education* is used to describe these practices.

In chapter 2 on yoga, you saw the evolution of Hanna's work with somatic yoga, but you can also try lying down and sensing your body's contact with the earth, as the following is considered a simple somatic practice. Remember, curiosity about what you are feeling is your constant focus while you engage in somatic practice. Is this healthy? Does this fit my needs? All excellent questions for exploration.

In Practice
A Six-Step Somatic Experience Exercise

Tune out of your surroundings for a moment and bring attention to your physical comfort in this short SE technique. Take your time with each of these steps, so that you spend at least 1 minute with the entire exercise.

Step 1: Take a grounding breath or two.

Step 2: What is going on inside of your body right now? What sensations are present at this moment? Perhaps there is constriction, anxiousness, or collapse. Is there more you can sense?

Step 3: Simply feeling the feelings will suffice to acknowledge them. Just check in with your emotions as they bubble up into your awareness.

Step 4: Let them express themselves by feeling them, as they are.

Step 5: Then, exhale and let them go.

Step 6: Take note of the sights, sounds, and fragrances around you. Or take note of other areas of your body that aren't feeling as intense.

I hope you found calm with this taste of a DIY SE technique and that you use it as needed. Remember what somatics teaches you: All emotions, even those that are suppressed and unexpressed, have physical effects. When you are able to experience and express the emotions held in your body, you are alleviating the incubation of illness. You are dispelling disease and inviting healing back in. Isn't that empowering to know?

7

Get Creative with Expressive Arts Therapies

I think music in itself is healing. It's an explosive expression of humanity. It's something we are all touched by.

BILLY JOEL

How do you feel when you hear your favorite song? It may evoke joy, memories, passion, and all kinds of emotions, unique to each of us. Music has been called many things, including the universal language, a great healer, even a reflection of the Divine. Kahlil Gibran called it "the language of the Spirit that opens the secret of life, bringing peace, abolishing strife." Music profoundly touches us all. It is a creative expression of humanity that is celebrated as something wonderful and loved throughout all cultures. "Across the history of time, music has been used in all cultures for healing and medicine," explains health psychologist Shilagh Mirgain. "Every culture has found the importance of creating and listening to music. Even Hippocrates believed music was deeply intertwined with the medical arts" (Mirgain 2019).

Music Therapy: What It Is and How It Works

Music therapy involves using our response and connection with music to encourage positive changes in our mood and overall well-being. Music therapy relies on this connection. This is what makes this type of intervention so effective. Using live music combined with psychotherapy, its practitioners offer an expressive therapy, are educated with master's degrees, and offer their services at some major hospitals these days. This established form of therapy is used in all kinds of settings with a variety of individuals to address physical, emotional, cognitive, and social needs. Music therapy experiences may include listening, singing, playing instruments, or composing music and playing it with others (AMTA 2010).

Clinical Music Therapy Defined

Officially, music therapy is the clinical and evidence-based use of music interventions to support you in meeting your individualized goals, such as reducing stress, improving mood, and self-expression. You can use it no matter your age and ability level within a therapeutic relationship. Officially that would be by a credentialed professional who has completed an approved music therapy program. In case you're interested for yourself or in this type of therapy, some such programs are Montclair State University, NYU, Drexel University, and Berklee College of Music. While musical skills or talents are not required for you, it is essential for music therapists to have at least a working knowledge of voice, piano, and guitar, along with a degree in psychotherapy.

History of Music Therapy

Even if you are new to the concept, music therapy is well-established in the health community. Formal music therapy was defined and first used by the US war department in 1945. It helped military service members recovering in army hospitals with occupational therapy, education, recreation, and physical reconditioning. It started with the nurses who sang to the soldiers when the soldiers were under their care.

Music Therapy at Metropolitan Hospital

You can see music therapy in use today with the largely uninsured homeless population in Harlem receiving short-term, psychiatric inpatient treatment at Metropolitan Hospital where Gabrielle Bouissou, creative arts therapist and supervisor, sees good results. She finds that music therapy transcends the defenses of her clients, helps them avoid violence, and gives

· · · · · ·
226

them an adaptive and socially acceptable release (Bouissou 2021). Here the homeless get dignified care. "They can beat the crap out of a drum. That expression is beautiful, productive, and celebrated. It allows people to be heard and can be used as a coping mechanism," said Bouissou. "It is a physical release that helps them avoid incarceration or being hospitalized. In the improv music groups we run, the music helps them conceptualize their frustrations, providing relief."

She says the blues is a popular genre at Metropolitan because it is low pressure. It also embodies the sentiment of the patients by saying *This sucks. I don't want to be here.* "It allows them to be heard, which is especially good for those who perseverate, or get stuck on their issues. In this way, they can freely express their feelings to avoid consequences. It's a healthy visceral release," says Bouissou. Throughout this chapter you will see these common themes repeated as benefits from music and expressive arts therapy in a variety of settings. Both help you transcend your defenses. Avoiding violence is an adaptive response. Channeling energy in a positive way is a coping mechanism. When you can freely express yourself without consequences, you are more likely to overcome maladaptive behaviors.

The Power of Rhythm

Bouissou finds that in music therapy and psychotherapy there is something innate, or built into the rhythm of it, that is grounding and that orients you to the beat. "Humans are musical beings in how we walk and talk. It connects us to the biological components of being human and the presence of melody is soothing." It is like the way a mother sings to her child to soothe them. Recent research indicates that rhythm such as drumming accelerates physical healing, boosts the immune system, and produces feelings of well-being. Rhythm is such a powerful tool because it permeates the entire brain, like all sound, which we will further explore.

It starts in the womb with the primordial thud of your mother's heartbeat. According to research by the American Music Therapy Association (AMTA), you begin your relationship with rhythm incredibly early in your development. As a prenatal infant, you could perceive and respond to simple rhythmic stimuli from very early in gestation, and you are aware of sound before you are born. This musical aptitude enabled you as a fetus to develop accustomed to uterine sounds, the voices of your parents, and the sounds of daily life.

Rhythmic awareness of the external environment is a powerful adaptive tool, enabling you as an infant to feel less stress post birth and most importantly, to enhance bonding with your parents. Your perception of rhythm is instinctive and ingrained. There are rhythms of nature and the earth and the cosmos. These are the cycles of life. "Life is about rhythm. We vibrate. Our hearts are pumping blood," said Mickey Hart, drummer of the Grateful Dead (Cerre 2015). Hart also shared how his grandmother with Alzheimer's had not spoken in a year but when he played the drums for her, she suddenly said his name.

Your Brain on Music

Your brain on music is a well-lit MRI brain scan. When stimulated by music, it would be seen to fire up every known part of your brain. Did you know that music also boosts brain chemicals? Listening to music increases the neurotransmitter dopamine, which is the brain's "motivation molecule" and an integral part of the pleasure-reward system. It's the same brain chemical responsible for the feel-good states obtained from eating chocolate, orgasming, doing drugs, and having runner's high. It helps you get high naturally.

Music Therapy Applications

Take the work of Dr. Oliver Sacks, neuroscientist and author of *Awakenings*, who finds that patients with neurological disorders who cannot talk or move are often able to sing, and sometimes even dance, to music. Sacks regards music therapy as a tool of great power in many neurological disorders, including Parkinson's disease and Alzheimer's disease because of its unique capacity to organize or reorganize cerebral function when it has been damaged.

Similar results have been found with a combination of personalized iPod soundtracks, daily dance and movement activities, and weekly musical performances at the memory care program of NYC Health + Hospitals/Coler. This 815-bed, skilled-nursing facility has seen music therapy bring a reduction in falls, violent behavior, and the use of antipsychotic medications among residents with dementia and Alzheimer's disease. The program is run by a designated team of staff who are certified, "Dementia Care Practitioners."

"When the music starts, lethargy becomes laughter, isolation becomes interaction, and we can break through and make a special connection with our residents with dementia and Alzheimer's," said Dr. Ram Raju, president and CEO. "I'm very proud of our expert team of doctors, nurses, and therapists at Coler for their innovative use of music to improve the quality of life of our most frail and elderly patients" (NYC Health + Hospitals 2016).

Brain Function and Human Behavior

Two University of Central Florida professors, neuroscientist Kiminobu Sugaya and world-renowned violinist Ayako Yonetani, are a husband-and-wife team who teach classes on how music impacts brain function and human behavior. How? By reducing stress, pain, and symptoms of depression as well as improving cognitive and motor skills (spatial-temporal learning). Your spatial-temporal ability is online when you read a map or a compass. It enables you to merge in traffic while driving, and determine how many objects can fit in a box. It also affects neurogenesis, the brain's ability to produce neurons, which helps your brain cells send and receive information.

Sugaya and Yonetani teach how those with neurodegenerative diseases such as Alzheimer's and Parkinson's also respond positively to music. "Usually in the late stages, Alzheimer's patients are unresponsive," Sugaya says. "But once you put in the headphones that play [their favorite] music, their eyes light up. They start moving and sometimes singing. The effect lasts maybe ten minutes or so even after you turn off the music" (Sugaya 2025).

Music Therapy Research

For a while, researchers believed that mainly classical music increased brain activity and made its listeners smarter, a phenomenon called the

Mozart Effect. Not necessarily true, according to Sugaya and Yonetani. In recent studies, they've found that people with dementia respond better to the music they grew up listening to. "If you play someone's favorite music, different parts of the brain light up," Sugaya explains. "That means memories associated with music are emotional memories, which never fade out, even in Alzheimer's patients" (Sugaya 2025). This means it all depends what the patient responds to rather than a specific genre of music.

"Music therapy helps speech, but also motor skills, memory, and balance. It is also emotionally uplifting," said Dr. Sanjay Gupta, American neurosurgeon and chief medical correspondent on CNN. Music therapy shows it may help psychologically, emotionally, physically, spiritually, cognitively, and socially. According to the Cleveland Clinic research, music therapy can be innovative in helping in these ways:

- reducing blood pressure and muscle tension

- improving memory and motivation

- enhanced communication and social skills through experiencing music with others

- self-reflection in observing thoughts and emotions

- self-regulation in developing healthy coping skills to manage your thoughts and emotions

- managing pain and increasing joy

Case Study: Music Therapy Brings Back Essence of Mother with Alzheimer's

Bouissou does private music therapy sessions at the home of a patient we will call Sandy (not her real name). Sandy was a school principal who was born Jewish in Austria during the Holocaust and escaped at a young age to the United States. She suffers from Alzheimer's disease, so the music therapy treatment plan is for memory care, degenerative disease, and as a forum for self-expression. "Since music engages the entire brain, an elderly person who has had a left-hemisphere stroke and loses their speech is still able to sing every word to their favorite song from their youth," explains Bouissou. Wow.

Walking into Sandy's apartment in Westchester, New York, everything is blue, which matches Sandy's bright eyes. Always dressed up and wearing lipstick and a necklace, courtesy of a vigilant home health aide, Bouissou and Sandy's sessions always start and end with an old-time favorite song that incorporates Sandy's name. The goodbye song is always "Good Night Irene" but replaced with *Sandy* rather than *Irene*, to which Sandy always lights up as she lifts her hands and exclaims, "Oh! Thank you!" Despite her memory challenges, she always knows her name. This always sparks recognition, which helps Sandy distinguish Bouissou among the other caregivers.

They have been sitting together over the past year in front of a big bay window where big trees mark the seasonal changes. Above them a placard hangs on the wall that reads *Because I said so!* Bouissou did some video sessions in COVID but came in person quickly to forge a connection. It's really about the all-important in-person connection. "Yes, I am facilitating psychotherapy but the music is the bridge to help patients engage with the family and the world. It helps us (therapist and family) connect with how Sandy is able to share the essence of who she is. My job is to tie in what is meaningful for her. As a former principal, we let Sandy teach us something so she is meaningfully contributing. It helps the family relate to her."

In over five years of therapy, Sandy's Alzheimer's has progressed to a word salad of loosely connected talk with the family. The music guides Sandy to a place where she can connect with others in the manner of which she can share. It's all about being present. There is a lot of laughter. It is a playful space. The goal is not to rehabilitate Sandy's memory but to provide a space to access her essence. "We are not pushing to fix her or reject her experience. We cannot correct the uncorrectable, but we can be present and engaged," said Bouissou. The goal is to connect with Sandy's current state and see her old brightness. It helps her family to see the mother who raised them.

Similarly, Bouissou incorporates music but in a different way with another Alzheimer's client who was a teacher and a strict disciplinarian.

This woman's disease is far less progressed, so she really enjoys being able to share her former profession. Bouissou laughs, "She just loves to share the performance part of the music and we stand up to perform the music. Mostly we do kids' songs. I ask her if the kids would like certain songs so she can give feedback. Her goal is to do all this in a way to keep the kids in line," laughs Bouissou.

Social and Emotional Studies

Just like with Sandy, another case study examining the use of music therapy with Alzheimer's patients and their caregivers found that patients showed proven relief with music therapy. Caregivers also got a lift to see an improvement in the social and emotional areas of their patients or loved ones. For example, an Alzheimer's patient unable to remember people often gets anxious and agitated, but with music therapy they were able to be physiologically and measurably calmer. The statistical tests showed significant positive differences in their before and after test scores on the Alzheimer's rating scales (Brotons 2003). How exciting!

Who Do Music Therapists Work With?

As you can see below, there are many who benefit from music therapy. People of all backgrounds, ages, and cultures can respond to music and to music therapy. Notable groups music therapists have helped include:

- military service members and veterans, as music therapy helps cope with trauma

- people with autism spectrum disorder (ASD), who are shown to learn best with consistency and predictability

- individuals with Alzheimer's disease, as it helps with memory and stimulates their mind because of predictability, familiarity, and feelings of security

- people in correctional settings, such as those who are incarcerated, in a mental health facility, in a halfway house, or in a group home can use this therapy to help improve their problem-solving, communication skills, relaxation, and in decreasing impulsivity

- victims of trauma and crisis who have experienced anxiety, stress, and pain found improved mood and confidence, and felt more in control with nonverbal outlets for their emotions

- those who are physically ill, which includes, but is not limited to, people with chronic pain, diabetes, cardiac conditions, cancer, headaches, recent surgery, and people in rehab

- individuals with mental health disorders can be helped with their communication and expression, to explore their thoughts and feelings, improve their mood and concentration, and develop coping skills

- people with chronic pain can experience decreased pain, anxiety, fatigue, and depression

- those who suffer with substance use disorders to increase their motivation and self-esteem, reduce muscle tension, decrease anxiety, improve self-awareness, and strengthen their coping skills

Music Therapy Settings

According to the AMTA, the current, most common settings for music therapy are hospitals, schools, nursing homes, outpatient clinics, mental health centers, and residences for individuals with developmental disabilities. Music therapists also go to juvenile detention facilities, schools, and private practices. Maybe you can think of even more settings beyond this!

Music Therapists for Preemies

Yes, music therapy works with all ages, even preemies! Singing or playing womb-like sounds in the neonatal intensive care unit (NICU) may help slow the heart rate and improve sleep and eating patterns of premature babies, as found in a new study. Infants with respiratory distress or sepsis (type of infection) generally fared better when their parents and caregivers sang lullabies to them or played noises that resembled their mother's heart-beat or fluid in the womb (Reuters 2015).

"We are learning from the literature and studies like this that premature infants do not necessarily grow best tucked away in an incubator. Neurologic function can be enhanced with music; vital signs can be enhanced through interactive sounds and music therapy," said Joanne Loewy, head of the Louis Armstrong Center for Music and Medicine at Beth Israel Medical Center in New York. Here, the care team utilizes live sound and music to replicate the auditory environment found in the womb. How? By re-creating a womb-like environment through sound and music, music therapy has been shown to deepen infant sleep-state. This is beneficial because it:

- supports infant self-regulation

- assists in the stabilization of breathing and heart rate

- enhances parent/infant bonding and soothes irritability

- reinforces feeding/sucking rhythms, weight gain, and promotes a sense of safety during painful procedures

Music Therapy Interventions

Premature infants hospitalized in the NICU due to complex medical needs receive music therapy interventions which may include:

- contingent singing, a sweet form of mother-infant vocal exchanges

- playing harmonic and melodic instruments to provide a "blanket of sound"

- tonal-vocal holding, an improvisational call and response exchange between mother and child

- songs sung by family and lullabies

These interventions provide comfort, stability, and promote bonding. They establish social connections, fosters healing through self-regulation, and addresses the developmental, physical, and emotional needs of infants. Music therapy may help with the following with children and adolescents:

- behavior disorders

- mood and anxiety disorders

- attention deficit hyperactivity disorder (ADHD)

- autism spectrum disorders (ASD)

- trauma

- substance use disorders (SUD)

Risks of Music Therapy

"Music therapy can be vigorous, as we are training to manage responses," said Bouissou. "Because music is so loaded and powerful, there are emotional and traumatic triggers. Music can call up repressed, bottled-up emotions that may then be released." That's why it is important to have a clinician guiding the experience, especially one versed in psychotherapy.

Nonclinical Music Therapy

Just so you are aware as you build your tool kit, there is a difference between Clinical Music Therapy and nonclinical applications. While these examples of therapeutic music are awesome and noteworthy, they are not of the clinical music persuasion.

- a person with Alzheimer's listening to their favorite songs on an iPhone with headphones

- groups like Bedside Musicians, Musicians on Call, Music Practitioners, and Sound Healers

- Music thanatologists are specialists whose musical modality unites music and medicine in end-of-life care using instruments such as flute or harp and voice at the bedside to serve the physical, emotional, and spiritual needs of the dying and their loved ones with prescriptive music. For example, my friend Natalie played flute at a hospice in a beautiful space called the "Angel Room," where people passed on.

- celebrities performing at hospitals and schools

- a piano player in the lobby of a hospital

- nurses playing background music for patients

- a high school student playing guitar in a nursing home

- a choir singing on the pediatric floor of a hospital

With that, we dive into another form of nonclinical music therapy.

Sound/Vibrational Healing

Like Einstein, quantum physics states that everything has a vibration and that even healing has a vibration. Vibrational healing (sound healing or sound therapy, all interchangeable labels) is gaining popularity all over the world as a way to find equilibrium. Sound healing does this by using various sound frequencies to treat physical, mental, and emotional conditions. This ancient healing technique uses sound pulsation to bring the body into a state of vibrational balance and harmony.

Although sound healing has grown in popularity in recent years, there is a history to it as a healing modality that dates way back. From vocal chanting to instruments such as Tibetan singing bowls and shamanic drums, there is some form of sound healing in every culture on Earth. It is said that sound healing can possibly be traced back 40,000 years to when Indigenous Australians used ancient didgeridoos for healing. Sound healing traces back to the sound chambers (architecture made for sound resonance) created by the ancient Egyptians in the pyramids.

As we know, our relationship with music is complex, but its effect on our emotional state is well-documented. Is it possible that nonclinical music therapy can go deeper still and actually heal our bodies and minds? If it lifts our spirits, connects us, and contributes to our well-being, then it is bound to be helpful, right?

Music Therapy at UCLA

Whether you're listening to music or playing a musical instrument, your brain and your body typically experience changes that are beneficial, explains Helen Lavretsky, MD, a geriatric psychiatrist and director of the UCLA Late-Life Mood, Stress, and Wellness Program. There, the specialty of music therapy has emerged to provide that healing experience for patients. Lavretsky notes that UCLA hospital physicians can now order music therapy for their patients in the same way that they might order physical or occupational therapy. She describes how music affects the body's ANS, the unconscious body functions such as heart rate, respiration, and digestion, as we discovered in chapter 1. Listening to music can improve the breathing rate and boost oxygen distribution throughout the body (Lavertsky 2018).

Sound Healing to Combat the Opioid Epidemic

For useful applications, combating the opioid epidemic is my favorite. A review by Cochrane, an independent network that examines the results of many different studies to support informed decision-making by healthcare professionals, found that music can help to reduce the amount of pain medication that a patient requires. Music seems to activate sensory pathways that compete with pain pathways. In the face of the current opioid epidemic, "there's quite a bit of interest in exploring non-drug options for pain reduction," Lavretsky notes.

Exciting new evidence obtained through scientific research now confirms that hearing a favorite piece of music will help your brain release natural opioids. First presented at the 2015 conference for the Society for Music Perception and Cognition by researchers at McGill University, the findings have also recently been published in scientific reports and are available on the website of the National Institutes of Health. Instead of painkillers, pain levels actually have been substantially lessened by using music to control pain instead of narcotics. Wow, that makes music a proven, effective form of pain management!

Other Positive Results

Another Cochrane review of studies with cancer patients found that listening to music positively affects not only pain but also anxiety, mood, and quality of life. Music has been used to reduce anxiety before and during surgical procedures and during chemotherapy and radiation treatments. It can improve cognitive and behavioral stimulation in older adults with co-occurring mental and physical disorders. Music therapy is on the rise in long-term care settings. Lavretsky asserts that the emotional nature of the universal musical reaction enables it to transcend cognitive limits in both young and old people. For instance, research suggests that music therapy can benefit children with behavioral difficulties and that it improves skills such as social interaction and communication.

UCLA Research: The Benefits of Chanting

Chanting or active singing also has major physiological advantages. In yogic thought, it is said that chanting is the highest form of breathing exercise. When stressed family caregivers of dementia patients practiced chanting meditation for eight weeks, in Lavretsky's research, their bodies' inflammatory responses decreased. Inflammation, a consequence of stress, aids in the development of age-related illnesses such as cancer, heart disease, arthritis, and Alzheimer's disease. The chanters also experienced improvements in their mood, cognition, and levels of cell-aging biomarkers. Lavretsky is currently researching the benefits of chanting meditation with older women (50+) who have cardiovascular risk factors and memory loss. Even for those who are gravely ill, sound can elicit happy emotions because it is the simplest and most traditional method, according to Lavretsky. We are connected to life by it.

For me, I saw my grandmother come alive with music on one of my last visits with her prior to her passing at 98. She was napping and woke up to tell me about the Doris Day song she remembered called "In a Shanty in Old Shanty Town." She was amazed when I found it on my iPhone and played it. She would say each line of the song just before it played, her eyes sparkling. It stirred up musical, family memories, and she was so excited to share them. As my son and I readied to leave, she even got up to walk us out and was fired up to walk around her garage (which she did for the even ground to avoid a fall). It was so neat to see the effect of music on her vitality.

Sound Healing Applications

Other organizations have used these methods in a plethora of ways. At the Sound Healing Institute in Sausalito, California, they offer a wide range of techniques using sound as a tool for change and specific to ailments in conjunction with hospitals. The Sound Healing Institute has four arms: the sound therapy center, an accredited college called the Globe Institute, a sound healing store, and the sound healing research foundation. Each have been developing projects to help bring sound healing and therapy more into the mainstream through hospitals and homes (Gibson 2022).

The Sound Healing Institute does this by distributing information and resources to develop new research projects and by disseminating information to the public in these ways:

- The use of chanting, toning, and overtone singing (a voice technique where one person sings two notes at the same time), as methods for resonating sound throughout the body.

- The use of natural sounds and natural instruments, such as crystal bowls and tuning forks, which resonate with specific healing frequencies and harmonics.

- They offer drumming and rhythm to corporations to release stress and build team consciousness and have found that Shamanic drumming takes people into altered states of consciousness.

- Binaural beat frequencies are used to draw you into very specific states of consciousness. This type of sound is used to alter brainwave states to help you with sleep disorders and facilitate creative expression.

Singing Bowl Research

Not only do I personally love singing bowls but I always get a good response when I share them in my classes and workshops. The National Center for Biotechnology Information agrees with a published study on the benefits of Singing Bowl Sound Meditation (Goldsby et al. 2017, 4016). This study examined the effects of sound meditation on mood, anxiety, pain, and spiritual well-being. Participants were a group of sixty-two women and men with an average age of fifty. As compared with pre-meditation, following the sound meditation participants reported significantly less tension, anger, fatigue, and depressed mood.

Vibrational Healing, aka Sound Bath Research

A relaxing soak in the tub isn't the only kind of bath that can have health benefits. Waves of soothing, echoing sound from traditional wind and percussion instruments, also known as a "sound bath," may help with stress, fatigue, and depression symptoms. In allowing the sound to "wash" over you and encourage a relaxed, meditative, or therapeutic state of mind, these forms of vibrational healing can have a direct effect on addressing the root causes for the increase in many ailments associated with those symptoms mentioned above.

Case in point is Heather Ross, from the Hands-On Healing chapter. An event took place as she was going through the immense stress and heavy feelings of an early breast cancer journey. With no expectations going in, Ross had a life-changing experience in a sound bath that led to a healing. The event was an immersive 3D experience of being on the beach, hearing the waves, birds, singing bowls, gong, and shamanic drumming. The instructor, Lindy Romez, created a sacred healing space that made her feel safe enough to go into a deep meditative place and stay there for close to an hour. From this emerged a vision.

"I was standing on a hill overlooking the land as a Native American warrior, seeing through those eyes, and connecting to a primal part of myself. I felt strong and powerful. The vision showed me I was able to connect with this most powerful part of myself." It was remarkable in that she walked into the sound bath feeling defeated but said she walked out with a new sense of permanent power. She knew from this vision that she had a powerful strength that stayed with her. Whatever is happening in her life, she can reconnect and immediately come back to it. She knew she would be okay.

There are other settings that also produce positive results. In hospital settings, sound baths for children and adults effectively reduced anxiety and stress and improved moods for both medical and surgical patients. This included patients in intensive care units. It has also been found that music therapy boosted empathy in caregivers without interfering with the technical aspects of the treatment. What seems evident then is that singing bowl/sound bath meditation may be a realistic, low-cost, low technology intervention for helping raise well-being.

Sound Healing Case Study #2: Detecting Cancer

Massachusetts Institute of Technology (MIT) has answered the call by developing a new method that involves simply passing sound waves through blood samples in order to diagnose and treat patients more quickly and effectively. Science has demonstrated that sound, or vibration, has a significant impact on substance.

Sound can be used in detecting cancer, as sound waves are sent and bounce back when they reach the organs. A device called a transducer turns the sound waves into images (Trafton 2015). The sound waves echo differently when bouncing off abnormal tissue compared to healthy tissue. This helps doctors detect potential tumors. The technique separates rare circulating tumor cells from billions of blood cells using sound waves. Precision medicine and cancer diagnosis, prognosis, and treatment are all aided by this "liquid biopsy."

Vibrational Healing: What to Expect

Whatever name you give sound healing experiences, it helps to know what to expect. Usually, you lie down and get really comfy. Your job is to do absolutely nothing but focus on the sound for the length of the treatment. The practitioner will often walk around the room if you're in a group or around your body while playing the instruments. Participation is simply to remain present, listen to the sounds being produced by the instruments being played, and relax as deeply as you can. What those instruments are depends on your practitioner. Often, a session does incorporate some sort of singing bowls, but I've seen people play harp, gongs, chimes, and different wind instruments.

While people have unique experiences, I know someone who had to take a break, as they felt overwhelmed. She was concerned the first time she tried that she might "pop out of her body." After another try, she was able to relax. Some people report feeling trauma triggers. There is no right or wrong reaction. From my experience and exploration, the vast majority of people lose track of time and report feeling transported and refreshed, which is what seems most typical. Some cry because they feel moved and as though they experienced healing.

Sound Meditation: Devotional Chanting/Kirtan

Although healing sounds can be produced by electronic brainwave music tracks, some feel the most effective way of generating them is live in person, by chanting. This ancient practice hails from India and is known as kirtan.

A kirtan is a call-and-response style song or chant, set to music, in which multiple singers recite or describe a legend, express loving devotion to a deity, or discuss spiritual ideas. This form of devotional music comes from chanting the sacred, ancient Hindu texts called the Vedas. Chanted in a very precise manner, this was passed from generation to generation of brahman, the priestly caste in India. Plain Vedic chant was embellished with vibrations and ornaments, creating kirtan. Music and religious experience are closely linked in Hinduism and is meant to affirm that God, or the Supreme Being, is accessible through sound and music. Steeped in the yoga community, kirtan is a popular community builder in the United States. Case in point is the growth of popular kirtan artists, such as Krishna Das and Deva Premal, who attract throngs of fans and play yoga festivals and venues across the country.

In Practice
Use the Mantra Om

When chanted, the sound of Om is said to vibrate at the frequency of 432 Hz. This is the same vibrational frequency found throughout everything in nature. As such, Om or Aum is the basic sound of the universe, so by chanting it, you are symbolically and physically acknowledging your connection to nature and all other living beings.

Author and yoga teacher Colleen Saidman has a podcast called *Talking Yoga*. In the episode "This Is Your Brain on Om," she interviews master teacher Jeff Masters. Masters has spent the last few years integrating yoga's ancient principles with modern science and medicine. By describing how the act of chanting Om soothes stimuli across the primary auditory cortex and interior components of the brain, including the thalamus, the hypothalamus, the hippocampus, and the amygdala, Master illustrates the biological processes that take place when you chant it.

Om, according to Masters, is a way that allows you to experience the absolute and a bridge that connects your internal perspective to your external perception. He feels that the story of your life is written in the tissues of your body. The practice of sounding Om allows you to lift the ink from all of those pages and gaze at it. It gives you the opportunity to either rewrite or erase those experiences, "scorching the seeds of those impressions so that they no longer impact your actions or dictate how you see the world." If that is the case, then it may be worth investigating. Could this be your experience? It's worth a try!

Think about what Om represents before chanting. Om is said to be the whole universe. It's considered to be the source of all creation. Om encompasses all time periods, from the past through to the present, and into the future. Om is eternal oneness of mind, body, and spirit with the Universe. Don't worry about chanting perfectly. Om is considered to be the vibration of the universe that no human voice can replicate exactly. The most important consideration is to chant in a relaxed way. Try to do this effort-lessly as possible without getting too wrapped up in the trying.

Step 1: Close your eyes and get into a relaxed, comfortable position.

Step 2: Take a few deep breaths as you pay attention to the sounds and vibrations in your body.

Step 3: Breathe in.

Step 4: As you breathe out, pronounce Om. Note that Om is com-posed of four sounds: "a," "u," "m," and the silence that follows. The "O" sounds like the "a" sound in the word "saw," combined with the "u" sound in the word "put." Blend the "m" into the end. These sounds should all merge together into a single sound similar to the "ome" in "home."

Step 5: Give equal measure to each sound.

Step 6: Breathe normally.

Step 7: Repeat Om in a slow, rhythmic way when you exhale.

You don't have to chant with every exhale. Match the length of each chant to the duration of your natural exhale. For instance, you may chant Om, take a breath or two and then chant again.

In Practice
DIY Music Therapy Technique

Use music to express your feelings. Music therapy encourages emotional release and self-expression, which enables you to share your deepest emo-tions through music. Did I mention this has been a bonding experience with my sons? There are no right or incorrect responses in this because it is subjective. Pick three songs that, in your opinion, best capture your current circumstances and emotions.

Answer the following questions for every song you selected. Just make the decision to be genuine. Always keep in mind that this is about using your own voice to convey yourself and your emotions.

- What are the titles of your songs?

- What comes to your mind when you hear the songs?

- How do they make you feel?

- What part of each song is the most important to you and why?

Trauma-Informed Expressive Arts Therapy

Arts therapy is action oriented and taps implicit, embodied experiences of trauma that can defy words and logic.

. . . .

DR. CATHY MALCHIODI, AMERICAN PSYCHOLOGIST, EXPRESSIVE ARTS THERAPIST, SPEAKER, WRITER, AND VISUAL ARTIST

If you long to express yourself through art, music, movement, or play and release those pent-up emotions with or without words, then expressive arts therapy might just be for you! The verbalization of thoughts and feelings is usually a key component of therapy in most cases. But in this approach, there is an option for unspoken expression. This may be the main form of communication in therapy for a child with limited language, an elderly person who has lost the ability to talk due to a stroke or dementia, or a trauma victim who may be unable to put their experience into words.

Expressive arts therapy, the combined use of art, music/sound (as we saw previously), dance/movement, enactment/improvisation, storytelling/narrative, play, and imagination provides a transformational outlet when words fail. Which is often the case in the shock of trauma. As you already know, this is significant because talking about trauma may cause re-traumatization because it persists in the brain. Through deliberate uses of self-expression and management, expressive arts therapy can be used as a response to pain and trauma. These modalities are often used to assist

. . . . . .

kids and adults in lowering hyperactivity and the stress reactions brought on by anguishing events. Imagine a therapy session that includes digging your hands into clay, painting, making a mask, creating a visual journal, or assembling a collage. In art therapy, the focus will be on the process rather than creating a finished art product. Plus, there is a wide range of art materials and processes from which to choose.

When I was a social worker working with young kids in Arizona, we always had crayons and paper on hand. I was directed to have the kiddos draw as part of their treatment plan. A child's drawing of their family, for instance, can reveal a lot to a therapist. Say there's a picture of three stick figures in the image of a mother, a brother, and a sister holding hands trumped by a large, shadowy figure with protruding teeth and a dark cloud surrounding them off to the side. This could be narrating the tale of a violent father or other individual. Talking points and information for use in therapy are made from this kind of material. My poet friend sees an expressive arts therapist and finds immense value in embodying her trauma in poems, collaging her feelings in her art, writing them as a type of narrative therapy, and a shamanic healing practice that utilizes psychodrama, which is coming up in chapter 8.

Narrative Therapy

Without knowing about this as an official form of therapy, I have been keeping diaries and journals and making books since I was seven years old. For my books, I folded copy paper and stapled it down the left side. They included pictures. The diaries I have had since that time lie in storage under my bed because there's no way I'd throw them out! They are a part of me—a record that I was here, breathing and taking up space on the planet.

Writing is a way for me to not only find my voice but to hopefully use it for good. It helps me see themes over time, such as when I realized I'd been writing about becoming a yoga teacher for five years and decided it was time to act! I see patterns that help me make more informed decisions. Recognizing patterns turns into wisdom. Writing enables me to feel like an expert in my own life and to live in a way that reflects my goals and values.

Narrative therapy can be beneficial for individuals, couples, or families. It enables you to see yourself as separate from your problems and any destructive behaviors. This form of therapy allows you to externalize your issues rather than internalize them. My ongoing DIY version of narrative therapy helps me rely on my internal compass, hone my skills, and create a sense of purpose to guide me through difficult times.

When you write, you get some distance from the difficulty you face. This helps you to see how it might actually be helping or protecting you, more than it is hurting you. With this shift in perspective, you feel more empowered to make changes in your thought patterns and behavior and "rewrite" your life story for a future that reflects who you really are, what you are capable of, and what your purpose is, separate from your problems. According to *Psychology Today*, narrative therapy was developed by Michael White and David Epston in the 1980s to reflect their thought that it is more helpful for you to see yourself as making a mistake, rather than seeing yourself as bad. You learn to be respectful of yourself and avoid pointing blame or judgment inward. A good narrative helps you to process and clarify what you experience.

In a nutshell, core aspects of narrative therapy are things like:

- deconstruction of your problematic and dominant storylines or narratives

- dividing your story into more manageable, smaller sections

- Rewriting the narratives of what is problematic can bring awareness of your prevailing plots. It might even open your perspective to move toward more wholesome plots. Known as the Unique Outcomes Strategy, this helps you understand your feelings and experiences.

I think a well-crafted story will also assist you in finding meaning and direction. It's like cleaning up your story like in SE and EMDR, you know?

DIY Narrative Therapy:
Your Life Story, Past, Present, and Future

Diving into the story of your life isn't just a stroll down memory lane; it's more like digging for hidden gems. This whole narrative crafting thing is like your personal therapy session, a chance to patch up any emotional bruises. Based on positive psychology, it's all about highlighting your strengths. Think of it as a road map to sort out your thoughts and kick-start some serious self-improvement. If you give this storytelling exercise a shot, you may find another layer of meaning in your life, which, in turn, may elevate your happiness.

Step 1: Write a story of your past. Be sure to describe challenges you have overcome and the personal strengths that allowed you to do so. Focus on your resilience. Where have you been able to turn your challenges into stepping stones?

Step 2: Describe your life now and who you are now. What are your strengths now? What challenges are you facing? In navigating the present, could any of your challenges be seen as opportunities?

Step 3: Picture your ideal future. How will your life be different than it is now? How will you be different than you are now? Are there fulfilling adventures, meaningful connections, and growth?

Brain-Wise Arts Intervention

Malchiodi created a program for treating traumatic stress called trauma-informed expressive arts therapy, which combines "brain-wise," arts-based interventions and embodied awareness ideas to aid in trauma healing (Malchiodi 2020). These techniques are the key psychotherapy techniques for traumatic stress. It also combines what is now known about how play and the expressive arts help you process and integrate any trauma with current best practices in trauma-informed care. It sounds like a cool combination to offset what otherwise might feel like a slog (Johnson-Welsh 2020).

IN PRACTICE
Art Therapy Exercise: Draw Someone Who Listens

- Grab paper and pencils or whatever medium you want and have on hand.

- Draw someone in your life who listens to you. It is all about reflecting on the importance of communicating with others and having your voice heard.

- Think about someone who makes you feel valued and supported. It doesn't matter much about your artistic ability, really, it's the feeling and the ensuing meditation on the power of relationships.

- Enjoy capturing their image with gratitude.

Expressive Therapy: Psychodrama Therapy
The body remembers what the mind forgets.

. . . .

JACOB MORENO, PSYCHIATRIST, EDUCATOR, FOUNDER OF PSYCHODRAMA, AND PIONEER OF GROUP PSYCHOTHERAPY

A woman sits in a therapy group where she chose two other participants to act as her pseudo parents. She directs them where she would like them to sit as they reenact a scene from her life. In it, she is telling these actor "parents" her deep, dark secret of how she was raped when she went abroad and has been too scared of their judgment to tell them in real life. Turns out she had always felt that they were cold to her, and it was a relief to finally share her sorrow without judgment in this setting. Each plays their part as the drama unfolds, and she finally gets to speak her truth with the supportive ending she always needed. She asks them to hug her at the end. She played out her story and got the validation and love she needed.

This is an example of psychodrama, an action-packed, experimental type of creative arts modality in which people explore issues by acting out events from their past. It was developed by Moreno, who also coined the phrase along with what is now known as group therapy and group psychotherapy.

The ABCs of Psychodrama

Psychodrama, aka drama therapy, is a form of expressive arts therapy in which clients use spontaneous dramatization, role playing, and dramatic self-presentation to investigate and gain insight into their lives. A psychodrama is best conducted and produced by a clinician trained in the method, aka a psychodrama director or a qualified professional such as a psychologist.

At its core, psychodrama uses deep action methods to explore and correct issues that have been identified in the group. Often a protagonist is chosen whose issue represents the main elements of the group. It's amazing to see how the protagonist brings up their drama and the members of the group are brought in as aids in the dramatic reenactment of the scene(s). Finally, the current scene is done again with alternate endings. Typically, these endings would empower the protagonist or correct the scene in some way.

What Differentiates Psychodrama

- First, spontaneity and creativity are the compelling forces in human progress so their use in therapy gives new alternatives of self-expression.

- Second, love and mutual sharing are powerful, indispensable working principles in group life, which creates connections often missing in the lives of traumatized people.

- Third, a dynamic community based on these principles can help create new techniques for mutual support and healing.

As an offshoot of psychoanalysis, Moreno saw psychodrama as "the next logical step beyond psychoanalysis." It was an opportunity to get into action instead of just talking, to take the role of the important people in your life to understand them better, and to confront them imaginatively in the safety of the therapeutic theater. Most of all, you can use it to become a more creative and spontaneous human being. Plus, you are embodying your healing in this dramatization with a more positive outcome.

Psychodrama Research

This isn't just psychobabble. A Smith College study concluded that psychodrama is a valuable therapeutic modality in the treatment of eating disorders (ED). The study found that the use of psychodrama with adolescents struggling with ED led to significant improvements in social skills and life satisfaction (Mertz 2013, 63–9). I find this impressive, given how prevalent and challenging this diagnosis can be.

IN PRACTICE
Act by Smiling on Purpose

If this sounds like something you'd like to explore, try this DIY version for yourself. Did you know that smiling initiates a complex shift of muscles, breath, and body chemistry? It releases endorphins that create a more positive mood. Plus, what you put out, others mirror back to you, feeding an increasingly positive emotional space. When you smile on purpose, it will affect all your interactions, whether in a meeting or on the phone or just walking by yourself.

Try it out! Today I invite you to smile on purpose. Start with your face and you might start to feel it in your heart.

8

Other Healing Modalities

*If you want to improve the world, start
by making people feel safer.*

**Dr. Stephen Porges, trauma pioneer, creator
of Polyvagal Therapy and the music-based
intervention called the Safe and Sound Protocol**

My research on healing trauma holistically would not be complete without including polyvagal theory because it clearly shows how your nervous system and social interactions are deeply connected. This understanding helps explain why you react the way you do, both emotionally and physically, and how your relationships play a role in healing. It offers a valuable perspective on how safety, connection, and self-awareness work together, leading to a deeper understanding of yourself and your path to recovery.

Polyvagal Theory

Since your mood and thoughts are intricately connected to your physiological state, shifting your nervous system into the safe position is one of the most powerful ways to positively impact your well-being. Based on neuroscience, the polyvagal theory applies the fight-flight-freeze-fawn reactions to the field of psychotherapy. The premise is you can operate more cognitively and intellectually when you feel safe. If not, higher functions become inactive as a result of perceived or real risk (Schwartz 2018). If this were to happen on a chronic basis, the brain gets stuck in the *on* position. It's stuck in the fight, flight, freeze, or fawn position. In other words, it's difficult to even imagine safety. This leads to:

- misreading the cues you are receiving from other people

- making it more likely you assume others are being aggressive or threatening

- perceiving anger all around you

- finding it nearly impossible to self-regulate when correct social cues are absent

Over time, this trend can create a dangerously false perception. You might see all people as a source of threat. This keeps the involuntary cycle going. You can't fight and you can't flee. That's when "freeze" kicks in, which causes shutdown.

The Vagus Nerve

Your CEO of calm is your vagus nerve, and it starts in your brain stem and travels through your neck, thorax, and belly. In fact, it is the longest cranial nerve in your body and the chief of the parasympathetic nervous system (PNS), controlling a variety of bodily activities, and relaying sensory information from external triggers to the rest of your body. Polyvagal theory focuses on the evolution of two of your body's systems. As a reminder, your PNS is your relaxation, or rest and digest response, which is connected to your vagus nerve.

The second is your sympathetic nervous system (SNS), which is the energize and act response that releases cortisol. Too much of this running through your nervous system can lead to autoimmune disease. Each has its own function and causes your body to react differently before, during, and after a traumatic or stressful event. If these two systems become damaged from excessive and recurrent trauma, a breakdown could occur and make you more vulnerable to mental illnesses such as PTSD and anxiety disorders.

Polyvagal Theory Basics

Since your PNS is linked to both relaxation and PTSD symptoms, poly-vagal theory helps you understand its dual role. It shows you how to use your "social nervous system" (how you engage with the world around you) to calm your "defensive system." It's a balance between activation and relaxation for better social engagement. When we enhance our connection with other people, we trigger neural circuits in our bodies that calm the heart, relax the gut, and turn off the fear response. This can reduce trauma symptoms and help you feel safe. Polyvagal therapy does this by guiding you out of the shutdown or freeze phase. It is all about relieving your symptoms. It helps you focus on your own social cues like:

- facial expressions

- vocal inflections

- body language

- eye contact

- vocal tone

The exercises you would do for calm in polyvagal therapy are specifically customized for you. The goal is to calm your vagus nerve through relaxation techniques like:

Meditation This may include humming meditation (like the bumblebee breathing from chapter 2).

Exercise Consider cardio, high-intensity weight training, and daily walking.

Socializing To get some laughter back into our lives!

Singing and Chanting Vocalizing either alone or with others.

Exposure to Cold This can range from splashing water on your face to taking an ice-cold shower.

Breathing Exercises These are a powerful component of self-regulation. Another particular form of this involves slow, deep breathing from your diaphragm (from the previous chapter).

Emphasis on a Longer Exhalation Used to engage the vagus nerve and recalibrate our responses.

Other Ways to Calm Your Nervous System

- massage, which can include a diaphragm massage and foot massages, is thought to be particularly effective (my personal favorite)

- foam rolling

- body scan exercises (at the end of this chapter)

- yin yoga

- sound healing

- eye movements to relax and strengthen the muscles around the eyes

Trauma compromises your ability to engage with others by replacing patterns of connection with patterns of protection. Polyvagal therapy is an antidote to that tendency that aims to teach you to find safety in your body.

IN PRACTICE
Polyvagal Therapy Body Scan Meditation

Since self-care begins at home, explore the physiology of self-regulation for yourself with this body scan meditation. Start by getting comfortable and take a few centering breaths.

Step 1: Bring awareness to your body by breathing in and out, noticing through touch and pressure where it makes contact with the seat or the floor. Throughout this practice, allow as much time as you need or want to experience and investigate each area of the body.

Step 2: When you're ready (no rush), intentionally breathe in and move your attention to whatever part of the body you want to investigate. You might choose to do a systematic body scan beginning at the head or the feet. Or you might choose to explore sensations randomly.

Step 3: Sensations might include buzzing, tingling, pressure, tightness, temperature, or anything else you notice. What if you don't notice any strong sensations or if you just feel neutral? You can simply notice that, too. There are no right answers. Just tune in to what's present, as best you can without judgment. You'll notice judgment puts a different spin on things.

The main point is being curious and open to what you are noticing, investigating the sensations as fully as possible, and then intentionally releasing the focus of attention before shifting to the next area to explore.

Emotional Freedom Technique: EFT Tapping

"Once your negative emotions, beliefs, and experiences have been processed and released, you are free to be positive again," asserts Nick Ortner in *The Tapping Solution*. This is the goal for a dark-haired man in his thirties as he sits on a chair across from an EFT therapist. The man is at a retreat where he came to work through the accidental death of his wife in a car while he was driving on the George Washington Bridge in New York City. As he processes his grief, tapping out the points on his body led by the practitioner, he makes statements about his guilt and trauma followed by a statement of self-acceptance as prescribed in using the EFT technique. When the therapist asks him to re-create how he exclaimed aloud in the moment of impact, he shouts "Oh my God!" before lapsing into tears. With repetition of the process over the course of the weekend, he states that his guilt lessened, his stress rating reduced, and he began to come to terms with his loss and that of his wife's five children.

Definition of EFT

EFT, also known as tapping or psychological acupressure, first hit the scene in the 1990s when developer Gary Craig published information about the therapy on his website. The practice involves tapping specific points on the body, mostly on the head and the face, in a particular sequence. While doing this, you focus on the issue that you wish to treat.

Uses of EFT

According to EFT International, the technique can be helpful for people with:

- performance and weight loss issues

- anxiety and depression

- chronic pain

- stress and trauma

EFT tapping is said to be one of the fastest and most efficient ways to address both the emotional and physical problems that tend to hamper many of our lives. It uses Chinese medicine energy meridians, or passageways, through which our qi or life-force energy flows through your body. You tap on specific points in the prescribed sequence of 1 through 9 acupressure points while focusing on particular negative emotions or physical sensations (Leonard 2019).

How EFT Works

The tapping helps calm the nervous system to restore the balance of energy in the body and in turn rewires the brain to respond in healthy ways. This kind of conditioning can help rid you of everything from chronic pain to phobias to addictions. Because of tapping's proven success in healing with a variety of problems, proponents of the technique recommend trying it on any challenging issue.

I loved that our high school taught the kids this technique. As you discover, neutralize, and eliminate the emotional baggage from specific events, you will have less and less internal conflict in your system that translates to higher levels of internal peace with less emotional and physical suffering," sums up Nick Ortner in his best-selling book *The Tapping Solution*. In my experience and on the OPLM network where I work, this technique is popular.

Use the SUD Rating Scale

The suffering is measurable too. How? Using the Subjective Units of Distress (SUD) Scale to convey levels of distress developed by Joseph Wolpe in 1969. The SUD scale is used as a way of getting in touch with and conveying how much anxiety you are feeling at the moment. EFT recognizes ten points on the scale, ranging from one (absolutely no stress) up to ten (maximum distress).

I like the way I can be scientific using the scale before and after practice to measure my results so I can see progress. This makes me feel like I am in control of regulating and working through my emotions.

Find the EFT Tapping Points

Here are the acupressure points used in EFT:

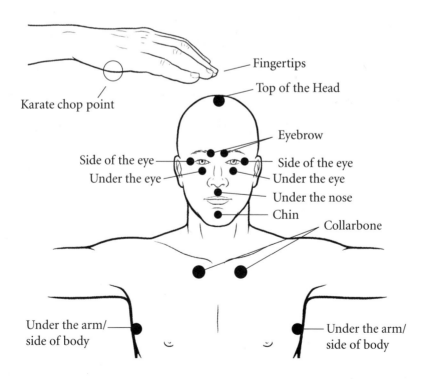

Fingertips

Top of the Head

Karate chop point

Eyebrow

Side of the eye

Side of the eye

Under the eye

Under the eye

Under the nose

Chin

Collarbone

Under the arm/ side of body

Under the arm/ side of body

The Steps of EFT Tapping Basics

For now, just familiarize yourself with the concepts. Find online videos to walk you through this tapping process.

Identify the Issue All you do here is make a mental note of what ails you. This becomes the target at which you "aim" the EFT tapping basic recipe. Examples might be: Sore shoulder, my father embarrassing me at my eighth birthday party, or hitting that high singing note. Be sure you are only targeting one issue at a time.

Test the Initial Intensity Here you establish a before level of the issue's intensity by assigning a number, as mentioned previously. This serves as a benchmark so you can compare your progress after each round of EFT tapping. If you start at an eight and eventually reach a four, then you know we have achieved a 50 percent improvement.

Useful Methods to Access Issues For emotional issues, you can re-create the memories in your mind and assess their discomforts. For physical ailments, you can simply assess the existing pain or discomfort. For performance issues, you can attempt the desired performance level and measure how close you come to it.

The Setup Phase This is a process you use to start each round of tapping. By designing a simple phrase and saying it while continuously tapping the KC point, you let your system know what you're trying to address.

When designing this phrase, there are two goals to achieve:

- Acknowledge the problem.

- Accept yourself in spite of it.

You do this by saying: "Even though I have this _____, I deeply and completely accept myself." The blank represents the problem you want to address. You can just insert things like:

This sore shoulder: "Even though I have this sore shoulder, I deeply and completely accept myself."

This fear of spiders: "Even though I have this fear of spiders, I deeply and completely accept myself."

This humiliation at my eighth-grade graduation: "Even though I have this humiliation at my eighth-grade graduation, I deeply and completely accept myself."

This difficulty making free throws: "Even though I have this difficulty making free throws, I deeply and completely accept myself."

Customizing EFT Phrases Not all of the issues will fit neatly into "Even though I have this _____." You will automatically choose something that represents your experience, your reaction, or a problem that you recognize as something that belongs to you. This is an important feature of the practice. Please note that you do not want to use EFT on someone else's problem. Rather than "Even though my daughter is addicted to drugs, I deeply and completely accept myself," it's better to focus on your own reaction, which might be "Even though I'm frustrated by my daughter's drug addiction..."

The Sequence This is the workhorse part of EFT tapping that stimulates/balances the body's energy pathways. To perform it, tap each of the points following the tapping sequence through the remaining tapping points starting at the eyebrow and ending at the top of the head. Eyebrow → Side of the Eye → Under the Eye → Under the Nose → Under the Mouth → Collarbone → Under the Arm → Top of the Head while saying a reminder phrase that keeps your system tuned in to the issue.

The Reminder Phrase This phrase is quite simple, as you only need to identify the issue with some brief wording. Depending on your issue, you might say the following at each tapping point:

- "This sore shoulder"

- "My father embarrassed me"

- "This difficulty in singing that high note"

Retest Finally, you establish an "after" level of the issue's intensity by assigning a number to it on a SUD scale. You compare this with the before level to see how much progress you have made. If you are not down to zero, then repeat the process until you either achieve zero or plateau at some level.

IN PRACTICE
EFT Tapping Simplified in Five Steps

These five basic steps are simplified, but practitioners state they are just as effective as the longer version.

Step 1: Assess Your SUD level.

Step 2: Insert the name of your problem into the set-up statement, "Even though I have a [*insert problem*], I deeply and completely accept myself."

Step 3: Tap continually on the karate chop (KC) point while repeating the statement three times.

Step 4: While repeating the reminder phrase, tap about seven times on the other seven tapping points.

Step 5: Test your results on a second level SUD rating.

Locating the Nine EFT Tapping Points

The Karate Chop (KC) Point Is located at the center of the fleshy part of the outside of your hand (either hand) between the top of the wrist and the base of the baby finger or, stated differently, it is the part of your hand you would use to deliver a karate chop.

Top of the Head (TOH) It is located at the very top, center of the head shown as the second tapping point but should be the last tapping point beneath Under the Arm (according to the sequence).

Beginning of the Eyebrow (EB) Is at the beginning of the eyebrow, just above and to one side of the nose.

Side of the Eye (SE) Is on the bone bordering the outside corner of the eye.

Under the Eye (UE) Is on the bone under an eye about 1 inch below your pupil.

Under the Nose (UN) Is on the small area between the bottom of your nose and the top of your upper lip.

Chin Point (CH) Is midway between the point of your chin and the bottom of your lower lip.

Beginning of the Collarbone (CB) To locate it, use an open palm and tap below the base of the throat between the collarbones.

Under the Arm (UA) On the side of the body, at a point even with the nipple (for men) or in the middle of the bra strap (for women). It is about 4 inches below the armpit.

In Practice
Tap in the Good

Opinions vary but according to my therapist and other experts I've learned from, EFT tapping can be used for both tapping out negative emotions and then tapping in positive intentions and affirmations. If this resonates with you, consider trying it with one or both of these options:

- Find a comfortable position.

- Option #1: Bring your hands crossed over one another just below your collar bones in Butterfly Hug (eagle mudra).

- Using bilateral stimulation (from EMDR in chapter 5) tap the fingers of your left hand and then your right hand under your respective collar bones, side to side.

- Option #2: Another position for this type of tapping is outside your fingernail beds on the outer right side. Start with your thumb, then index finger, middle, ring, then pinkie fingers as you make affirmations, visualizing what you would like to happen. Maybe it's a number on the scale, that jump shot, or a picture in your mind.

- Here are some starter affirmations to tap in or create your own.

  » I am the power, the master, and the cause of my attitudes, feelings, emotions, and behaviors.

  » It is healthy to take time to heal.

  » My best is good enough.

  » With my own healing my family gets stronger.

  » My creativity heals myself and others.

  » I am 100 percent powerful and decisive in everything I do.

  » I have perfect self-control and self-mastery in everything I do.

  » There is a divine plan of goodness for me and my work.

  » As I create and listen, I will be led.

Positive Psychology

"The aim of positive psychology is to catalyze a change in psychology from preoccupation with repairing the worst things in life to also building the best qualities in life," says Martin Seligman, an American psychologist, founder of positive psychology, educator, and author. As a conscious creator, you want to focus on what you want rather than what you don't want in your life, right? Therein lies the rub and the long-standing problem with psychology, that it disproportionately focused on treating mental illness rather than promoting mental health.

Who wants to focus entirely on the negative side of human experience? Seligman was recruited by the army to help soldiers, and it helped them to spotlight overcoming adversity by embracing resilience and growth rather than treating chronic disease. Add to that the modern challenges of the pandemic, recent reports on the earth crisis, and ongoing wars, which may lead you to wonder, what can you do to flip the negativity script and focus on what you do want? The answer is happiness. Everyone just wants to be happy. One alternative for doing that is with this relatively new form of psychology that emphasizes the positive influences in your life. It supports my intuitive notion that I want to manifest in the positive. It was also something Mother Theresa said. When asked, she didn't want to attend an anti-war march, but she was happy to be at a pro-peace rally instead.

Positive Psychology: The Study of Happiness

This entire subfield is a deep dive into the art of human happiness by concentrating on the productive events and influences in life, including uplifting experiences such as joy, inspiration, and love. Also of importance are the useful states and traits of gratitude, resilience, and compassion (*Psychology Today* 2019). These include your character strengths, optimistic emotions, and constructive institutions. The belief is that happiness is derived from both emotional and mental factors, and the aim is to help you identify happiness from moment to moment.

Seligman also suggests that if you are able to maintain a growth mindset, you will be better able to demonstrate resilience and actually grow from the traumatic experience in the long run. This is what inspired Seligman to concentrate on assisting soldiers who had just returned from combat. He helped them to change their attribution style, the manner in which they explain the origin of events in their lives. The stories they tell. Specifically, he found it useful for them to move from a fixed to a development mentality, a mindset where they see the negative experiences as brief and particular. This better enabled them to make adjustments and cultivate effective coping mechanisms.

What is essential to keep in mind is that post-traumatic growth is not a direct result of trauma but instead is related to how you work to grow as a result of the trauma. Not only is positive psychology proven to help soldiers, it is even known to be more effective than CBT in dealing with major depression for anyone (Asgharipoor et al. 2012, 33–41).

Techniques Used in Positive Psychotherapy

If you think this sounds like something you'd like to apply in therapy or your own life, note that happiness may be broken down into three more manageable components:

Positive Emotions focusing on and purposefully cultivating constructive, helpful feelings and resources.

Engagement finding, getting involved and invested in things you love. You know, the thing that you become so immersed in that it causes you to lose track of time.

Meaning looking for purpose in your life's events and your interpretation of them.

The exercises in positive psychotherapy are used to enhance as many parts of your life as possible. Say you want to boost positive emotions, you could try the best possible self exercise. In it, you use your imagination to picture your life after everything has gone as well as it possibly could. It's like creating a vision board in your mind. Imagination can take you everywhere!

I like to do a version of this at night in bed while meditating before drifting off to sleep. It's a process I learned from the Abraham Hicks deliberate creation teachings. You say, wouldn't it be nice if_____? Fill in the blanks with the best-case scenario. I imagine wonderful outcomes in all my life and that of my family and friends. It definitely makes for a better night's rest. It has been shown that imagining an act can activate and strengthen regions of the brain involved in its real-life execution, which improves your performance. For instance, imagining playing piano can boost neural pathways in regions related to the fingers.

Not only can you practice in your mind but you can also imagine feeling as if it is already done. I call this anticipating how it will be to bask in the afterglow, to feel how full your heart will be as if it is happening in real time or once the event is over. For me, I might get stressed when preparing to host a party but afterward my heart feels full and warm. That is what I call basking in the afterglow. I can anticipate I will feel good during and after the party too. It's just work to get it set.

Short-Term Sampling

Some other techniques used in this form of therapy involve examining your daily activities. Short-term sampling is one practice using an app or texts on your phone. Therapists may, if given consent, remind you to record your everyday experiences. These are self-reported, random samples where you and your therapist are gathering data to keep track of when you are experiencing being in the zone or a flow state, a mental state of complete focus and immersion in a task. It could be something like *Beep!* "Tell me something good!" This is a simplistic example.

Some therapists might ask more specific questions like how effective is the conversation you are having, how much do you enjoy the conversation, where are you and how does that effect your well-being? See how it could also be used to examine how you are using your behavior modification techniques from therapy? It's about noticing what you are doing in your daily life. It brings awareness to how you are using your tools. It can show you how to reframe your perspective and modify your behaviors. It helps you apply techniques and gives your therapist data on targeted behavior. These records can be expanded upon as daily entries are added to describe the details of your past day. They are then evaluated with long-term appraisals.

Short-term sampling can focus on having affirming experiences add up. It can be inspiring and worth tracking since they help produce the desired results. You already heard that both positive psychology and CBT are effective in reducing symptoms of depression through studies. One in particular examined the difference between the two approaches and found that positive psychotherapy was more effective than CBT at boosting happiness because it increased the overall happiness of those with depression (Azar 2011).

Defensive Pessimism

The positive psychology approach is thought to be less helpful and possibly ineffective when used in the treatment of certain serious or chronic mental health issues. You can go out on a limb and see that being optimistic and positive may not benefit everyone. Some people, who can be termed "defensive pessimists," thrive on the fact that they approach situations from a negative viewpoint. These people are better able to achieve success by first anticipating possible setbacks. From there, they work to avoid failure. If this sounds like you this approach may better help you cope with anxiety. It may also assist certain people to adapt more quickly and outperform strategic optimists (Skedel 2021).

The point is everyone is different, which is why you want to explore which approach works for you. Eeyore is a fun example of a defensive pessimist. Even though he's one of the most notoriously pessimistic cartoon characters, the beloved donkey from A. A. Milne's *Winnie the Pooh* still can bring a few laughs every so often. Case in point, this gloomy, yet still slightly optimistic quote:

"It's snowing still," said Eeyore gloomily.

"So it is," answered Pooh.

"And freezing," said Eeyore.

"Is it?" asked Pooh.

"Yes," said Eeyore. "However," he said, brightening up a little, "we haven't had an earthquake lately."

Toxic Positivity

On the opposite end of the pessimism spectrum is the extreme of toxic positivity. I have always considered myself an optimist and been told as much. When I first encountered the term, I was surprised yet validated to learn what I have felt in going through hard times; that slapping a smile on or covering up something that hurts just makes matters worse. You can term this as toxic positivity because it may deny you the authentic support that you need to cope with what you are facing (Carmichael 2021).

Sure, we are all aware of the benefits of a positive view on life for mental health. The issue is that things in life aren't always good. We all experience terrible feelings and issues as a human living on Earth. Even though these experiences are frequently unpleasant, those feelings are necessary and need expression. It helps if they are handled freely and honestly. Positive thinking is taken to an overly broad extreme in toxic positivity. This mindset reduces and ignores all traces of human emotions that aren't strictly pleasant or positive in addition to emphasizing the value of optimism.

Toxic positivity can be harmful in these ways (Cherry 2024):

- When it is humiliating. It is important for someone who is suffering to understand that their emotions are valid and that their friends and family may offer them support and affection. Telling them that their emotions are inappropriate is poisonous.

- When it results in guilt. If it avoids real human feeling, it suggests that you are doing something wrong if you are unable to maintain your optimism in the face of tragedy. Toxic optimism can be used as a defense. It's possible that people act in this way to stay out of awkward or upsetting emotional situations. But if we minimize, reject, and ignore these damaging ideas, we might internalize them and turn them against us. Done that, been there.

- If it hinders development.

The phrase "good vibes only" might be particularly grating when you're going through a really painful emotional moment. It might sound incredibly harsh to be told to "look on the bright side" when facing challenges such as financial difficulties, job loss, illness, or the loss of a loved one. In spite of trying circumstances and obstacles, optimism is achievable. However, it's not helpful to feel criticized for not keeping up appearances. You don't need to be urged to remain optimistic when you are going through trauma.

How to Avoid Toxic Positivity

Consider these steps to take if toxic optimism has hurt you or you recognize this kind of attitude in yourself. There are actions you can take to develop a better, more constructive mindset. Some ideas are:

- Manage your negative emotions rather than ignoring them. Negative emotions can cause tension if they are unchecked, but they can also reveal important details that might help you make life-changing decisions.

- Be realistic about how you "should" feel. Avoid "shoulding all over yourself." It's common to experience anxiety, worry, or even fear when faced with a challenging situation. Letting oneself have a little leeway is sometimes the best self-care. Your emotions are all legitimate.

- Multiple emotions are okay. It's common to feel both hopeful that you'll win and anxious about the future when faced with a challenge. The situation is difficult, and so are your sentiments. Be reassured that everything will work out.

- Consider other people's perspectives and offer your assistance. Avoid using harsh generalizations to silence someone who is expressing a difficult emotion. Comfort them instead that you are here to listen to them and that their feelings are normal.

- Keep an eye on your emotions. Following "positive" social media profiles may occasionally be beneficial for inspiration, but be mindful of your feelings afterward. It could be wiser to take a media break if reading "uplifting" content makes you feel bad or ashamed.

Take-Home Message

Positive psychology has shown that your well-being and satisfaction can blossom through your efforts and intentional activities. It takes practice, it might not always be easy, but it will be worth the effort. When looking to increase happiness, well-being, and life satisfaction, experts agree the key is to be proactive and energetic in your pursuit.

IN PRACTICE
Three DIY Positive Psychology Interventions

Here are examples of positive psychology interventions with tangible action items. Applying them need not entail huge changes in your lifestyle. Start small with one or two tips that can change your habits. Or use them just to start rewiring your brain for better health and wellness.

> **Start a Gratitude Journal** It's a great buffer and reframe against negative emotions such as envy, hostility, worry, and irritation. It involves a focus on the present moment and appreciating what is instead of focusing on what could be. Once I start writing, I sometimes surprise myself that I am able to fill pages with gratitude even after a challenging day.

> **The Gratitude Letter** This entails writing a letter with specific examples to someone who has gone out of their way to help, inspire, and/or uplift you. This is someone who has made a difference in your life. This practice of gratitude is especially effective

when expressed directly to another person and the effects of doing so last. Add your own twist.

Best Possible Self Exercise This helps you to see explicitly your own understanding of what self-actualization might mean in your case. Consider your most significant goals in the different areas of your life: professional, social, romantic, physical, or any other category of your choice. Then imagine your life after everything has gone as well as it possibly could:

- What would you be doing?

- Where would you be living?

- How would your days look?

- How would you feel?

Make It Your Own

Add your own twist to these practices. Not a writer? Create pictures, songs, memes, or whatever medium you want. Make them your own. Notice the impact these exercises have. Be scientific about it. Note how you felt while you were doing them and how you feel after the exercise. Can you rate your experiences? How long did it last? How are you going to continue your gratitude practice?

Happiness Is Not a Constant

To be clear. It's neither appropriate nor realistic to feel happy all the time, and some will always face more challenges than others. Dear friend, please remember it's not a failure when you're feeling down. That is part of the ebb and flow of emotions. However, if you are always as content as you can be in the situation you find yourself in, isn't that the most you could ask for anyway?

IN PRACTICE
Positive Psychology Meditation on Happiness

Meditation can make a huge impact on your happiness by teaching you present-moment awareness instead of worrying about the future or obsessing over the past.

- Get comfortable and close your eyes or soften your gaze. Breathe slowly and deeply. Breathe in relaxation and a sense of ease. Let go of any tension as you exhale. Let the warmth of relaxation flow through your whole body, from your head all the way down to your feet.

- Find your own way to the still, quiet center of your being, with your body relaxed, your emotions calm, your mind peaceful and spacious.

- Think of a time when you experienced great joy and well-being, perhaps when you were in a beautiful place or with a good friend.

- Recall your experience with as much detail as you can. If possible, bring an image of that moment to mind. What was happening? What was the environment like? Were you alone or with others? What sights or sounds can you remember?

- Remember how the experience of well-being or joy felt in your body. Did your body feel light? Energetic? Expansive? What did joy feel like in your mind? Did your mind feel open? Present? Clear? Take a few moments to let your awareness feel the sensations in your body and the mood in your mind. Let them fully register as you breathe in this feeling of well-being. Relax into it with each exhalation.

- Practice calling up this image and the feelings of well-being regularly each day for one week. At times, you may find you can simply invoke and sustain those feelings of well-being without having to re-create the specific memory.

Use this practice whenever you are feeling stuck and want to shift to a more uplifted state of mind, or when you simply want to open yourself to joy.

Positive Psychology Subfield: The Strengths-Based Psychology Approach

When was the last time you felt empowered to create a positive change in your life while someone is only pointing out your flaws or lack of potential? Probably never. That would be like arduously trying to climb a mountain while rocks are thrown at you. You've heard the adage "Your value doesn't decrease based on someone's inability to see your worth." Well, a strengths-based approach is about finding your self-worth. It values the capacity, skills, knowledge, connections, and potential in you and your community. Focusing on strengths does not mean ignoring challenges or simply spinning struggles into strengths. If you were to choose a practitioner who worked with you in this way, it would be a collaboration, helping you to do things for yourself. The aim is for you to become a coproducer of support, not a passive consumer of it (Beadle-Brown et al. 2021, 401–22).

Standards in the Strengths-Based Approach

If your interest is piqued, here's what to look for in a therapist who uses the strengths-based approach. Researchers Rapp, Saleebey, and Sullivan offer these standards for judging what constitutes a genuine strengths-based approach, so you can look for these benchmarks in deciding.

Goal Orientation Strengths-based practice is goal oriented, since we know the central and most crucial element of any approach is the extent to which you yourself set goals you want to achieve in your life.

Strength Assessment The primary focus is not on your problems or deficits. Instead, you should feel supported to recognize the inherent resources you have at their disposal, which you can use to counteract any difficulty or condition.

Resources from the Environment Strength proponents believe that in every environment there are individuals, associations, groups, and institutions who have something to give that you've found useful, and that it may be the practitioner's role to establish links to these resources.

"Everyone has strengths and when a client hears positive feedback about what's right, they light up. Many of my clients only hear about the negatives, the problems, and they feel guilt and shame," says Margret Greene, a LCSW in private practice in Wilton, Connecticut. "When you amplify the well part of a client or family, you can literally see a client's face transform and they are open to listening, case planning, and moving forward" (Greene 2021).

Greene went on to say she sees there is a bit of self-fulfilling prophecy happening in this scenario as well. If you are told you are a good mother, you often will act like a good mother. There is an old saying that she has in her office that said, "If you treat people how they ought to be treated, they will act as they should." Likewise, notice how you feel when you practice self-love, focus on your strengths, and project self-respect.

Strengths-Based Approach for Addiction

Evidence suggests that strengths-based approaches can improve retention in treatment programs for those who misuse substances. Greene cited this example. If a person relapses but they were sober for five months, their sobriety is acknowledged and the focus would be on what was working and how to get back on track. Rather than punishing them, which could lead to more guilt and ultimately a full-blown relapse. The conversation would instead be about how they were able to keep it together for five months and see if they can build on that.

With this approach, they embrace self-worth, develop power and control over their addiction, separate themselves from past issues, and begin to form new relationships with loved ones and their greater community. In trauma work, a strengths-based approach looks to understand how the behavior makes sense, given a person's distress and limited resources. This approach accepts a person as is. It recognizes the desperation and extreme states of emotion that unhealed trauma creates and affirms their need for care and resources. Conversely, improved social networks and enhanced well-being also contribute to connectivity, which is a key to resilience and healing.

IN PRACTICE
Strengths-Based Psychology Questions Journaling

These questions are used to "combat the relentless pursuit of pathology that instead helps one discover hidden strengths that contain the seeds to construct solutions to otherwise unsolvable problems," says social work scholar Clay Graybeal. Pick your top three (or all) that speak to you:

1. What do you like to do in your spare time?

2. What energizes you?

3. What do you feel good about?

4. Describe a successful day. What made it successful?

5. What are you really proud of?

6. What do you like about yourself?

Trauma Healing Trifecta: Radical Acceptance, Buddhist Meditation, and Psychotherapy

It was Dr. Tara Brach's longing to be at peace that drew her into psychotherapy, first as a client, then clinician, and then to the Buddhist path. If you aren't familiar with her, Brach is an American psychologist, author, proponent of Buddhist meditation, and guiding teacher/founder of the Insight Meditation Community of Washington, D.C. "In the weaving of these traditions I discovered what I now call *Radical Acceptance,* which means clearly recognizing what we are feeling in the present moment and regarding that experience with compassion" (Brach 2011).

Radical Acceptance

One of the options you have for any problem is "radical acceptance," says Marsha Linehan in her 1993 research. Radical acceptance is steeped in Buddhist tradition and is about accepting life on life's terms and not resisting what you cannot or choose not to change. Radical acceptance is about saying yes to life, just as it is. What does this mean? I've struggled with applying radical acceptance, but I have found a tactic that helps. For me this entails acting "as if" I chose it in order to accept it, like it was a soul contract or a lesson my soul wanted to learn. When I am able to accept everything that is happening right now as if I chose it, it seems my life makes some kind of miraculous shift. For me it is a reframe. I am here to learn lessons and figure this must be part of it. My way of embracing this idea to avoid working against reality and try to work with it. I show myself compassion by saying to myself as I go about my day, "you are doing a good job." In other words, radical acceptance is the ability to accept situations that are outside of your control without judging them, which in turn reduces the suffering that is caused by them. It takes more effort to fight against them. Rather than being attached to a painful past, radical acceptance suggests that nonattachment is the key to overcoming suffering.

> **Nonattachment** When in denial many may think, I can't stand this. This isn't fair. This can't be true. Or it shouldn't be this way. It's almost as if I think refusing to accept the truth will keep it from being true, or that accepting means agreeing. Accepting is *not* agreeing. The battle against reality is draining, I know. It also doesn't work to refuse to accept things, such as the fact that your friend cheated you, that you were fired for something you didn't do, or that you didn't get into the college you wanted to go to. All of these do nothing to improve the situation and only make you feel worse.

Accepting Reality Of course, accepting reality is so hard when life is painful. No one wants to experience pain, disappointment, sadness, or loss. Yet those experiences are a part of life. When you attempt to avoid or resist those emotions, you add suffering to your pain. You may build the emotion bigger with your thoughts or create more misery by attempting to avoid the painful emotions. You can ease suffering by practicing acceptance.

Brach finds that using a combination of both psychotherapy and meditation practices with radical acceptance can lead to profound healing and spiritual transformation in traumatized clients. Another version of this idea comes from the late, great Carl Rogers, who said, "The curious paradox is that when I accept myself just as I am, then I can change." Not before. Brach feels that in her inner work and in working with her psychotherapy clients and meditation students, she sees over and over that radical acceptance is the gateway to healing wounds and spiritual transformation. When you can meet your experience with profound acknowledgement, you discover the wholeness, wisdom, and love that are your deepest nature. How amazing to discover your true nature is well-being.

Buddhist Meditation

Buddhist meditation practices and psychotherapy contribute to radical acceptance in distinct and complementary ways. "With Buddhist mindfulness training we learn to be aware of what is happening inside us with a clear, non-judging attention," explains Brach. "Specific practices to develop compassion cultivate our capacity to hold with kindness painful or intense experiences that are arising within us." Brach finds that when there is deep wounding, the presence of the therapist and the tools of psychotherapy provide a safe and supportive container in which memories and associated feelings can gradually come into consciousness.

In Brach's experience, if the process of including difficult emotions in awareness stops at the level of cognitive understanding without a fully embodied experience, the genuine acceptance, insight, and inner freedom that are the essence of true healing will not be complete. She went on to share that if the client can only access and open up to strong feelings in the presence of the therapist, they will not have the tools or confidence to continue on a path of personal and spiritual transformation independently. Again, we see the strength of a holistic approach using therapy and complementary healing modalities that work together. To me, it also sounds similar to the steps of observing and describing in DBT with self-compassionate mindfulness, or moment-to-moment awareness without judgment, that along with the intention to attend to how you are feeling.

Facing Trauma

In his book *The Trauma of Everyday Life*, Harvard-trained psychiatrist and Buddhist monk Mark Epstein makes a strong case that the best course of action is to address trauma head-on and find a way to cope with it. It sounds straightforward. Epstein provides a welcome reminder that experiencing trauma—whether it be the death of a loved one, the loss of a career, a bodily injury, or illness—is not a failure or an error in any way (Epstein 2013).

Using the realistic view school of Buddhism, which maintains that trauma is not something to be ashamed of, not a sign of weakness, and not a reflection of inner failing. It is merely a reality. This is a realistic view. "It's impossible to find the inner peace we're searching for if we don't take a realistic view of the trauma that confronts us," Epstein explains. He challenges the way Western psychology teaches that if we understand the cause of trauma, we might move past it, while many drawn to Eastern practices see meditation as a way of rising above or distancing themselves from their most difficult emotions. He uses his own experience as well as that of his patients to illustrate the truth of what the Buddha taught.

According to Epstein, both miss the point that trauma is a necessary component of life and can be a driving force for development of a deeper comprehension of change. When you view trauma from this angle, realizing that pain is illogical and universal, your suffering becomes more fundamentally connected to the rest of the world. Through agony there is relief. The Buddha would agree and say, "There will be no end to grief." While it is never static, Epstein affirms that it is not a single phenomenon (or even a five-stage one, a theory developed by Elisabeth Kübler-Ross). He adds that there is no reason to think it will go away permanently and no need to feel bad about oneself if it doesn't. Grief keeps repeating itself. Like us, it is colorful, startling, and alive.

Epstein says it makes us more human, caring, and wise to realize that we all share in trauma and that throughout that trauma, if it doesn't destroy us, it has the power to awaken us to both our minds' own capacity and to the suffering of others. It can be our greatest teacher, our freedom itself, and it is accessible to all of us. Grief comes up a lot for caregivers of those who are struggling or who have passed. It seems that grief is the most intense, primal, and painful form of love. It is an understandable, sane, and natural response to loss.

Radical Acceptance Coping Affirmations

Try repeating one of the following phrases to practice radical acceptance of a situation that challenges you:

- It is what it is.

- You have no power over me.

- This is how it has to be.

- I can't predict the future.

- I am strong, I will survive the present crisis.

- I can't go back in time.

- I can't change or control the past.

- Everything in the past has led up to this moment.

- Right now, everything is as it should be based on past events.

- I have no control over other people.

- I will not always agree or like it and that's okay.

Or create your own mantra. You may prefer to use phrases from a favorite song or spiritual text.

IN PRACTICE
A Buddhist Mantra to Try

Mantras are often repeated as a calming, grounding, or self-soothing technique. One example is the Tibetan Buddhist mantra for compassion, *Om Mani Padme Hum*. It translates to "behold the diamond in the lotus." I see it as a place of purity within our hearts, a refuge to which we can retreat during the trying times. The idea is that within all of us is the lotus flower, it's just covered up by a lot of mud and muck.

Reciting this mantra over and over again, with the right intention, is believed to get rid of the mud and muck until we are as sparkling, pure, compassionate, and wholesome as the lotus flower itself. Or as the Dalai Lama interprets, "the mantra transforms your impure body, speech, and mind into the pure body, speech, and mind of a Buddha."

- Sit comfortably in a quiet, private space, where you won't disturb anyone.

- Breathe deeply for a minute to clear your mind.

- Then begin reciting the mantra OM MANI PADME HUM slowly in a low quiet voice.

- When thoughts intervene, return to focusing on the mantra.

CONCLUSION

It is said that the condition of the world reflects that of our collective consciousness, our set of shared beliefs, ideas, and moral attitudes that operate as a unifying force within society and that is able to change organically. With the challenges we face, the hovering black clouds of collective consciousness may stress our nation and might sometimes terrify or even traumatize us. At other times, the collective can have the opposite effect. Like when we heal ourselves, we heal our family and the greater family.

We can, likewise, create a ripple effect of positivity and raise our energy so that collective consciousness reflects the light, love, and change we want to see in the world. We can tap into the collective consciousness through our healing modalities, religion, art, music, dance, and the other universals that represent it. While these are all ways of expressing yourself, they also connect you to the greater whole. When you create or are in the flow state, you are tapping into the creativity of the Universe. Awareness of unity consciousness is healing and can also validate you and what it means to be human. As humans, we have a shared experience. We all want to be happy, we will all die, and along the way we will experience the ups and downs of life here on Earth. Together, the individual and then the group consciousness provide the context from which we can recognize our inner strength and begin to heal.

Likewise, its union of the same duality in exploring and using psychology and complementary healing modalities for holistic healing of anxiety and trauma. We see the utility of the connection of the mind-body and how both approaches can be integrated to provide a full set of tools at our disposal. That is if we can open our awareness and proactively explore our options. With conscious national, generational, and individual healing, we can work through the reservoir of accumulated unresolved pain. Using our discernment, we can draw from all these methods and decide what works for us.

Our individual and collective trauma can look like a dark cloud over us, but when we choose love over fear and work on self-care and healing, we are truly working for the greater good. In turn, this can attune us to the power of community in making change. I envision the black cloud of our collective consciousness in this way transforming into a sparkling shield of light. I believe our challenges are here for transcendence in this most opportune juncture of history.

Dear reader, if you are here on Earth now, that makes you a divine warrior with an important part to play and a mission to accomplish in your own unique way. If I had a manifesto, it is that we come here as extensions of the divine healing intelligence to learn lessons and discover the missions we planned before we were born. As we work to heal our trauma or fear, it is possible we can use these obstacles as stepping stones even as we realize that our obstacles are the path.

I used to be disturbed that my best wasn't good enough to save my loved ones until I changed my perception. I can honor the dead by living fully in the present. Moreover, my best is definitely good enough. When I lay my head down on my pillow at night, if I did my best, that is good enough no matter what. Come what may. My lesson in this life is to never give up, so my goal is to distill what I have learned in my healing journey so that you may find what works for you. My wish for you is that this synthesis of trauma practices provides you with a toolbox of offerings to use at your disposal. When you are fighting for your life, you are most likely to heal if you stop at nothing to discover your healing combination. It is up to us to save ourselves and find it. In the words of the Buddha, "May you be happy, healthy, safe, and at peace."

Thank you for going on this journey with me.

Namaste,

Jackie

BIBLIOGRAPHY

Agarwal, Ankit, Shanmugavel Karthik, Nivedita Nanda, Gopal Krushna Pal, and Pravati Pal. 2014. "Slow Yogic Breathing Through Right and Left Nostril Influences Sympathovagal Balance, Heart Rate Variability, and Cardiovascular Risks in Young Adults." *North American Journal of Medical Studies* 6 (3): 145–51. https://www.ncbi.nlm.nih.gov/pmc/articles/PMC3978938/.

AMTA (American Music Therapy Association). 2010. "Music Therapy Research." https://www.musictherapy.org/research.

Asgharipoor, Negar, Hamidreza Arshadi, Aliasghar Asgharnejad Farid, and Ali Sahhebi. 2012. "A Comparative Study on the Effectiveness of Positive Psychotherapy and Group Cognitive-Behavioral Therapy for the Patients Suffering from Major Depressive Disorder." *Iran J Psychiatry Behav Sci.* Autumn-Winter; 6 (2): 33–41. https://pmc.ncbi.nlm.nih.gov/articles/PMC3940016/.

Azar, Beth. 2011. "Positive Psychology Advances, with Growing Pains." *Monitor on Psychology.* 42 (4): 32. http://www.apa.org/monitor/2011/04/positive-psychology.

Beadle-Brown, Julie, James Caiels, and Alisoun Milne. 2021. "Strengths-Based Approaches in Social Work and Social Care: Reviewing the Evidence." *Journal of Long-Term Care* (2021): 401–22. https://DOI: 10.31389/jltc.102/.

Bergman, Brandon, Bettina Hoeppner, John F. Kelly, Corrie Vilsaint, and William White. 2017. "Prevalence and Pathways of Recovery from Drug and Alcohol Problems in the United States Population: Implications for Practice, Research, and Policy." *Science Direct* 181: 162–9. https://www.sciencedirect.com/science/article/abs/pii/S0376871617305203.

Boussiou, Gabrielle, music therapist from Metropolitan Hospital in Harlem, New York. Phone interviews September 29, 2021; October 26, 2021; and November 2, 2021.

Brach, Tara. 2011. "Integration of Buddhist Meditation and Psychotherapy." https://www.tarabrach.com/integration-of-buddhist-meditation-and -psychotherapy-2/.

Brotons, Melissa, and Patricia Marti. 2003. "Music Therapy with Alzheimer's Patients and Their Family Caregivers: A Pilot Project." *Journal of Music Therapy* 40 (2):138–50. https://doi.org/10.1093/jmt/40.2.138.

Brown, DA, RP Ciraulo, PL Gerberg, RB Saper, and CC Streeter. 2012. "Effects of Yoga on the Autonomic Nervous System, Gamma-Aminobutyric-Acid, and Allostasis in Epilepsy, Depression, and Post-Traumatic Stress Disorder." https://doi.org/10.1016/j.mehy.2012.01.021.

Burg, Matthew, Rachel Friedman, Rachel Lampert, Forrester Lee, and Pamela Miles. 2010. "Effects of Reiki on Autonomic Activity Early After Acute Coronary Syndrome." *Journal of the American College of Cardiology*, 56 (12): 995–6. https://doi.org/10.1016/j.jacc.2010.03.082/.

Calhoun, Lawrence, Arnie Cann, Emre Senol-Durak, Kanako Taku, and Richard Tedeschi. 2017. "The Posttraumatic Growth Inventory: A Revision Integrating Existential and Spiritual Change." *Journal of Traumatic Stress*, 1: 11–18. https://doi.org/10.1002/jts.22155.

Carmichael, Chloe. 2021. "What Is Toxic Positivity? Being Optimistic Has Its Benefits, But Anything Can Be Taken to An Extreme." *Psychology Today*. https://www.psychologytoday.com/us/blog/the-high-functioning -hotspot/202107/what-is-toxic-positivity.

Cerre, Mike. Mickey Hart's Rhythm of Life on PBS My Generation. Produced by Mike Cerre and GLOBE TV. AARP, June 24, 2012. Broadcast on PBS.

Chapman, Alexander L. 2006. "Dialectical Behavior Therapy: Current Indications and Unique Elements." *Psychiatry (Edgmont)* 3 (9): 62–8. https://pmc.ncbi.nlm.nih.gov/articles/PMC2963469/.

Cherry, Kendra, MSEd. 2024. "Why Toxic Positivity Can Be Harmful. It's Not Always Helpful to Look on the Bright Side." Very Well Mind. www.verywellmind.com/what-is-toxic-positivity-5093958.

Cleveland Clinic Staff. 2021. "What Is Reiki? And Does It Actually Work?" Health Essentials. https://health.clevelandclinic.org/reiki/.

Cleveland Clinic Staff. 2022. "Dopamine Deficiency." https:// my.clevelandclinic.org/health/articles/22588-dopamine-deficiency.

Collier, Lorna. 2016. "Growth After Trauma: Why Are Some People More Resilient Than Others—And Can It Be Taught?" *Monitor on Psychology* 47 (10): 48. https://www.apa.org/monitor/2016/11/growth-trauma.

Columbia Presbyterian Staff. 2017. "Healing with Reiki." *Health Matters.* https://healthmatters.nyp.org/healing-with-reiki/.

Corliss, Julie. 2014. "Mindfulness Meditation May Ease Anxiety, Mental Stress." Harvard Health Publishing. https://www.health.harvard.edu /blog/mindfulness-meditation-may-ease-anxiety-mentalstress-20140 1086967.

Crane-Godreau, Mardi, Peter Levine, and Peter Payne. 2015. "Somatic Experiencing: Using Interoception and Proprioception as Core Elements of Trauma Therapy." *Frontiers in Psychology,* 6: 93. https://doi.org/10 .3389/fpsyg.2015.00093.

Cronkelton, Emily. 2022. "Energy Therapy: What to Know." *Medical News Today.* https://www.medicalnewstoday.com/articles/energy-therapy.

DailyHistory.org. 2021. "What was the Spartan Training called the Agoge?" https://www.dailyhistory.org/What_was_the_Spartan_Training_called _the_Agoge.

Dispenza, Joe. 2016. "Blessing of the Energy Centers." Aired on Rewired Series through Gaia TV. https://www.gaia.com/video/blessing-energy -centers.

Dixon, Elizabeth. 2021. "Breaking the Chains of Generational Trauma, We Don't Have to Pass Down Everything We Inherit." *Psychology Today.* https://www.psychologytoday.com/us/blog/the-flourishing-family /202107/breaking-the-chains-generational-trauma.

Eichenseher, Tasha. 2022. "What You Need to Know About Somatic Yoga." *Yoga Journal.* https://www.yogajournal.com/practice/somatics-yoga/.

Eisenberg, Marla, Katie A. Loth, Dianne Neumark-Sztainer, and Melanie Wall. 2010. "Yoga and Pilates: Associations with Body Image and Disordered-Eating Behaviors in a Population-Based Sample of Young Adults." *International Journal of Eating Disorder,* 44 (3): 276–80. https://onlinelibrary.wiley.com/doi/10.1002/eat.20858.

Emerson, David, and Elizabeth Hopper. 2011. *Overcoming Trauma Through Yoga: Reclaiming Your Body.* North Atlantic Books.

BIBLIOGRAPHY

Emerson, David, Alison Rhodes, Joseph Spinazzola, Laura Stone, Michael Suvak, Bessel van der Kolk, and Jennifer West. 2014. "Yoga as an Adjunctive Treatment for Posttraumatic Stress Disorder: A Randomized Controlled Trial." *Journal of Clinical Psychiatry*, 75 (6): 559–65. https://doi.org/10.4088/jcp.13m08561/.

Emerson, David. 2022. "Find a Facilitator." TCTSY—Trauma Center Trauma-Sensitive Yoga. https://www.traumasensitiveyoga.com/facilitators.

Emerson, David, Serena Choudhry, Rita Sharma, and Jen Turner. 2009. "Trauma-Sensitive Yoga: Principles, Practice, and Research." *International Journal of Yoga Therapy*, 19 (1): 123–8. https://doi.org/10.17761/IJYT.19.1.H6476P8084L22160.

Epstein, Mark. 2013. *The Trauma of Everyday Life*. Penguin Press.

Field, Barbara. 2022. "What Is Embodiment: The Body Mind Connection." *Very Well Mind*. https://www.verywellmind.com/what-is-embodiment-5217612.

Finger, Alan. 2005. *Chakra Yoga: Balancing Energy for Physical, Spiritual and Mental Well-Being*. Shambhala.

Gibson, David. 2010. "The Sound Healing Center." https://soundhealingcenter.com/.

Gibson Ramirez, Lacey. 2020. "Yoga's Energy Centers: What Science Says About the Chakras." Yoga U. https://www.yogaonline.com/yoga-research/yogas-energy-centers-what-science-says-about-chakras.

Goldsby, Tamara, Michael Goldsby, Mary McWalters, and Paul Mills. 2017. "Effects of Singing Bowl Sound Meditation on Mood, Tension, and Well-Being: An Observational Study." *Journal of Evidence Based Complementary Alternative Medicine*. 22 (3): 401–6. https://doi.org/10.1177/2156587216668109.

Gonzales, Matt. 2022. "PTSD Statistics." The Recovery Village. https://www.therecoveryvillage.com/mental-health/ptsd/.

Greene, Margret. 2021. Medical Social Worker with Yale New Haven Health. Interview and email on November 21, 2021. For more info on Greene visit here: https://margretgreene.com/.

Hanley Defoe, Robyne. 2022. "Humour: A Pillar of Resiliency." *Psychology Today*. https://www.psychologytoday.com/us/blog/everyday-resilience/202207/humour-pillar-resiliency.

Hicks, Esther. 2004. *Ask and It Is Given: Learning to Manifest Your Desires.* Hayhouse.

Interlandi, Jeneen. 2014. "A Revolutionary Approach to Healing PTSD," *The New York Times Magazine.* Health Issue. https://www.nytimes .com/2014/05/25/magazine/a-revolutionary-approach-to-treating -ptsd.html.

Iyengar, B.K.S. 2008. *B.K.S Iyengar Yoga: The Path to Holistic Health.* Dorling Kindersley.

Jared, Jenny. 2015. "United We Om Yoga and Meditation Nonprofit-By-Donation Yoga, Practice to the Underserved." United We Om. https://www.unitedweom.org/.

Johnson-Welsh, Emily. 2020. "Trauma-Informed Expressive Arts Therapy." https://www.trauma-informedpractice.com/.

Judith, Anodea. 2015. *Anodea Judith's Chakra Yoga.* Llewellyn Publications.

Judith, Anodea. 2017. *Eastern Body, Western Mind: Psychology and the Chakra System as a Path to the Self.* Jaico Publishing.

Kelder, Peter. 1998. *The Ancient Secret of the Fountain of Youth.* Harmony.

Kelloway, Rhonda. 2019. "Five Somatic Experiencing Exercises for Grounding," *Life Care Wellness Blog.* March 19, 2019. https://life-care -wellness.com/5-somatic-experiencing-techniques-that-anyone-can-use -to-stay-grounded/.

Keltner, Dacher. 2010. "Hands on Research: The Science of Touch." *Greater Good.* https://greatergood.berkeley.edu/article/item/hands_on_research.

Keyes, Raven. 2012. "Dr. Sheldon Marc Feldman at 2012 New York Reiki Conference, Part 1." *Columbia Surgery.* https://columbiasurgery.org /news/2012/10/12/dr-sheldon-marc-feldman-2012-new-york-reiki -conference-part-1.

Keyes, Raven. 2017. *The Healing Light of Angels: Transforming Your Past, Present & Future with Divine Energy.* Create Space Independent Publishing Platform.

Keyes, Raven. 2012. *The Healing Power of Reiki: A Modern Master's Approach to Emotional, Spiritual & Physical Wellness.* Llewellyn Publications.

Keyes, Raven. 2021. *Medical Reiki: A Groundbreaking Approach to Using Energy Medicine for Challenging Treatments.* Llewellyn Publications.

Keyes, Raven. 2024. "Medical Reiki Works." https://www.medicalreikiworks
.org/.

King, Dominic. 2023. "Brrr! What to Know About Cold Plunges." https://
health.clevelandclinic.org/what-to-know-about-cold-plunges.

Lavretsky, Helen. 2018. "The Sound of Healing," *UCLA Health Vital Signs
Issues*. 80: 11. https://www.uclahealth.org/sites/default/files/publication-
pdfs/bf/Vital-Signs-Fall-2018.pdf?f=bf3b79fa.

Lee, Frank, Walter Lubeck, Arjava Petter, and William Rand. 2001. *The
Spirit of Reiki: From Tradition to the Present Fundamental Lines of
Transmission, Original Writings, Mastery, Symbols, Treatments, Reiki
as a Spiritual Path in Life, and Much More.* Lotus Press.

Lee, Jennie. 2016. *True Yoga: Practicing the Yoga Sutras for Happiness &
Spiritual Fulfillment.* Llewellyn Publications.

Leonard, Jayne. 2019. "A Guide to EFT Tapping." *Medical News Today.*
https://www.medicalnewstoday.com/articles/326434.

Levine, Peter. 2015. *Trauma and Memory: Brain and Body in a Search for
the Living Past: A Practical Guide for Understanding and Working with
Traumatic Memory.* North Atlantic Books.

Loizzo, Joseph. 2016. "The Subtle Body: An Interoceptive Map of Central
Nervous System Function and Meditative Mind-Brain-Body Integration."
Annals of the New York Academy of Sciences 1373 (1): 78–95.
https://doi.org/10.1111/nyas.13065/.

Malchiodi, Cathy. 2020. "What Is Trauma-Informed Expressive Arts
Therapy?" *Psychology Today.* https://www.psychologytoday.com/us
/blog/arts-and-health/202005/what-is-trauma-informed-expressive
-arts-therapy.

Mata Amritanandamayi (The Hugging Saint). 2019. https://amma.org/.

Mayo Clinic Staff. 2018. "Post-Traumatic Stress Disorder." *Patient Care and
Information.* https://www.mayoclinic.org/diseases-conditions/post
-traumatic-stress-disorder/symptoms-causes/syc-20355967.

McLeod, Saul. 2024. "Erik Erikson's Stages of Psychosocial Development."
Simply Psychology. https://www.simplypsychology.org/erik-erikson.html.

Mertz, Corrine. 2013. "The Effectiveness of Psychodrama for Adolescents
Who Have Experienced Trauma." Master's Thesis Smith College: 63–9.
https://scholarworks.smith.edu/theses/947/.

Mirgain, Shilagh. 2019. "The Healing Power of Music." *University of Wisconsin Health.* https://www.uwhealth.org/news/the-healing-power-of-music.

National Council on Community Behavioral Health. 2024. "How to Manage Trauma." Infographic: 1-2. https://www.brighamandwomens.org/assets /bwh/womens-health/connors-center/pdfs/how-to-manage-trauma -infographic.pdf.

Neff, Kristen. 2021. *Fierce Self-Compassion: How Women Can Harness Kindness to Speak Up, Claim Their Power, and Thrive.* Harper.

Neff, Kristen. 2015. *Self-Compassion: The Proven Power of Being Kind to Yourself.* William Morrow.

Neff, Kristen. 2024. "What Is Self-Compassion?" https://self-compassion.org/.

Nichols, Hannah. 2022. "Alternate Nostril Breathing: Benefits, How To, and More." *Healthline.* https://www.healthline.com/health/alternate-nostril -breathing#risks.

NYC Health + Hospitals Staff. 2016. "Music and Memory Program at NYC Health + Hospitals' Skilled Nursing Facility Improves Quality Outcomes for Residents with Dementia." https://www.nychealthandhospitals.org /pressrelease/music-and-memory-program-at-nyc-health-hospitals-skilled -nursing-facility-improves-quality-outcomes-for-residents-with-dementia/.

Ortner, Nick. 2014. *The Tapping Solution.* Hay House.

Patanjali. 2022 edition. *The Yoga Sutras of Patanjali.* Translated by Sri Swami Satchidananda. Independent Publication.

Pope, Timothy. 2018. "Chakras and the Endocrine System." https://www .timothypope.co.uk/chakras-endocrine-system/.

Positive Psychology Staff. 2019. "Positive Psychology." https://www .psychologytoday.com/us/basics/positive-psychology.

Psychology Today Staff. 2018. "Trauma-Focused Cognitive Behavior Therapy." https://www.psychologytoday.com/us/therapy-types/trauma-focused -cognitive-behavior-therapy.

Reuters Staff. 2015. "Lullabies, Other Music May Help Sick Preemies." Fox News Children's Health. https://www.foxnews.com/health/lullabies -other-music-may-help-sick-preemies.

Schwartz, Arielle. 2018. "The Polyvagal Theory and Healing Complex PTSD." *Center for Resilience Informed Therapy.* https://drarielleschwartz .com/the-polyvagal-theory-and-healing-complex-ptsd-dr-arielle-schwartz/.

Sears, Matthew. 2024. "The Fearful Secret at the Heart of Ancient Sparta." *Slate*. https://slate.com/news-and-politics/2024/01/sparta-300-warriors -history-slavery.html.

Segal, Inna. 2010. *The Secret Language of Your Body*. Beyond Words.

Skedel, Renee. 2021. "Defensive Pessimism: Definition and Effectiveness." *Choosing Therapy*. https://www.choosingtherapy.com/defensive -pessimism/.

Stelter, Gretchen. 2023. "A Beginner's Guide to the 7 Chakras and Their Meanings." *Healthline Media*. https://www.healthline.com/health /fitness-exercise/7-chakras.

Stone, Alyson. 2019. "90 Seconds to Emotional Resilience." https://www .alysonmstone.com/90-seconds-to-emotional-resilience/.

Sugaya, Kiminobu, and Ayako Yonetani. 2025. "Your Brain on Music: A Popular Class Breaks Down How Our Brain Responds to Music." Pegasus, University of Central Florida. Accessed May 8, 2025. https://www.ucf .edu/pegasus/your-brain-on-music/.

Sullivan, Debra. 2023. "Grounding Mats: Your Questions Answered." *Healthline Media*. https://www.healthline.com/health/under-review -grounding-mats#how-it-works.

Thich Nhat Hanh. 2021. "Thich Nhat Hanh On How to Deal with Strong Emotions." Plum Village. https://plumvillage.app/thich-nhat-hanh-on -how-to-deal-with-strong-emotions/.

Trafton, Anne. 2015. "Using Sound Waves to Detect Rare Cancer Cells: Acoustic Device Can Rapidly Isolate Circulating Tumor Cells from Patient Blood Samples." *MIT News Office*. https://news.mit.edu/2015 /sound-waves-detect-rare-cancer-cells-0406.

Treleaven, David. 2018. *Trauma-Sensitive Mindfulness: Practices for Safe and Transformative Healing*. W.W. Norton & Company.

Tribole, Evelyn, and Elyse Resch. 2003. *Intuitive Eating: A Revolutionary Program that Works*. St. Martin's Griffin.

University of Pennsylvania's Positive Psychology Department Staff. 2019. "Resilience Training for the Army Program." *Positive Psychology Center*. https://ppc.sas.upenn.edu/services/resilience-training-army.

U.S. Department of Veteran Affairs. 2024 National Veteran Suicide Prevention Annual Report. https://www.mentalhealth.va.gov/docs/data-sheets/2024 /2024-Annual-Report-Part-2-of-2_508.pdf.

van der Kolk, Bessel. 2018. "Overcome Trauma with Yoga." YouTube video. 5 minutes and 45 seconds. https://www.youtube.com /watch?v=MmKfzbHzm_s.

Virtue, Doreen. 2004. *Archangels and Ascended Masters.* Hay House.

Warren, Sarah. 2019. "Combining Your Clinical Somatics and Yoga Practices." *Somatic Movement Center.* https://somaticmovementcenter.com/somatics -yoga/.

Warren, Sarah. 2023. "New Study Shows Pandiculation Relieves Lower Back and Neck Pain." *Somatic Movement Center.* https://somaticmovement center.com/clinical-somatics-research-study/.

Webster, Angie. 2016. "Quick Tip: Breath Sweep." Reiki Rays. https://reikirays .com/30646/quick-tip-breath-sweep-to-clear-your-energy/.

Weintraub, Amy. 2012. *Yoga Skills for Therapists: Effective Practices for Mood Management.* W. W. Norton & Company; 1st edition.

Wolf, Ben. 2011. "Reducing Anxiety: The Light Stream Technique." *Hope and Healing for Life.* https://hopeandhealingforlife.com/2011/08 /reducing-anxiety-the-light-stream-technique/.

INDEX

To Write to the Author

If you wish to contact the author or would like more information about this book, please write to the author in care of Llewellyn Worldwide and we will forward your request. Both the author and the publisher appreciate hearing from you and learning of your enjoyment of this book and how it has helped you. Llewellyn Worldwide cannot guarantee that every letter written to the author can be answered, but all will be forwarded. Please write to:

Jacqueline Jackson
℅ Llewellyn Worldwide
2143 Wooddale Drive
Woodbury, MN 55125-2989

Please enclose a self-addressed stamped envelope for reply or $1.00 to cover costs. If outside the USA, enclose an international postal reply coupon.

Many of Llewellyn's authors have websites with additional information and resources. For more information, please visit our website:

WWW.LLEWELLYN.COM